New Jersey for Kids

New Jersey for Kids

Patrick Sarver

AN IMPRINT OF RIVERGATE BOOKS
New Brunswick, New Jersey, and London

LIBRARY OF CONGRESS CATALOGING IN PUBLICATION DATA
Sarver, Patrick
  New Jersey for kids / Patrick Sarver.
     p.   cm.
  Includes indexes.
  ISBN 978-0-8135-5165-4 (pbk. : alk. paper)
  1. New Jersey—Guidebooks. 2. New Jersey—Description and travel. 3. Children—
    Travel—New Jersey—Guidebooks. 4. Family recreation—New Jersey—
    Guidebooks. I. Title.
  F132.3S27 2011
  F974.9—dc22

                                                                2011010851

         A British Cataloging-in-Publication data record for this book is available
                               from the British Library

                   Visit our Web site: http://rutgerspress.rutgers.edu

                     Manufactured in the United States of America

Contents

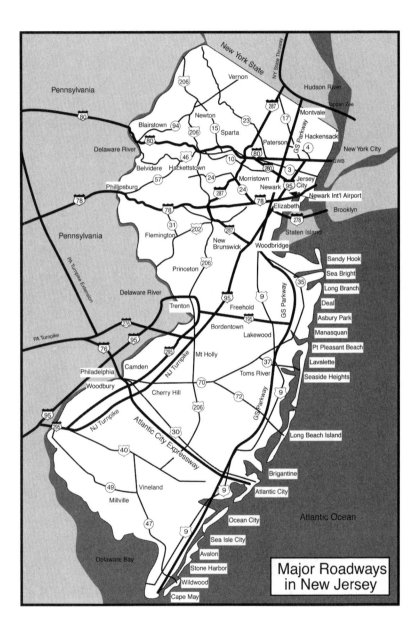

Major Roadways
in New Jersey

Preface

This new edition, *New Jersey for Kids*, grew out of a general travel guide to the Garden State called *New Jersey Day Trips*, which is also published by Rutgers University Press. That book, which was originally credited and written by Barbara Hudgins, is now in its twelfth edition. It includes kids' activities and interests but only in the wider context of a general travel guide to the state. While some material in this edition is based on *New Jersey Day Trips*, this book starts with the premise that there are activities that children are interested in that are much different from the adult perspective.

The one common element, besides covering the same state, is that the chapters are divided into subject categories, such as amusement parks, animals, creative fun, museums, sports, and so forth. This approach allows parents to search for places by activities that would be suitable for their children. There is also an index in the back of the book that lists places by county so that you can find things close to home.

This book is designed to provide an overview of what each listing offers, a handy guide that will help you save a lot of time in locating fun and educational activities for children. Other than listings like state parks or amusements or historic sites, this edition is not so much a read-and-go guide as it is designed to help you get started in getting your children involved in creative, fun activities in the Garden State.

This book is not designed to be a complete catalog of all activities of interest to kids in New Jersey. What it does do is provide a wide sampling of quality venues and activities, with an emphasis on the creative, the educational, and the unique. You may, for example, know of a dance studio or sports camp close to your home that is not included. If such a place is not included here, it is not a reflection on that organization. The emphasis here has instead been on including those places that seemed particularly noteworthy.

Please note that while every effort has been made to include the latest phone numbers and websites with each listing, these can change at any time. Also, because many of the listings are small organizations and businesses, a few are unfortunately bound to go out of business or perhaps change their names while this edition is in print. Because the majority of listings in this book offer classes or special events, visiting websites and then calling is a virtual necessity.

Finally, the author and editors of this edition hope that you will find activities in this volume that will help enrich the life of your child, perhaps helping him or her discover things that will develop into lifelong interests. There is a wide variety of fun things for kids to do in New Jersey, and if you and your children find places to visit and to become involved in, this edition will be a worthwhile addition to your family's library.

Prices, Abbreviations, and Hours

Exact prices are not included in this edition since they change so quickly from year to year. In addition, a large number of listings have a single fee covering multiple class sessions, or charge a camp or semester tuition. In many instances, a facility may have different course fees for different classes, and courses change from semester to semester as well. For this reason, any price information would be quickly out of date, so they are not given for those entries.

For listings that do have a simple entrance fee, however, the range of prices is indicated by the following codes:

$	=	up to $5
$$	=	$5.01 to $10
$$$	=	$10.01 to $15
$$$$	=	$15.01 to $25
$$$$$	=	$25.01 to $35
$$$$$$	=	$35.01 and above

ABBREVIATIONS

(BP) = Birthday Parties (including other themed parties)

(SC) = Summer Camp (typically day camps as well as other summer programs)

HOURS

Because classes often list numerous times, the hours provided are often general, such as "after-school and Saturdays." When a facility is seasonal, the months or seasons are listed. While the hours of operation were accurate when this edition went to press, they can change at any time—and often do. So, too, do the names and content of classes and special programs and events. *Readers are strongly encouraged to check a listing's website and to telephone first.*

New Jersey for Kids

Theme Parks and Amusements

While Six Flags Great Adventure in Jackson is known for its big roller coasters, there are also plenty of traditional amusement rides like the large Ferris wheel as well as several areas with children's rides. *(Photo by Patrick Sarver)*

Six Flags Great Adventure

Six Flags Great Adventure, the largest theme park in the state, seems to be headed in two directions. There seem to be more children's rides on the one hand, and bigger and faster roller coasters to attract teenagers, on the other. Four areas are for smaller children, including Bugs Bunny National Park, Loony Tunes Seaport, Wiggles World, and the Golden Kingdom. A dozen coasters, from Kingda Ka, at 456 feet the tallest and fastest coaster on earth, to El Toro, at 188 feet high the second tallest wooden coaster in the U.S., can be found here. Because the park is owned by Warner Brothers, one whole area is called Movietown. There's Batman, the Ride, a double-track inverted coaster based on the Batman and Robin movie. There's also the Dark Knight indoor coaster that runs in the dark. Another section is called Boardwalk, featuring an all-American amusement park theme. Here you will find games of chance, some small rides, and Superman, The Ride, and the Great American Scream Machine. At the other end of the park, Frontier Adventures has a vague Western theme and the Bizarro coaster. The section encompasses the Super Teepee for gifts, the Runaway Mining Train, and a barbeque palace next to the splashing log flume.

There are variety shows, festivals, and the central Fort Independence arena where the dolphin show reigns. Also on site are tiger and other wild animal shows as well as the original carousel, a large Ferris wheel, and a few other tame entertainments. Acrobat and circus acts can usually be found. The Grandstand at the Lake hosts Saturday night fireworks. If you want to spend your time on rides and not lines, you have a better chance with smaller, midway-style amusements.

Bring along towels—there are still flume rides that drench you! Lockers are available. And of course there are plenty of shops, drink vendors, and concession stands. Six Flags also has lengthened its season with a Halloween Fright Fest in October. The rides, ghoul shows, and the atmosphere are designed for teens and almost-teens.

LOCATION: Jackson Twp. (Ocean County). N.J. Turnpike, Exit 7A, then Rt. 195 to Exit 16. **HOURS:** Early Apr.–mid-June, call or check the website for hours. Late June–Labor Day, daily, 10:30–10. Open weekends, Sep., Oct. **ADMISSION:** $$$$$$ (safari $$ more). Discounts: Children 54 inches & under. Under 3 free. Parking extra. Season tickets available. **PHONE:** 732-928-1821. **WEBSITE:** www.sixflags.com.

Hurricane Harbor

Hurricane Harbor, a separate water park at Six Flags Great Adventure, has its own hours and prices. This place is large, and you can buy a combo ticket to both parks even though you may not be able to handle both parks in a single day.

Hurricane Harbor consists of 45 acres of wave pools, high-flying water slides, and roving rivers. Six Flags has spent a lot of money to create the look of a tropical hideaway. One section has a theme of a shipwrecked inventor on a tropical island. For families there is Discovery Bay, a large wading pool that features a giant bucket that pours 1,000 gallons of water onto the waiting crowd below. The park also keeps adding more multicolored, sky-high water slides each year. The newest is the Tornado, a seven-story-high ride that sends rafts plummeting down a tunnel, hurls them into a giant funnel, and spins them around its 60-foot diameter.

There are also slides for passenger rafts and bodysurfers plus chutes for the popular enclosed rides. And the big wave pool, Blue Lagoon, lets everybody get into the act with the cycles of the wave machine (five minutes on, seven off).

Taak It Eez Ee Creek is a long, meandering tube ride that has a bit more swirls and eddies than the usual ones. It also acts as a transportation river between one part of the park and another, so it offers a fun way to get around. For younger kids, there are all sorts of climbing nets and water gadgets. Bring suntan lotion, hats, towels, and swim sneakers if you have them. Changing rooms and showers are provided; lockers are extra.

LOCATION: See Six Flags entry for location and telephone.
HOURS: Late June–Labor Day, daily, 10:30–7;
Memorial Day–mid-June, weekends. **ADMISSION:** Adults, $$$$$$.
DISCOUNTS: Children 54 inches & under. Under 3 free.

Mountain Creek Waterpark

Mountain Creek consists of a water park, a mountain biking park, and a ski area in winter. At Mountain Creek Waterpark, there are more than two dozen rides, slides, and pools. More adventurous rides are emphasized, but there are moderate rides as well. The Wild River Canyons area includes the Colorado River Ride, a 1,600-foot white-water adventure. Thunder Run and the Gauley are major white-water tube rides. Adventure Ridge features the Alpine Pipeline, Vortex, and Vertigo tube speed coasters in the dark. And then there's the H2-Oh-No!, a speed slide that drops you down 99 feet in mere seconds, and High Anxiety, a two- to four-passenger tube ride that drops you down four stories.

Moderate rides include an area called Kids World, featuring the Spraygrounds, an interactive water play fort, the relaxing Lost Island River, and a wading pool. Elsewhere, there are rubber tube rides that twist and turn, straight slides that jackknife you into the water, closed chute rides, and the Tarzan Swing water hole, where you just jump in from a swinging rope. The High Tide wave pool is comparatively tame, but it can get crowded.

> **LOCATION:** Rt. 94, Vernon (Sussex County). Rt. 80 to Rt. 23 North to Rt. 94; go north for 4 miles. **HOURS:** Early June–Labor Day, generally 11–7, but hours vary for water park and mountain biking. Call or see website. **ADMISSION:** Water park, people 48 inches & taller, $$$$$. Discounts: Seniors, children 48 inches and under. Under 3 free. **PHONE:** 973-864-8444. **WEBSITE:** www.mountaincreekwaterpark.com.

Clementon Park

Set on 40 acres about 12 miles southeast of Camden, this venerable amusement park has rides that range from an old-fashioned carousel to a large log flume for families. Newer rides include the Thunder Bolt, Flying Pharoah, Inverter, Samba Tower, and Turtle Whirl. There is an interactive playport for kids, plus traditional kiddie rides. More relaxing rides include the Clementon Belle mini steamboat, the C. P. Huntington Train, and the ten-story Giant Ferris Wheel. The biggest ride by far, though, is the Hellcat wooden roller coaster, one of the largest in the state.

Splash World, a 13-acre water park alongside the amusement park, has a separate entrance, so you can enter it alone or buy combination tickets. Splash World includes a Pirate Ship, set in a pool for the little ones. Laguna Kahuna is a large splash, slide, and play area for kids. For the more adventurous, there are the 700-foot enclosed chutes of the Black Viper or the Sky River Rapids, with their three sets of water slides and three splash pools. Besides the other curling and straight slides, one can always find the level 1,200-foot Lazy River, a tube ride that eddies through scenic waterfalls and rock formations. Changing rooms, showers, and lockers available.

> **LOCATION:** 144 Berlin Rd. (Rt. 534) off Rt. 30 or 42, Clementon (Camden County). **HOURS:** Late May–June, Thu.–Sun., 12–9; June, Thu.–Sun., 12–10 (Splash World, 12–8); Memorial Day–Labor Day, daily, 11–9 (Splashworld, 11–7). Times vary on weekdays in May, June, and Aug. Closed occasionally for private parties. Check seasonal schedule on the website. **ADMISSION:** Combination pass, $$$$$$.

Discounts: Seniors, children under 48 inches tall. Under 3 free. Individual parks, $$$$. **PHONE:** 856-783-0263. **WEBSITE:** www.clementonpark.com.

Land of Make Believe

This amusement park, set in rural Warren County next to Jenny Jump State Park, encompasses 30 acres and every year brings bigger and new attractions. There are two sections: the water park and the amusement rides, but this park is small enough that you can easily do both in a day. And many of the dry rides are definitely for younger kids.

Pirate's Cove water park includes a lazy river ride and several midsized water slides. There is a giant wading pool for youngsters, with a life-sized pirate ship in the middle. This one squirts water and has a simple slide. Parents can sit on lounge chairs around the pool and watch. The river tube ride can be used by children and parents alike and is fairly mild. A covered water slide called the Black Hole is geared to older kids (you must be at least 8 years old to use it), while other new water slides like Pirate's Plunge, 400-foot-long Pirate's Peak, and Pirate's Cannonball are geared to the faster crowd. Lockers and changing rooms are available.

On the amusement park side there is a carousel, Sidewinder, Jump Around Frog, Tilt-A-Whirl, Tornado, miniature train ride, hayride, and a number of small kiddie rides. Many young children also like putting on costumes and becoming part of the show at the Middle Earth Theater or going to simple attractions like the petting zoo and the maze. The park also still has free parking.

LOCATION: Rt. 80, Exit 12. Two miles south to Hope (Warren County), then follow signs. **HOURS:** Mid-June–Labor Day, daily, 10–6. Call for May, Sep. hours. **ADMISSION:** $$$$. Discounts: Seniors. Under 2 free. **PHONE:** 908-459-9000. **WEBSITE:** www.lomb.com.

Wild West City

This northern New Jersey version of a Dodge City comes complete with marshal, cowboys, the Sundance Kid, shoot-outs, and a posse of kids. On a dusty street flanked by stores and a blacksmith shop, you can lean on the hitching post and watch cowboys twirl ropes and go through a series of lasso tricks. But the big deal of the day is when the bad guys rob the bank or the stagecoach on its way down Main Street. The sheriff "deputizes" all the kids to help round up the villains.

There are also educational shows, such as a frontier cook - ing demonstration, Native American dances, mountain men get-togethers, and other nonviolent events. However, the main theme here is the Wild West as imagined in dime novels and Hollywood.

Many of the stores along the street sell real Western goods and plenty of toy guns. There are others that display relics of the Old West, such as an old-time barber shop, a working blacksmith shop, and a real jail cell. You can take an authentic stagecoach ride down the main street or the miniature train ride that circles the town (extra fee for these). And don't be surprised if there's a holdup on the way. You can also pan for gold, visit the petting zoo or chuck wagon, or play miniature golf.

> **LOCATION:** I-80 to Rt. 206 North (Exit 25) to 50 Lackawanna Dr., Netcong (Sussex County). **HOURS:** Mid-June–Labor Day, daily, 10:30–6. Shows start at 11. May–Columbus Day, open weekends. Special events Oct. and Nov. **ADMISSION:** $$$. Under 2 free. Rides extra. **PHONE:** 973-347-8900. **WEBSITE:** www.wildwestcity.com.

Blackbeard's Cave

This recreation park south of Toms River includes a variety of activities, from a miniature golf course and bumper boats that travel through caves to batting cages and a driving range. For small kids, there's the Adventure Station, a park with numerous kiddie rides and activities, including a mini Ferris wheel, a mini coaster, and a mini train ride. Older kids have an archery range, Water Wars (water balloons), Eurobungy trampoline, climbing wall, and a quarter-mile Formula 1 Go-Kart track. An unusual form of jousting and Splatter Zone (a paintball arena) are also on hand, as well as an arcade.

> **LOCATION:** 136 Rt. 9, Bayville (Ocean County). **HOURS:** May–Oct., daily, 10 A.M.–midnight; hours vary rest of year. **ADMISSION:** Pay per ride. **PHONE:** 732-286-4414. **WEBSITE:** www.blackbeardscave.com.

Bowcraft Amusement Park

Set alongside Route 22, this small park has been modernizing over the years. Its thirty-plus rides and attractions include a swing carousel, a miniature train ride, and several other kiddie rides such as a mini coaster, bumper cars, Tilt-a-Whirl, and Frog Hopper. A video arcade and game room keep older kids busy. With a larger coaster and a flume ride, the trend here is to provide more for early teens, but the emphasis is still on smaller kids.

> **LOCATION:** 2545 Rt. 22 West, Scotch Plains (Union County). **HOURS:** June–Aug., daily; Apr.–May and Sep.–Oct., weekends only. Hours vary; see website for schedule. **ADMISSION:** Free parking and admission; pay per ride. **PHONE:** 908-389-1234. **WEBSITE:** www.bowcraft.com.

Storybookland

This well-known children's park has small structures in the shape of the Gingerbread House, the Old Woman's Shoe, Noah's Ark, and the like. The petting zoo, miniature train ride, antique car ride, and numerous kids' rides are all included in the admission price. It was built for the summer crowd, but special events also include a Halloween event, and a large, popular Christmas light display from mid-November to Christmas.

LOCATION: 6415 Black Horse Pike (Rt. 40/322), Egg Harbor Twp. (Atlantic County). **HOURS:** July–early Sep., 10–5:30; spring and fall, shorter hours. Special afternoon and evening Christmas hours. **ADMISSION:** $$$$. Under 1 free. **PHONE:** 609-641-7847. **WEBSITE:** www.storybookland.com.

Tomahawk Lake

This old-fashioned family picnic lake is combined with a new-fashioned kiddie water park, making for an interesting combination. The setting is an 18-acre freshwater lake with sandy beach. The low admission fee includes parking, lake use, and a tot-sized water world. Several larger water slides, the bumper boats, and miniature golf are available for an extra fee.

LOCATION: Tomahawk Trail (off Rt. 15), Sparta (Sussex County). **HOURS:** Memorial Day–mid-June, weekends only; mid-June–Labor Day, daily. **ADMISSION:** $$$; weekdays, $$. **PHONE:** 973-478-7490. **WEBSITE:** www.tomahawklake.com.

The Funplex

There are two locations for this amusement center, one in East Hanover and another in Mount Laurel. They are similar. There's an arcade, laser tag, motion simulator, bumper cars, electric go-karts, bumper boat ride, miniature golf, batting cages, outdoor go-karts, and the like. There's also MagiQuest, Foam Frenzy (with foam balls), and the XD Theater at East Hanover and bowling at Mount Laurel. Both sites are very geared to parties for youngsters.

LOCATIONS: 3320–24 Rt. 38, Mount Laurel (Burlington County), and 182 Rt. 10 West, East Hanover (Essex County). **HOURS:** Daily, 10–9, until 10 on Fri. Hours vary by season and day. **ADMISSION:** Pay per ride or a variety of wristband packages. **PHONE:** 856-273-9666 and 973-428-1166. **WEBSITE:** www.thefunplex.com. (BP)

Eagleswood Amusement Park

This modest park, which lies inland from Long Beach Island, features kiddie rides and go-karts along with an arcade, restaurant, batting cages, and driving range. There's kiddie rock climbing, a giant slide, bungy trampolines, kiddie go-karts, Sky Glider, Tornado, and Free Fall. Two eighteen-hole miniature golf courses round out the attractions.

LOCATION: 597 Rt. 9, Staffordville (Ocean County). **HOURS:** Apr.–Oct., Mon.–Thu., 12–9; Fri.–Sat., 12–10; Sun., 10:30–9. Arcade and driving range open all year. **ADMISSION:** Pay per ride or a wristband package. **PHONE:** 609-978-6606. **WEBSITE:** www.eagleswoodamusementpark.com.

Sahara Sam's Oasis

This 58,000-square-foot indoor water park features eleven rides and water amusements. The Cyclone Flow Rider is an uphill surf simulator that lets you test your boogie board skills. Tim-Buk-Tu Tree Fort is a multiple water play area with a giant tipping bucket. There's also a water basketball court, a 410-foot river ride, a family raft ride, as well as other slides, pools, and geysers. Outside the water area, there's a large arcade and video game shop. Showers and lockers on site.

LOCATION: 535 N. Rt. 73, West Berlin (Camden County). **HOURS:** Tue.–Thu., 1:30–7; Fri., 1:30–8:30; Sat., 10–8:30; Sun., 10–6:30. **ADMISSION:** $$$$$. Under 3 free. **PHONE:** 856-767-7580. **WEBSITE:** www.saharasams.com.

CoCo Key Water Resort

The rides and the layout are different from Sahara Sam's, but this 55,000-square-foot indoor water park nonetheless shares many of the same types of features. It offers three 40-foot body and raft slides, Parrot's Perch interactive play island, an adventure river, activity pools with water basketball and a lily-pad walk, and a wading pool and baby bungee for toddlers. Outside the water area, kids can enjoy an arcade. Showers and lockers on site.

LOCATION: Mount Laurel Marriott, 915 Rt. 73, Mount Laurel (Burlington County). **HOURS:** Sun.–Thu., 10–8; Fri.–Sat., 10–9. Shorter hours Mon.–Thu. off-season. **ADMISSION:** $$$$$$. Discounts on weekdays. **PHONE:** 856-802-3988. **WEBSITE:** www.cocokeywaterresort.com.

Funtime America

An indoor amusement park with 40,000 square feet of rides, games, and other amusements. Rides include a Himalaya mini coaster, the Magic Ring carousel, bumper cars, a mini-train ride, and a helicopter amusement ride. There's a two-story-tall laser tag arena where

Parrot's Perch interactive play island is the centerpiece at the indoor CoCo Key Water Resort in Mount Laurel, which also features several large water slides and smaller play and wading pools.
(Photo by Patrick Sarver)

up to twenty-four can play at a time. The Venturer motion simulator gives you the feeling of climbing, diving, and tilting. There's also a 20-foot-high rock-climbing wall. The soft-play castle is a four-story play area with plenty of tubes, slides, ladders, and rope climbs. Besides the usual amusements, there's also an arts and crafts area where kids can build their own plush animals or paint ceramic pieces, and an animal center that features exotic animals in a miniature habitat, with boa constrictors, monitor lizards, turtles, and iguanas. And, of course, there's a large video arcade.

LOCATION: 111 Rt. 35 South, Cliffwood (Monmouth County). **HOURS:** Mon.–Wed., 10–9; Sun. and Thu., 10–10; Fri., 10 A.M.–11 P.M.; Sat., 10 A.M.–midnight. **ADMISSION:** Rides and features priced separately; packages available. **PHONE:** 732-583-4600. **WEBSITE:** www.funtimeamerica.com. (BP)

Jeepers!

More than seventy family-oriented arcade games, including driving games, redemption and skill games, and sports games. There are also bumper cars, a kids' train, a Himalaya-style ride, and jet-abouts. Plus there's a parrot habitat featuring live parrots and gemstone "mining." The latest addition is a Wild Earth simulator ride that takes you on a photo safari across the African plains. Plus there's a 4-D movie theater with a wildlife theme.

LOCATION: 635 Kapkowski Rd., Elizabeth (Union County).
HOURS: Mon.–Thu., 11–9; Fri.–Sat., 11–10; Sun., 11–8.
ADMISSION: Point card system for rides and amusements.
PHONE: 908-289-9454.
WEBSITE: www.jeeperselizabeth.com. ⓑⓟ

Space Odyssey USA

A members-only (you join for a fee) high-tech party and amusement center that blends high-tech games, fun parties, game shows. There's glow-in-the-dark bowling, laser tag, paintless paintball, inflatables, a high-tech arcade, a spaceship/alien train ride. Sports include soccer, basketball, dodgeball, broomball hockey, and scooters. Spaceship is a three-level indoor playground with an adventurous alien train. There are two inflatables for lots of bouncing fun called Castle Fun and Wacky World.

LOCATION: 491 Dean St., Englewood (Bergen County).
HOURS: 10–9. **ADMISSION:** By membership. Guest trial
memberships available. **PHONE:** 201-567-3810.
WEBSITE: www.spaceodysseyusa.net. ⓑⓟ

Laser Park

Kids and their teammates navigate a maze of barriers with fog flowing along the ground, dodging laser beams, sometimes attacking their foes and defending their base. There's also an arcade as a change of pace from the laser tag.

LOCATION: 45 Everett Dr., Bldg. C, Princeton Junction
(Mercer County). **HOURS:** Wed.–Thu., 4:30–7; Fri., 4–10; Sat., 11–10;
Sun., 12–7. **ADMISSION:** $$ per game. **PHONE:** 609-936-1800.
WEBSITE: www.laserpark.com. ⓑⓟ ⓢⓒ

BOARDWALK AMUSEMENT AREAS

Boardwalks up and down the Jersey Shore offer a wide range of traditional and not-so-traditional amusement rides and activities. Rides are generally on a pay-as-you-go basis, with multi-ride booklets and bracelets available. Water parks, on the other hand, have general admission fees, sometimes with time limits or late-in-the-day discounts. And, of course, there are arcades, wheels of fortune, and skill games at booths in addition to an abundance of novelty shops and eateries along the way. They are usually open seasonally from late March to early November, although some indoor businesses are open year-round.

Keansburg

This is an older area that has been revitalized with new rides. The boardwalk runs about four or five blocks and includes plenty of kiddie rides plus several concessions and arcades.

Across from the amusement area is a block-long water park called **Runaway Rapids** that definitely gives class to the area with its eighteen large water chutes and slides. A high-speed slide and double-wide slides for tubes make the 10- to 12-year-olds happy. A newer corkscrew slide puts a new twist on the downhill motion. The park also has two spa pools. A lazy river ride and a kiddie pool with giant bucket offer an alternative to the slides. You buy bracelets for 2- or 3-hour sessions.

> **DIRECTIONS:** Garden State Parkway to Exit 117, then Rt. 36 to Laurel Ave. **PHONE:** Amusements, 732-495-1400. Water park, 732-495-5240. **WEBSITE:** www.keansburgamusementpark.com.

Point Pleasant Beach

Jenkinson's Amusements at 300 Ocean Avenue dominates the boardwalk here, featuring four indoor arcades and three miniature golf courses for the family crowd. The amusement-ride section includes around thirty rides, with half strictly for younger kids. The rides are mostly midsize, for both kids and adults, and they cover several blocks. On the northern end of the amusement area, Jenkinson's Aquarium is open year-round and offers something for rainy days. Special events, such as fireworks and concerts, take place on the beach, usually Wednesday or Thursday nights.

> **DIRECTIONS:** Garden State Parkway to Exit 98 South to Rt. 34 South to Rt. 35. **PHONE:** 732-892-0600. **WEBSITE:** www.Jenkinsons.com.

Seaside Heights

Seaside is one of the largest boardwalk amusement centers, with lots of amusements and concessions along the boardwalk and the piers. Weekly fireworks go off on Wednesday nights.

The **Casino Pier** (800 Boardwalk) features forty rides, including many large ones like the Ferris Wheel, Skyscraper, and the Pirate Ship, plus an assortment of bumper cars, a log flume, and kiddie rides as well as a Haunted House ride. The indoor section features an authentic 1910 American-made wooden carousel. Along the boardwalk there are numerous indoor arcades, such as Coin Castle, that include air hockey games and food stands along with the usual Skeeball and video games. Rides are active all day. **PHONE:** 732-793-6488. **WEBSITE:** www.casinopiernj.com. Just north of the pier is a half-mile long skyride (Fee: $) that takes you to the far northern end of the boardwalk.

Across from Casino Pier is **Jenkinson's Breakwater Beach** (800 Ocean Terrace). This is a full-sized water park that offers water slides, Patriots Plunge, Krazy Krick, the Cannonball, and an interactive children's play area called the Perfect Storm. **ADMISSION:** $$$$$. Three-hour and twilight admissions are less. **PHONE:** 732-793-6488. **WEBSITE:** www.casinopiernj.com/breakwaterbeach.

About a mile down the boardwalk is **Funtown Pier** (1930 Boardwalk, Seaside Park). Rides here include the Tower of Fear, a looping coaster, and the old Giant Wheel. Altogether there are forty rides, half for kiddies. All-day (12–6) prices on summer weekdays. **PHONE:** 732-830-7437. **WEBSITE:** www.funtownpier.com.

> **DIRECTIONS:** Garden State Parkway to Exit 82 to Rt. 37 East through Toms River to bridge; keep left for Seaside Heights.
> **WEBSITE:** www.seasideheightstourism.com.

Beach Haven

A small cluster of amusements caters to families on Long Beach Island. On the square block at Bay and Taylor Avenues, you'll find **Thundering Surf,** which is a combination of six curling water slides, the Crazy Lazy River, and a small kids area called Cowabunga Beach, with dancing fountains and a Super Soaker Waterworks. Next to it is Settler's Mill, a fancy miniature golf complex complete with waterfall (609-492-0869; www.thunderingsurfwaterpark.com). A block away, at 7th Street, is the Victorian-themed **Fantasy Island,** which includes a small coaster, kiddie rides, Ferris wheel, carousel, arcades, and an old-fashioned ice-cream parlor. The most adventurous ride here is Max Flight, a flight simulator that rotates 360 degrees in all directions. (609-492-4000; www.fantasyislandpark .com.)

Atlantic City

Directly across from Trump's Taj Mahal (Virginia & Boardwalk) is the **Steel Pier,** which is open during the warm-weather season (609-345-4893; www.steelpier.com). Coasters, flume ride, go-karts, Ferris wheel, carousel, the Rocket, a roller coaster with spinning cars, and many kiddie rides combine with cotton candy and hot dogs.

The venerable Central Pier (1400 Boardwalk) has been renovated after a 2009 fire and hosts a large video arcade, paintball, and go-karts. Most casino hotels along the boardwalk have at least one video arcade room available.

Ocean City

The piers here are actually on the inland side of the boardwalk. A giant Ferris wheel dominates the skyline at **Gillian's Wonderland Pier** (Boardwalk & 6th; 609-399-7082, www.gillians.com). This amusement park has a few adult rides, such as a log flume and a small coaster, but the majority of the thirty-five rides and attractions are for the smaller set. There's also an indoor area with a monorail and kiddie rides for inclement weather. **Playland's Castaway Cove** (Boardwalk & 10th; 609-399-4751, www.boardwalkfun.com) offers arcade games and more than thirty rides, many for younger children. **Gillian's Island Waterpark** (Boardwalk at Plymouth Place) has a wide range of water slides, a children's water-play area, and a lazy river packed into a relatively small space. And Playland's Pier 9 (Boardwalk & 9th) features a go-kart track under the boardwalk.

> **WEBSITE:** www.oceancitynj.com.

Wildwood

New Jersey's largest boardwalk stretches almost 2 miles from North Wildwood through Wildwood itself. In addition to the numerous games of chance, arcades, food stands, and souvenir shops, there are three large amusement piers. **Morey's Surfside Pier** (Boardwalk & 25th St., N. Wildwood) at the northern end is the most visible because of the really high AtmosFear, Sky Scraper, and Condor rides. This pier offers all sorts of amusements, including a double log flume and the Doo Wopper coaster with spinning cars. There are go-karts, too, as there are on all the three Morey piers. There's also a complete water park (Ocean-Oasis) at the end of the pier. It includes a kids' area with a dumping water bucket, an endless river, and plenty of turning, twisting waterslides.

The middle pier, **Mariner's Landing** (Boardwalk & Schellenger), includes a Raging Waters park with plenty of water slides, raft run, rope swing, endless river, activity pool, and other water fun for kids. A total of thirty thrill and smaller rides are all packed onto this pier and offer plenty of variety for everyone.

The **Adventure Pier** (Boardwalk & Spencer) on the south has the fewest rides, but there are still more than a dozen rides here.

> **ADMISSION:** Pay as you go with tickets or get passes for rides on all three piers ($$$$$$), a waterparks-only pass, or a combination pass.
> **PHONE:** 609-522-3900. **WEBSITE:** www.moreyspiers.com.

The Zoom Phloom at Morey's Surfside Pier in Wildwood is one of the longest, tallest, and steepest log flumes on the East Coast. *(Photo by Patrick Sarver)*

Across the boardwalk from Mariner's Landing is a separate water park, **Splash Zone.** It has plenty of speed slides and chutes, body flumes, giant water blasters, and a big raft ride as well as a shaded wading pool and a lazy river. Hurricane Island is an interactive play area with blasters, sprays, and other fun stuff for kids.

HOURS: Memorial–Labor Day; call or check website for hours.
ADMISSION: $$$$$. Limited-time rates available.
DISCOUNT: Under 48 inches. **PHONE:** 609-729-5600.
WEBSITE: www.splashzonewaterpark.com.

MINIATURE GOLF COURSES

There are miniature golf courses in almost every corner of the state, from the simple and traditional to those that look like they were designed for DisneyWorld to indoor courses that feature fluorescent scenes illuminated by black light. The greatest concentrations are along Jersey Shore boardwalks and at other Shore towns. What follows is a partial list of miniature golf courses that are especially notable and appeal the most to children.

Atlantic City Miniature Golf

Located at the center of the Atlantic City Boardwalk, this eighteen-hole course features numerous bronze sculptures, miniature waterfalls, fountains, and a scenic colonnade for a backdrop. Kennedy Plaza is on the National Registry of Historic Sites. There's also a picnic circle, amphitheater, and the JFK Memorial Courtyard surrounding the course. The course offers elevated greens with realistic contours, roughs, and sand traps.

> **LOCATION:** I Kennedy Plaza, Atlantic City (Atlantic County), across from Boardwalk Hall. **HOURS:** Apr.–Oct., Sun.–Thu., IO A.M.–II P.M.; Fri.–Sat., IO A.M.–midnight. **ADMISSION:** $$. **PHONE:** 609-347-1661. **WEBSITE:** www.acminigolf.com.

Goofy Golf

The course is rather simple and small, and the greens could use a little repair. What makes this interesting are the fun figures that younger kids will like. There's a Teenage Ninja Turtle, a large brontosaurus, and a number of colorful animal figures. This is an old-fashioned shore miniature golf course that has a certain novelty quality to its "scenery" that overcomes any shortcomings in the actual golfing experience.

> **LOCATION:** 920 Boardwalk, Ocean City (Cape May County). **ADMISSION:** $$. **PHONE:** 609-398-9662.

Dynamite Falls Adventure Golf

This eighteen-hole course includes putting into an ore car, unique water features that carry your ball to different levels, and a hole with fountain explosions. Lots of rocks as well as water features create an attractive course. This course also has baby-putters for really little kids and will give them quick lessons in put-put golf if you ask. In addition to the mini golf, there's a Gemstone Mining Adventure in which kids can pan for gold just like in the Old West while learning about the history of the gold rush. They also get a bag of mining ore. Everyone gets to keep the gems they pan and they can learn about each one. Part of a complex that also includes Funtime Junction play center.

LOCATION: 400 Fairfield Rd., Fairfield (Essex County).
HOURS: Apr.–Oct., Sun., 11–6; Mon.–Thu., 3–8; Fri., 3–10; and Sat., 10–10. **ADMISSION:** $$. Under 3 free. **PHONE:** 973-808-0300.
WEBSITE: www.dynamitefalls.com.

Congo Falls Adventure Golf

Three courses can be found here: Congo Queen, Solomon's Mine, and the all-indoor Lost City. A towering King Kong, waterfalls, unusual rock formations, caves, and special effects highlight this Disney-style layout along the boardwalk. The area is well landscaped, with large figures—including King Kong and a giant lizard—as underground greens. There are lots of water features, rock work, and old timbers as well as a cave and a snake pit. These eighteen-hole courses have plenty to appeal to young and old alike.

LOCATION: 1132 Boardwalk, Ocean City (Cape May County).
HOURS: 8 A.M.–midnight. **ADMISSION:** $$. **PHONE:** 609-398-1211.
WEBSITE: www.congofalls.com.

Monster Mini Golf

This is a national franchise chain, and there are currently two locations in New Jersey, each taking a somewhat different spooky look. These all-indoors eighteen-hole courses are set in black-light fluorescent landscapes filled with monsters, goblins, and other Halloweenish figures. You might hit your ball through a haunted tree or bump into a robed skeleton as you negotiate the angles of your hole.

LOCATION: 194 Rt. 46 East, Fairfield (Essex County), and 49 East Midland Ave., Paramus (Bergen County). **HOURS:** Tue.–Thu., 2–9; Fri., 2–10; Sat., noon–10; Sun., noon–8. **ADMISSION:** $$.
PHONE: 973-244-0026 and 201-261-0032.
WEBSITE: www.monsterminigolf.com.

Cape May Miniature Golf

This course is combined with Cocomoe's Ice Cream Parlor, which puts a happy touch to the end of a round of miniature golf for kids and offers a view of the course from the back deck. The well-groomed eighteen-hole landscaped course features a waterfall, rock formations, a play-through cave, and real sand traps. The theme is mostly rock garden.

LOCATION: 315 Jackson St., Cape May (Cape May County).
HOURS: Summer, daily, 10:30–10:30. **ADMISSION:** $$.
PHONE: 609-884-2222. **WEBSITE:** www.capemayminigolf.com.

You might hit your ball through a haunted tree or bump into a robed skeleton as you negotiate the holes at Monster Mini Golf in Fairfield and Paramus, among the new wave of indoor black-light courses. *(Photo courtesy of Monster Mini Golf)*

Pirate Island Golf

Journey through theme-park-style attractions with animated pirates, caves, waterfalls, suspension bridges, and pirate ships filling the landscape as you negotiate an eighteen-hole course. There are a variety of interesting water features, old timbers, and large ships to enhance the nautical theme and create a fun atmosphere for all ages.

> **LOCATION:** 33rd St. & Landis Ave., Sea Isle City; 27th St. and Dune Dr., Avalon; and 112 9th St., Ocean City (Cape May County).
> **HOURS:** 9 A.M.–11:30 P.M. in season; until 11 in Ocean City.
> **ADMISSION:** $$. **PHONE:** 609-263-8344; 609-368-8344; 609-398-9938.
> **WEBSITE:** www.pirateislandgolf.com.

Playland's Golden Galleon Pirate's Golf

This course features two nineteen-hole layouts. The theme here is pirates, with a 20-foot-high cutlass-bearing pirate and a pirate ship forming the centerpieces of this boardwalk course. A giant octopus sprawls above the entrance and there's a miniature lighthouse. The holes here also offer some challenging angles on shots.

> **LOCATION:** 1120 Boardwalk, Ocean City (Cape May Country).
> **HOURS:** 8 A.M.–11 P.M. **ADMISSION:** $$. **PHONE:** 609-399-3186.
> **WEBSITE:** www.oceancityfun.com/pirategolf.asp.

Under the Sea Miniature Golf

A Sponge Bob–like theme of under-the-ocean creatures, shipwrecks, pirate chests, and the like is designed to appeal to younger kids. You play a couple of holes downstairs by the entrance, then head upstairs to a large room illuminated in black light. The entrance is a little hard to find, tucked away at the back of an outdoor food court.

LOCATION: 744 Boardwalk, Ocean City (Cape May County).
HOURS: Daily, 9 A.M.–11 P.M. **ADMISSION:** $. **PHONE:** 609-398-0300.

Duffer's Miniature Golf

A compact but nicely landscaped adjunct to a restaurant/ice cream shop that features an ocean theme and singing animatronic pelicans. With statuary of colorful fish, an octopus, a wrecked pirate ship, and an undersea castle, this is definitely a course designed to entertain the kids before they get their ice cream.

LOCATION: 5210 Pacific Avenue ,Wildwood (Cape May County).
Call for hours and prices. **PHONE:** 609-729-1817.
WEBSITE: www.dufferswildwood.com.

Pirates of Wildwood Miniature Golf

Another indoor course that is illuminated by black light, it features glowing figures and the greens outlined in fluorescent colors. The theme here is pirates, and the atmosphere is a lot like a fun house, especially since you wear 3-D glasses to enhance the depth of the wall art.

LOCATION: 3400 Boardwalk, Wildwood (Cape May County).
HOURS: Summer, daily, 9 A.M.–midnight; shorter hours in spring and fall. **ADMISSION:** $. **PHONE:** 609-602-4354.

Willowbrook Golf Center

Some courses seem dedicated to water, others to flowers, still others to cute figures. With large reddish cliffs, red gravel landscaping, caves, and some strategically placed boulders, these two courses are definitely dedicated to the world of rock. In fact, for New Jersey, it looks quite Southwestern, which is what gives it an unusual appeal.

LOCATION: 366 Rt. 46 Service Road East, Wayne (Passaic County).
At intersection of Rt. 23. **HOURS:** Vary by season; call.
ADMISSION: $$. **PHONE:** 973-256-6922.
WEBSITE: www.willowbrookgolfcenter.com.

Branchburg Family Golf Center

Two eighteen-hole courses offer a fun challenge amid cascading waterfalls and beautiful landscapes. The course is well designed to appeal to players of all ages, and the entire facility was recently refurbished and relandscaped. There are also batting machines and a driving range next to the miniature golf courses, and golf lessons are offered.

LOCATION: Rt. 22, Branchburg (Somerset County).
HOURS: Daily; hours vary with season. **ADMISSION:** $$.
PHONE: 908-541-0465. **WEBSITE:** www.branchburggolf.net.

Pleasant Valley Golf Center

A pleasant blend of traditional miniature golf and contemporary design, with lots of flowers and gazebos combined with such classic touches as a Liberty Bell, statuary, a lighthouse, and a railroad "crossing."

LOCATION: 93 Rt. 73, Voorhees (Camden County). **HOURS:** 10–9, vary with season. **PHONE:** 856-767-2167. **WEBSITE:** www.pvminigolf.com.

Fox Meadow Golf Center

A relaxing and well-landscaped eighteen-hole course filled with waterfalls, streams, and smooth greens. The emphasis here is on the water and the greenery. A driving range and golfing lessons are also offered at this facility.

LOCATION: 2880 Rt. 73 North, Maple Shade (Burlington County).
HOURS: Peak season, 8 A.M.–11 P.M.; off-peak, until 9 P.M.
ADMISSION: $$. Children 12 and under, $. **PHONE:** 856-755-3555.
WEBSITE: www.foxmeadowgolfcenter.net.

Hyatt Hills Golf Complex

A picturesque waterfall cascading down a boulder "mountain," wandering streams, bridges, and ponds highlight this nicely landscaped eighteen-hole course. The greens at the "Mt. Hyatt" course are large, and the facility is attractive and well maintained with plenty of water features in a parklike setting. A driving range and golf lessons are also available.

LOCATION: 1300 Raritan Rd., Clark (Union County).
HOURS: Summer, daily, 7 A.M.–10 P.M.; shorter hours in spring and fall. **ADMISSION:** $$. Children 16 and under, $.
PHONE: 732-669-9100. **WEBSITE:** www.hyatthills.com. (BP)

Creative Fun

Acting classes at the Mayo Center for the Arts in Morristown cover acting skills, stage presence, and character development, culminating in a live performance. *(Photo courtesy of the Mayo Center)*

THEATER ARTS
Mayo Center for the Arts

Children's theater classes here run 14 weeks and work toward an open class performance. During the school year, there are after-school and longer Saturday classes. Classes are taught in a number of categories. Musical Theater offers classes for ages 5 to 18, starting with basics of singing, movement, acting, and stage presence and developing those talents through six age levels. There is a similar progression for acting classes (6–18 in four age levels), including acting skills, stage presence, character development, and improvisation. Also offered are two levels for singing technique, with vocal coaches teaching proper vocal techniques and performance.

> **LOCATION:** 100 South St., Morristown (Morris County).
> **HOURS:** Weekdays, 4–8:30, and Sat., 9–2. See website for specific class times. **ADMISSION:** Semester tuition. **PHONE:** 973-539-0345. **WEBSITE:** www.mayoarts.org.

Brightest Star Performing Arts

A broad range of classes for kids interested in theater are held at the Bickford Theatre at the Morris Museum. Students participate in group activities led by art professionals in weekly classes for ages 1 and up. Moms & Tots Music sessions are filled with singing, movement, stories, games, and instrument playing. Rhythm & Rhyme Showtime offers games, music, dance, improvisation, and fairy tales. Creative Drama & Song has kids bringing featured storybooks to life with music, movement, and dramatic components. Dance Party Fun covers beginning dance techniques. The flagship program, Musical Theatre Workshops, gives kids a chance to develop singing, acting, and dancing skills and ends with a musical theater presentation.

> **LOCATION:** At Morris Museum, 6 Normandy Heights Rd., Morristown (Morris County). **HOURS:** Vary.
> **ADMISSION:** Semester tuition. **PHONE:** 973-971-3726.
> **WEBSITE:** www.morrismuseum.org/static/bickford/star.html. (BP)

Growing Stage

Classes for preschool to high school are offered that are fun and engaging, taught by professionally trained teaching artists. One-hour classes include Creative Dramatics for preschool to grade 3, which introduces kids to the theater arts as an extension of their imaginations and role playing through creative games, story dramatization, and improvisation. Performing Arts Workshops for 4th through 8th graders teaches kids the basics of stage performance, including warm-up techniques for voice and body, improvisation, theater games, stage direction, and scene work. The Actor Speaks for 7th to 9th graders introduces children to the basic elements of playwriting, including character, plot, and setting; they develop their own scenes, which they rehearse for a final performance. Musical Performance Lab, grades 4–6 and 7–9, focuses on song interpretation, movement, and performance in both a solo and group setting, including performing for a live audience. There's also a course on Blacklight Puppetry, in which students adapt a piece of mythology into script, create a storyboard, construct two-dimensional puppets, and use them for a presentation to family and friends. Classes typically run an hour on Saturdays for 10 weeks.

LOCATION: Historic Palace Theatre, Rt. 183, 7 Ledgewood Ave., Netcong (Morris County). **HOURS:** Sat., classes 9:30–1. **ADMISSION:** Semester tuition. **PHONE:** 973-347-4946. **WEBSITE:** www.growingstage.com. (SC)

All Children's Theatre

Children ages 4–17 can gain experience with comedy, creative dramatics, and singing and dancing for musical theater as well as scenery design. All programs end with a performance on the last day. Programs for elementary and middle school grades are held on Saturday mornings and afternoons. A special program offered for ages 4–5 on Saturday afternoons includes acting, singing, and dancing.

LOCATION: Parsippany Theatre, 1180 Rt. 46 West, Parsippany (Morris County). **HOURS:** Primarily on Sat. **ADMISSION:** Varies with class. **PHONE:** 973-335-5328. **WEBSITE:** www.allchildrenstheatre.org. (SC)

Front & Center for Performing Arts

Three large studio rooms, a private voice room, homework room, and more are the setting for a rounded curriculum including dance, acting, vocal training, and musical theater. There are many performance opportunities, including a full musical production in January and a year-end revue in May. Musical theater sessions are set up by age group, from age 2½ up. The youngest sessions, Broadway Babes and Show Time Jr., introduce kids to the world of creative movement and theater. There are games, storytelling, development of motor skills, and song. Show Time for kids 5–9 provides fundamental dance and vocal skills as well as acting techniques through games, improvisation, and sight-singing. There's also a performing version focusing on preparation for a choreographed number at a competition. The Production class (ages 6–12) leads to a small production of a Junior Show. Musical Theatre (age 10 and up) provides instruction in singing, acting, and dancing. The Drama Classes (5 and up) starts with Acting Out, with acting games, storytelling, and basic theater terms. Creating Drama (7 and up) teaches through theater games and improvisation, self-expression, and basic scene work. The Production class leads to a small production at a Junior show. Scene Study is for more experienced students, with in-depth focus on scenes and monologues. There's also a Voice course and numerous classes in dance, from Hippity Hop and Ballet to Lyrical and Tap.

> **LOCATION:** 95 Victory Rd., Springfield (Union County). **HOURS:** Class times vary; check website for schedule. **ADMISSION:** Varies with class. **PHONE:** 973-258-1123. **WEBSITE:** www.front-n-center.com. ⑤ⓒ

Playwrights Theatre of New Jersey

In the PTNJ's Creative Arts Academy, classes are taught by practicing theater artists, including working actors, writers, and directors. Students work with one another, creating characters and telling stories. Class content varies based on the school year of each student. There's Creative Play for K and pre-K featuring storytelling, drama exercises, and other creative activities. Playmakers for grades 1–3 includes theater games, pantomime, and improvisation. Musical Performance for grades 4–6 explores sound and movement and playing imaginative theater games. In Acting Lab for grades 4–6, kids act, play, and develop play-building skills. Playwriting Lab for kids 4–6 teaches the basic elements of playwriting, including characters, dialogue, and building scenes and stories. There's also Musical Performance for grades 7–9. There are ten sessions in each course.

> **LOCATION:** 33 Green Village Rd., Madison (Morris County). **HOURS:** Classes are after school and on Saturdays; see website for schedule. **ADMISSION:** Semester tuition. **PHONE:** 973-514-1787, ext. 21. **WEBSITE:** www.ptnj.org. ⑤ⓒ

Theatre School at Paper Mill Playhouse

This school at the Paper Mill, the state theater of New Jersey, generally offers around ten classes a semester for kids aged 4–12 in which they can learn singing, acting, and dancing. Classes typically are an hour and run for 18 to 20 weeks. Classes include Musical Theatre Workshop, focusing on acting through songs; Acting & Improv, with theater games and improvisation exercises for novice actors; Acting for the Camera, which leads kids through the commercial audition process; Theatre Tots, which brings fairy tales to life; Broadway Tap & Jazz, which teaches the language of dance through Broadway choreography; and Creative Drama I and II, in which students participate in theater games, improvisation, and scene studies and then advance to scenes, songs, and performing a scripted play in costume.

LOCATION: 22 Brookside Dr., Millburn (Essex County).
HOURS: Weekdays after school and Sat. mornings.
ADMISSION: Semester tuition. **PHONE:** 973-376-4343.
WEBSITE: www.papermill.org.

Arts Maplewood/What Exit? Theatre Company

The Performance Classroom put on by What Exit? Theatre Company at the Burgdorff Center for the Performing Arts introduces and teaches children about theater. There are creative music theater classes for grades K–4. Music Theater for grades 1–3 has students collaborating with teaching artists to create original stories and write songs while learning basic musical theater techniques. The Performance Playhouse, for grades 2–4, lets kids have the fun of putting on a show. They learn elements of acting, dance, and singing. Classes run 12 weeks, one hour each.

LOCATION: 10 Durand Rd., Maplewood (Essex County).
HOURS: One-hour classes Monday after school.
ADMISSION: Tuition by semester. **PHONE:** 973-378-2133 and 973-763-4029. **WEBSITES:** www.artsmaplewood.org and www.whatexittheatre.com. (sc)

Kelsey Theatre at Mercer County Community College

The Kelsey Kids Playshops provides classes in theater arts for grades K–7. PlayTime for K–2 is a one-hour course held at 10 on Saturday mornings in which kids explore movement and storytelling while dramatizing stories. Playing Around With Theatre for grades 3–5 meets for 8 weeks later on Saturday as students create their own improvisational scenes. The PlayShops Master Class for grades 5–7 is a 2-hour course that meets for 26 weeks in which students create, script, rehearse, and present an original play.

LOCATION: 1200 Old Trenton Rd., West Windsor (Mercer County).
HOURS: Sat. mornings. **ADMISSION:** Semester tuition.
PHONE: 609-570-3333. **WEBSITE:** www.kelseytheatre.net. (sc)

Strand Theater School of the Arts

This musical theater program is designed for students aged 4 and up and is held at a historic theater. Daily rehearsals and specialized games and activities focus on teamwork, movement, vocal techniques, and acting. The 10-week sessions are taught by professional instructors in musical theater, art, acting, vocals, and more. Classes are held after school and evenings, with added Saturday workshops. There's a Junior Musical Theater Workshop for children aged 4–7 in which kids learn appropriate movement and song as well as acting basics. The Youth Musical Theater Workshop for ages 8–12 combines acting, singing, and dancing with basic scene work. There's also an advanced version that continues on from there. The Strand also offers an acting and improvisation class as well as Broadway Voices, in which students study voice and diction, song analysis, and audition technique.

> **LOCATION:** 400 Clifton Ave., Lakewood (Ocean County).
> **HOURS:** Weekdays after school and Sat. mornings.
> **ADMISSION:** Semester tuition. **PHONE:** 732-367-7789.
> **WEBSITE:** www.strand.org/SSOA.aspx. (sc)

Essex Youth Theater

This specialized program uses custom scripts to provide equal roles for a specific number of students. Each class includes acting exercises, theater games, and improvisation to develop dramatic skills. There are four age levels. Elves (ages 4–5) participate in plays like the *Teddy Bears' Picnic*, providing animal characters for nonreaders who love to play-act and pretend. Fauns (6–8) get into scripts like *If Kids Ruled the World*, in which they play weekly theater games and exercises. Centaurs (8½–12) practice theater magic in *The School for Witches & Wizards*, enhancing their dramatic skills and creativity. In Creative Dramatics (7–11) kids create a play and their own characters and scenes. There are improvisations, lots of theater games, and monologues. It ends with kids performing their play at the Studio Playhouse. All classes run ten to twelve sessions.

> **LOCATION:** Montclair Operetta Club, 494 Valley Rd., Upper Montclair (Essex County). **HOURS:** Vary with class.
> **ADMISSION:** Semester tuition. **PHONE:** 973-746-3303.
> **WEBSITE:** www.essexyouththeater.com. (sc)

Performers Theatre Workshop

Theater arts classes are provided at this organization for children aged 3 and up. This center offers more than eighty classes in voice, song interpretation, musical theater, jazz/hip-hop, tap, ballet/modern, stage acting, acting for TV, and comedy and improv. Private lessons are also available. Many classes put on end-of-the-semester shows. There are three age groups. Broadway Kids (3–5) combines imaginative play, singing, acting, theater games, dance, and movement to create the building blocks of the performing arts. There's also a beginner's ballet class. The Junior Division (5–7) has four one-hour classes. The Jr. Jr. Division integrates jazz and tap dancing, acting, and singing. There's also a continuing ballet and a Jazz/ Hip-Hop class and a Glee singing class using songs from the TV show. For kids 9–18, classes are divided into acting, dancing, and singing, with such classes as Group Acting, TV Commercials & On-Camera Acting; Jazz/Hip-Hop, Tap, and Ballet; and Group Voice, Glee, and Sight-Singing. Classes last ten sessions each.

> **LOCATION:** One Pierson Rd., Maplewood, and 70 Mt. Pleasant Ave., Livingston (Essex County). **HOURS:** Weekday classes in Maplewood; Saturday classes in Livingston. **ADMISSION:** Course tuition. **PHONE:** 973-992-3034. **WEBSITE:** www.ptwonline.com. (SC)

The Music Shop Performing Arts Center

The Musical Theatre workshops at this center combine vocal, dance, and acting training with audition technique and performance preparation. Classes include Introduction to Dance, in which kids learn basic dance steps for musical theater dancing. Musical Theatre Vocal Fundamentals focuses on good singing and healthy vocal technique. Improvisation and Acting teaches acting skills through improvisation and role playing. Musical Theatre Workshop is a comprehensive class combining acting, singing, dancing, and character development. Classes are for twelve sessions. A number of different levels and types of music programs are also offered. There are private lessons, Kindermusik, musical theater, a music technology lab, and jazz studies for experienced saxophonists.

> **LOCATION:** 56 Fanny Rd., Boonton (Morris County).
> **HOURS:** After school; see website for schedule.
> **ADMISSION:** Semester tuition. **PHONE:** 973-334-8484.
> **WEBSITE:** www.themusicshop.com. (SC)

Annie's Playhouse

This school for the performing arts offers musical theater, acting, singing, dancing, gymnastics, and private lessons. Musical Theatre classes include Broadway Babies, Mini-Musical Theatre, Musical Theatre Jr., Musical Theatre Workshop, and Musical Theatre Masters. Acting classes include Creative Drama, Theatre Production, TV Commercial and Film Acting, and Acting & Improv. Dance includes Tap, Jazz/Hip-Hop, Ballet, Pre-Ballet/Tap, and Tumbling. For career-oriented students, there are also audition-only classes, competition dance, musical theater companies, and on-camera training.

> **LOCATION:** Far Hills Mall, 35 Rt. 206, Far Hills (Somerset County).
> **HOURS:** After school and Sat. classes. **ADMISSION:** Semester tuition.
> **PHONE:** 908-658-3002. **WEBSITE:** www.anniesplayhouse.com. (BP)(SC)

Acting with Emily

Eight-week courses are provided in theater, TV, and commercial training for kids aged 3 and up. Parents can find out if their children have what it takes to be on TV and if they are ready for a professional acting career. Each class uses video playback and authentic scripts from TV shows, movies, and commercials to help train kids to feel comfortable in front of a camera. They learn how to audition, meet new people, and be confident. A professional photo shoot is included. Parents attend their own workshops to get the technical details. In Acting for the Camera, students work on camera with scripts (handpicked for each student) with modified TV, movie, and commercial scripts for emergent readers. On-camera Scene Study helps students aiming for the school play or Broadway realize their full potential as actors. In Acting for Commercials, students work individually and in groups to improve their on-camera presence. Creative Drama allows students to develop original characters and plot lines based on stories existing or imagined by the class. In Introduction to Musical Theatre, popular and age-appropriate Broadway songs are learned in a class specifically designed for young voices. Improvisation helps younger kids loosen up on stage and screen and in auditions, sharpens their listening skills, and teaches them how to create characters. For the youngest children, classes combine modified theater games, on-camera exercises, and simulated on-camera auditions. Kids are grouped by school grade.

> **LOCATION:** 94 Baker St., Maplewood (Essex County).
> **HOURS:** After school and weekend sessions.
> **ADMISSION:** Semester tuition. **PHONE:** 973-232-6679.
> **WEBSITE:** www.actingwithemily.com. ⒝ⓟ

Cresskill Performing Arts

Around twenty different classes are offered that are related to dancing, singing, art, and acting. Classes include Once Upon a Time (ages 4–7), where kids act out fairy tales and have a related craft activity; Kids Concoctions to Make and Take (8–12), with unusual art/craft items; Ballet Beginnings (4) covers ballet basics. There's also Intro to Jazz & Tap (5–7); Theater Games & Acting (5–9), a beginning acting class; Preteen Hip-Hop, with current music and latest dance moves; Preteen Acting, with preparation for success in monologues and scenes; and Intro to Musical Theater, with singing, acting, and dancing. Classes run September to June.

> **LOCATION:** 300 Knickerbocker Rd., Suite 110, Cresskill (Bergen County), and 260 Grand Ave., Englewood (Bergen County).

HOURS: Weekdays after school/evening and Sat.; Tue.–Wed. only in Englewood. **ADMISSION:** Class tuition. **PHONE:** 201-390-7513. **WEBSITE:** www.cresskillperformingarts.com. (BP)

Algonquin Arts Theatre Performing Arts Academy

Drama and music classes at this academy run for 9 weeks for ages 6 and up. Creative Dramatics (ages 6–8) teaches role playing and make believe by using theater games and improvisation. The Independent Film Maker (11 and up) explores the craft of making a film from a story idea, shooting, and editing. Acting for Young Actors (11 and up) strengthens young actors' skills through improvisation, movement, voice, character, and story creation. The Broadway Singer I and II and Broadway Dancer I and II teach basics as well as personal interpretation and then provide more experience. Musical Theatre I, II, and III is a sequence that helps kids learn vocal, dance, and acting techniques as part of a musical cast. There's also the Algonquin Glee Singers and the School of Rock (11 and up), which explore their respective genres from the basics and beyond.

LOCATION: 60 Abe Voorhees Dr., Manasquan (Monmouth County). **HOURS:** Weekday evenings. **ADMISSION:** Semester tuition. **PHONE:** 732-528-3735. **WEBSITE:** www.algonquinarts.org.

ART

Art-4-All

Designed for beginners to learn the creative processes behind making art step by step, lessons cover the use of line, shape, form, texture, and color and media from pencil, pastel, and painting to collage and clay. The emphasis is on originality and creativity. All classes meet for ten sessions, once a week. Classes include Art for the Preschooler (ages 3–5), where kids explore color, texture, line, and shape with tempera, watercolor, markets, collage, printmaking, and clay. Basic Art Skills (6–9) is a multimedia class with an emphasis on drawing and painting with various media to help children develop a personal style. Drawing & Painting (9–13) teaches drawing skills to encourage personal expression by experimentation with various media. Pottery & Ceramics (6 and up) emphasizes hand building with coil, slab, and modeling clay in a variety of approaches. Art for Parent and Child (3–5) allows sharing of the creative process and explores colors, lines, and textures with a variety of materials. Ceramics for Parent and Child (6 and up) lets kids and parents explore working with clay together to create decorative and functional forms.

LOCATION: 265 Main St., Somerville (Somerset County).
HOURS: Tue., Thu., Sat. **ADMISSION:** Semester tuition.
PHONE: 908-725-4490. **WEBSITE:** www.art-4-all-inc.com. (BP)

Artisan Studio

This studio offers a variety of art classes for preschoolers and up in which they learn the basics while having fun. Sessions include KinderArt, Mommy & Me, Young Artisans, Famous Artists, Petite Painters, Clay Today, Multi Cultural Arts, Green Scene, and Origami. There's also Basic Drawing, Cars & Toons, Kartoon Kids, and Draw and Paint for Kids. Other classes are designed for both children and adults, such as Papier Mache Away. Plus there are three levels of Helping Hands art classes that are designed for special needs children.

LOCATION: 9 N. Main St. (Rt. 79), Marlboro (Monmouth County).
HOURS: Mon.–Thu., day and evening classes; Fri. and Sat., daytime classes. **ADMISSION:** Varies with class; monthly fee.
PHONE: 732-294-0234. **WEBSITE:** www.artisanstudio9.com. (BP)(SC)

Bass Art Studio

Students aged 4–13 playfully explore and experiment with a variety of media in 12-week sessions. Painting, Drawing & Mixed Media, for ages 4–10 in three age groups, teaches kids about the concepts of line, value, proportion, rhythm, and color through projects that cover a spectrum of media such as paint, pen and ink, printmaking, collage, and clay. There's also Painting & Drawing I for kids 11–14, in which they learn the fundamentals of drawing, painting, and composition as well as paint mixing, color theory, and space and line. Sculpt It! (8–12) provides kids with a chance to work with clay, plaster, cardboard, wood, wire, and found objects as well as modeling, carving, and mold making. And Drawing Basics (9–14) shows them how to translate the world of 3D onto a picture plane.

LOCATION: 202 Park St., Montclair (Essex County).
HOURS: Mon. and Wed.–Fri. after school. **ADMISSION:** Class tuition.
PHONE: 973-509-7588. **WEBSITES:** www.bassartstudioofnj.com and www.fernbass.com. (BP)(SC)

Creative Kids Place

This studio offers weekly classes in painting, drawing, sculpting, and design for kids ages 3–9. Children explore a new experience in art each week, using different art materials to make their own works while learning different art elements such as color, lines, shape, and techniques. One week may be clay; the next could be painting.

After-school and summer camp art classes at the Hunterdon Art Museum in Clinton cover a wide range of art subjects and media. *(Photo courtesy of the Hunterdon Art Museum)*

Classes generally run eight weeks. Kids paint landscapes, design T-shirts, do chalk rubbings, create clay sculptures, and more—all with a sense of fun.

LOCATION: 33 Railroad Pl., Hopewell (Hunterdon County).
HOURS: Weekdays; hours vary with class; see website for schedule.
ADMISSION: Course fee. **PHONE:** 609-466-KIDS.
WEBSITE: www.thecreativekidsplace.com. (BP) (SC)

Hunterdon Museum of Art

An extensive listing of classes is offered for preschoolers on up. For preschoolers, there's Art for Two (ages 2½–4; five sessions), Art Start: Colorful Creations (3½–5) in two 5-week sessions, and Kinder-Art for 10 weeks. Little artists explore color and creativity in a wide range of materials in each session. After-school classes are set up by age, and there are around twenty courses to choose from. They run the gamut from 2D/3D Art Studio, Glass Fusing; Draw, Paint & Sculpt; and Comic Book Creation to Van Gogh and Friends, Japanese Anime & Superheroes; Claymation Nation; and Sculpture Studio. There are also special workshops on Sundays from time to time. And in ArtZone, families with young children who are visiting the museum for the day can make art (free with admission).

LOCATION: 7 Lower Center Rd., Clinton (Hunterdon County).
HOURS: Museum: Tue.–Sun., 11–5. Classes Tue.–Fri. after school and
Sat. morning, with preschool classes also during weekdays.
ADMISSION: Course tuition. **PHONE:** 908-735-8415.
WEBSITE: www.hunterdonartmuseum.org. (BP)(SC)

PlayArt Creative Learning Center

A variety of art classes are available here for toddlers to teens.
PlayArt with Mommy (ages 1–3) provides toddlers with a hands-on
program that promotes creative development by creating a "masterpiece," including cooking up all-natural play dough, large-scale
painting, making masks, and creating collages. Four and eight-week
sessions. PlayDate is designed for fun with friends, using a wide variety of materials to create with. These sessions range from mural
painting and scribbling to using clay crayons, creative crafts, and
more. StudioArt is the next level, and kids choose the subjects they
like and get an art history lesson as well as have hands-on fun
exploring different materials, from beading to jewelry making to
mad science. There's also PlayArt Family Night on the third Thursday of the month (6–8 P.M.), with a wide variety of art activities for
children and their families, including mural painting, sand exploration, and crafts.

LOCATION: 27 Chestnut St., Ridgewood (Bergen County).
HOURS: Times vary; see website for schedule.
ADMISSION: Course tuition. **PHONE:** 201-857-2084.
WEBSITE: www.myplayaart.com. (BP)(SC)

The Messy Artist

This studio at the Kaleidoscope Center for the Arts focuses on sensory exploration and the process of art for kids. Children can use
materials in any way they want. Even at age 2, kids express themselves through art, and an open-ended approach encourages in -
dependence and self-esteem. There are Caregiver & Me sessions for
children ages 1½ and older, and drop-off classes for kids 4–6. For
older kids (grades 1–5), there are drawing and painting classes with
more structure and depth. Storybook Art takes kids on a journey
through the world of literature. Each week a class reads a book, and
the book's story and illustrations inspire a project related to the plot
and pictures in the book. Beginning reading, comprehension, and
writing skills are part of this fun class. For Foundations in Art, students explore a variety of materials, including acrylic paint, charcoal,
pencil, clay, pastels, and more. Projects include still-life drawing,
self-portraits, and a variety of abstract and sculptural work. Students

also learn such concepts as color theory, perspective, and the design and use of patterns in art. Classes last 10 weeks.

LOCATION: 60 Valley St., Rear Entrance, South Orange (Essex County).
HOURS: Mon.–Fri., 9:15–5:15. Later on Fri. **ADMISSION:** Semester tuition. **PHONE:** 973-378-2425. **WEBSITE:** www.themessyartist.com. ⓑ ⓢ

Visual Arts Center of New Jersey

Kids Art for ages 3 and up explores a wide variety of media, from drawing and painting to ceramics, sculpture, printmaking, and three-dimensional work. Most classes run 10 weeks except for the 4-week Mommy & Me sessions that introduce kids 3 and up to many art media. There are more than two dozen classes in all, with popular ones repeated at different times. They range from art sampler classes, comic book art, and introduction to drawing and painting to exploring sculpture, ceramics for kids, and fashion illustration. Students are generally grouped into two- or three-year age groups. There's a lot of hands-on fun and learning for everyone.

LOCATION: 68 Elm St., Summit (Union County).
HOURS: Mon.–Fri. after school and on weekends.
ADMISSION: Semester tuition. **PHONE:** 908-273-9121.
WEBSITE: www.artcenternj.org. ⓢ

Appel Farm Arts & Music Center

Classes and workshops are offered in visual arts, drama, and music, with the main focus on art. From the Young at Art parent and child class for kids aged 2–3 to evening cartooning for children 9–12, there are a dozen art class selections. There's Art Starts, with finger painting, collage, and sculpture projects inspired by illustrations in children's literature. Or the DaVinci Drawing Studio, with charcoal, colored pencils, and pastels used in learning techniques of the Renaissance artist. Or Play with Clay, in which kids create fun objects with hand building and the pottery wheel. There is also a series of craft-style workshops, from making wire sculpture to tunnel book art to basketry and porcelain flower making.

In addition to art, there are also drama classes, including Big Theater, an intro to theater via games and dramatic play, with voice, movement, and storytelling. Fantastic Music Theater starts with storytelling and songwriting, then leads into character development with ensemble work, improvisation, and scenes. And there's a percussion class focusing on the basics of rhythm. Most classes are held on Saturdays, but there's Friday for preschoolers and a few weekday evening sessions. Classes run about 10 weeks.

LOCATION: 457 Shirley Rd., Elmer (Salem County). **HOURS:** Vary with class; see website for schedule. **ADMISSION:** Course tuition. **PHONE:** 877-394-6274 **WEBSITE:** www.appelfarm.org.

Express Yourself Studios

Six-week art classes include Mixed Media Workshop (ages 5–8), which covers many techniques and diversity of projects made through painting, drawing, collage, sculpture, clay, and mixed media. Drawing and Painting Workshop (9–12) helps kids develop their art skills and discover their own style and be introduced to specific drawing and painting fundamentals. Cartoon Workshop explores the fundamentals of cartooning and graphic storytelling as kids work on creating their own comic strips. Sculpture involves using clay and hand building through pinching, coiling, slab construction, and modeling. There's also a drop-in art workshop for toddlers on Thursday and Saturday mornings.

LOCATION: 1912 Springfield Ave., Maplewood (Essex County). **HOURS:** Tue.–Fri., 4:30–5:30. **ADMISSION:** Class tuition. **PHONE:** 973-763-5256. **WEBSITE:** www.expressyourselfstudios.com. **(BP)**

Perkins Center for the Arts

This facility is dedicated to providing a wide range of creative classes for ages 3 and up. There are classes in visual and performing arts, a conservatory that offers individual music lessons, and other services. There are classes in art, drama, and pottery. Art classes include Art Exploration; Comic Book Illustration; Little Picasso; Mermaids, Monsters & Pets; The Da Vinci Art Club; Mixed Media; Painting Studio; and Jungle Arts. Pottery includes A Taste of Pottery for parent and child, Exploring Clay, and Welcome to Pottery.

Music classes include Music and Movement for Parents and Children, Puddle Jumpers, and Rise Up Singing. Dance classes include Ballet, Classically Creative Dance, Garden Ballerinas, Jazzy Jam & Jive, Modern Ballet, and Princess Dancers. Drama classes include Acting and Drama, Comedy, and Improvisation. Classes in all categories differ in the two locations.

LOCATION: 395 Kings Hwy., Moorestown (Burlington County), and 30 Irvin Ave., Collingswood (Camden County). **HOURS:** Mon.–Fri. after school and Sat.; see website for schedule. **ADMISSION:** Course tuition. **PHONE:** 856-235-6488 and 856-833-0109. **WEBSITE:** www.perkinscenter.org. **(SC)**

Creative Hands Art Studio

This studio provides professional instruction in drawing, painting, sculpture, ceramics, and pottery wheel for ages 3½ and up. Classes for children aged 3–6 show kids how to have fun while creating their own works of art and include Mommy & Me classes to Kindergarten Kids. These meet for 10 weeks and combine different media, including drawing, painting, sculpture, and ceramics. Classes for ages 6 and up are grouped in specific age ranges, covering the basics of drawing, various types of painting, sculpture, and ceramics. There are foundational classes combining different media as well as more specialized sessions in specific media.

> **LOCATION:** 14 Kings Rd., Madison (Morris County).
> **HOURS:** Weekdays and Sat. **ADMISSION:** Class tuition.
> **PHONE:** 973-604-0773. **WEBSITE:** www.creativehandsartstudio.com.
> (BP) (SC)

COOKING

Kitchen Kapers Culinary Academy

Hands-on cooking classes for kids aged 6–12 focus on skills appropriate for younger chefs. (Ages 12–16 have their own teen classes.) Students get to sample all dishes prepared in class. A little history, science, and math also get mixed into the cooking lessons. There's often a seasonal theme tied into a class, and some sessions are set up for parent and child. Classes last 1½ to 2 hours. Kids' classes include such topics as Gingerbread for the Family, Family Cooking, Comfort Foods, Bake Christmas Cookies, The Cupcake Corner, Delicious Desserts, Movie Night Munchies, and Quick Breads. A tasty time, indeed, for young chefs.

> **LOCATION:** East Gate Square Shopping Center, 1341 Nixon Dr.,
> Moorestown (Burlington County). **HOURS:** Most classes on Sun.,
> but also on holiday Mon. and weekday evenings.
> **ADMISSION:** $$$$$$ per session. **PHONE:** 856-778-7705.
> **WEBSITE:** www.kitchenkapers.com. (BP)

Young Chefs Academy

This cooking school for children aged 3 and up teaches culinary skills to kids, including how to cook properly and make delicious and nutritious meals. Each class includes hands-on participation in recipe preparation. The kids taste the food they make and discuss the results. Recipes are always changing, and children learn about food history, nutrition, and modifying recipes. They also learn kitchen safety, proper food handling, food preparation, cooking techniques, presentation, table setting, and more. KinderCooks for ages 3–5 incorporates recipes, age-appropriate culinary skills, nutrition, and movement in 1–1½ hour classes set up in monthly units.

Jr. Chefs for ages 5–12 offers a well-rounded approach to teaching cooking skills, incorporating creativity with culinary techniques. Themes include such topics as Harvest Festival, Bake the Season Bright, and Sweets for the Sweet. There are also one-time 1½-hour workshops, with such palate-pleasing subjects as Super Soups, Give Pizza a Chance, Chocolate Lovers Delight, and Happy Chinese New Year.

LOCATION: 712 Ginesi Dr., Morganville (Monmouth County), and 5 Jill Ct., Bldg. 14, Suite 4, Hillsborough (Somerset County). **HOURS:** Weekdays after school and Sat. morning. **ADMISSION:** Course tuition. **PHONE:** 732-536-7777 and 908-281-2433. **WEBSITE:** www.youngchefsacademy.com. (sc)

Ridgewood Culinary Studio

This year-round cooking studio offers 12-week sessions of one hour each. Among the classes are Pre-Kindergarten Drop-off (ages 4–6), which introduces kids to fun recipes. Kindergarten–2 Grade shows kids how to prepare recipes; 3–5 Grade teaches kids about the importance of healthy food choices, how to understand nutrition labels, and how to follow recipes and create their own; 5–8 Grade shows kids how to make exciting recipes using all the tools in the kitchen.

LOCATION: 223 Chestnut St., Ridgewood (Bergen County). **HOURS:** Mon.–Thu., 3:45–4:45. **ADMISSION:** Class tuition. **PHONE:** 201-447-2665. **WEBSITE:** www.ridgewoodculinarystudio.com. (BP) (SC)

CRAFTS

Just Bead Yourself

Kids can learn to design their own jewelry with the help of these beading specialists. Special events include Afternoon Tea with my Doll and Me, in which kids make matching necklaces for themselves and their dolls. There are also afternoon bead classes for kids ages 7–16. Bead Basics shows how to design, string, and crimp as well as finishing techniques and the creation of a beaded bracelet. Wire Wrapping Earrings & Pendants, Coiled Wire Bead Bracelet, Interweave Flower Bracelet, and other classes are also offered. In addition to classes, walk-in workshops are also available.

LOCATION: 113 Central Ave., Westfield (Union County). **HOURS:** Shop hours, 10:30–4:30; until 5:30 Wed., 6 on Fri., 6:30 Thu. Also Mon. and Tue. school holidays until 2:30. **ADMISSION:** Workshops: $$$$$. Classes vary. **PHONE:** 908-232-3411. **WEBSITE:** www.justbeadyourself.com. (BP) (SC)

Montclair Beadworks

A make-your-own jewelry studio that includes one-on-one bead-making classes as well as a special Children's Class in which kids learn to design and finish two bracelets using soft flex wire, crimp beads, and a clasp.

LOCATION: 43 Church St., Montclair (Essex County).
HOURS: Tue.–Sun., 11–6; until 7 on Fri. and 5 on Sun.
ADMISSION: $$$$$. PHONE: 973-744-3202.
WEBSITE: www.montclairbeadworks.com. (BP)

Glassworks Studio

This make-your-own glass art studio specializes in fused (kiln-formed) glass and sandblasting (etched glass). Kids can make a fused glass or sandblasting project whenever they want to come in. For fused works, they pick their projects, create their designs, and decide on the texture. The staff then fires, processes, and wraps the piece ready for pickup in a week. For sandblasting, kids choose a glassware item, cover it with an assortment of stickers, tape, or custom stencils, and watch while the staff blasts the item and peels away the mask to reveal an artistic creation. Designs can range from figures to abstracts, from simple to complex, and from table items to those that can hang on walls. Private lessons are also available.

LOCATION: 151 South St., Morristown (Morris County). Entrance in rear of building. HOURS: Sep.–June: Tue.–Sun., 12–6; Fri., 12–9; July–Aug.: Mon.–Fri., 12–6, Sat., 11–4. ADMISSION: $$ plus materials. PHONE: 973-656-0800. WEBSITE: www.umakeglass.com. (BP)(SC)

Hot Sand

Glassblowing is available at this studio for kids ages 9 and up, where they can work with a glass artist to create their own, unique glass works. They can blow an ornament with one color and a twist and a loop. Or they can blow a glass bubble, a drinking glass, a pumpkin or apple, a Valentine heart, Easter egg, sun tile, and other projects. These are as much works of art as they are functional pieces. There are also hands-on instructional glassblowing workshops from time to time.

LOCATION: 1200 Ocean Ave., Asbury Park (Monmouth County).
HOURS: Walk-in hours, Fri., 3–8; Sat., 11–8; Sun., 11–7.
ADMISSION: $$$$$$. PHONE: 732-927-5475.
WEBSITE: www.hotsandap.com.

All Fired Up!

A paint-your-own pottery studio, with more than four hundred different designs and pieces to choose from. Kids can paint piggy banks, covered boxes, cats, dogs, pirate banks, dragons, turtles, and frogs. Infants can make footprint and handprint ceramics. This cozy yet contemporary setting emphasizes the fun of creating pottery designs. Throughout the summer, there's a Paint 'Til You Drop Kids Club, with no sitting fees. Summer Arts on Fire workshops on Tuesdays and Thursdays for kids have ceramics, glass fusing, and mosaics projects for kids. A glass-fusing class is also available from time to time. And there's Storytime on Wednesday, Thursday, and Saturday mornings for preschoolers that includes handprint and simple ceramics painting projects. The studio also has a play area with toys for kids to occupy themselves when parents are finishing their own projects.

LOCATION: 602 Haddon Ave., Collingswood (Camden County). At the LumberYard Condos. **HOURS:** Tue.–Thu., 11–9; Fri., 11–10; Sat., 10–10; Sun., 12–5. See website for classes and workshop times. **ADMISSION:** $$. **PHONE:** 856-833-1330. **WEBSITE:** www.paintallfiredup.com. (BP)

Brushes & Bisque

Special classes are offered for kids ages 5 and up on Wednesday afternoons. Activities include painting T-shirts, stuffing animals, making mosaics, creating glass bead necklaces, tie-dyeing, playing with clay, painting plates with different animal themes, fingerprinting flowerpots, painting with sand, decorating mugs, and glasswork. Kids can also paint their own ceramics during walk-in hours.

LOCATION: 45 Broadway, Denville (Morris County). **HOURS:** Tue., Wed., Sat., Sun., 11–6; Thu., Fri., 11–9. Classes, Wed., 3:30–5. **ADMISSION:** $$$$ per class; walk-in studio fee, $$. **PHONE:** 973-627-6292. **WEBSITE:** www.brushesandbisque.net. (BP)(SC)

Color Me Mine

This chain of paint-your-own pottery studios offers a relaxing atmosphere and more than five hundred different unfinished ceramic pieces to choose from. Kids can paint ceramics or do an art project with a similar theme. There are clayful critter hand-building parties where kids work with moist clay to create their own animals or people, including press molds, then they paint their critters. They can also make custom hand and foot prints on plates or they can work with mosaics. This is primarily a drop-in and paint franchise, but some locations also offer weekly classes for kids.

LOCATIONS: Bernardsville (Somerset County), Denville (Morris County), Freehold (Monmouth County), Princeton (Mercer County), Ridgewood (Bergen County), Summit (Union County), Toms River

(Ocean County), and Voorhees (Burlington County). **HOURS:** See individual websites for hours. **ADMISSION:** Studio fee, $$. **PHONE:** 908-598-0248. **WEBSITE:** www.colormemine.com. (BP)

Git' Fired Up!

It calls itself a pottery playhouse and features ceramic pottery painting, glass fusing, hand building with clay, and pottery wheels. All tools, from brushes and stencils to design books are provided. Ceramic pieces include plates, mugs, piggy banks, tiles, and figurines, which stay at the studio for a week to ten days to be glazed and fired after they're decorated. The ceramics studio operates largely on a walk-in basis. Glass-fusing classes are also offered in which kids aged 7–14 can making plates, plaques, jewelry, suncatchers, and more. Kids can also create Paint-Me T-shirts and decorate them. There are also Kids N Clay classes for children aged 7–14 in which they can learn to make pots on a pottery wheel and glaze them, as well as hand-building projects like jack-o'-lanterns.

LOCATION: 626 Bay Ave., Point Pleasant Beach (Ocean County) and 92 Lawrence Ave., Ocean Grove (Monmouth County). **HOURS:** Wed.–Mon., 10–5; Fri.–Sat. until 6. **ADMISSION:** $$ plus ceramic piece cost. **PHONE:** 732-892-7529 and 732-897-0007. **WEBSITE:** www.gitfireduppottery.com. (BP)(SC)

Island Studio

A paint-your-own pottery studio that also offers glass fusion and mosaics. There's a large selection of all three types of projects to choose from. There are vases, picture frames, dishes, mugs, figurines, magnets, and more. Instructors help in creating a unique project, including choosing colors and designs. There are glass-fusing classes for ages 8 and up, including Basic Glass Necklace, Deluxe Glass Necklace, Glass Fused Coasters, Glass Fused Nite Lite, Glass Fused Plates or Bowls, Glass Fused Ornament, and Funk Glass Tile. There are also mosaic classes in which kids pick their own projects. Classes include instruction, mosaic pieces for the top surfaces, and glue, grout, and tool use.

LOCATION: Harbor Square Mall, 261 96th St., Suite 118, Stone Harbor (Cape May County). **HOURS:** Seasonal; call for hours. Closed in winter. **ADMISSION:** Varies with class and piece. **PHONE:** 609-368-6500. **WEBSITE:** www.islandstudio.org. (BP)

Art Attack

A place to paint high-quality bisque ceramics and to create glass fusion projects. Children choose from a variety of home decor items, kids' figurines, jewelry, and more. Designs are sketched, stenciled, stamped, or sponged onto the project. Then kids paint their pieces, with the staff assisting as needed. With glass fusion, kids choose a project and base glass and decorate the base with colored glass and lightly glue it on, then the staff will fuse and slump the design in a kiln. Glass and ceramics are ready in seven days. There are also workshops and special events, such as mother-daughter glass-fusing night, and Paint with Santa.

LOCATION: 14 Commerce St., Flemington (Hunterdon County).
HOURS: Wed.–Fri., 12:30–5:30; Sat., 10–6; Sun., 11–5.
ADMISSION: Based on project. **PHONE:** 908-284-0587.
WEBSITE: www.artattackfun.com. (BP)

Earth, Paint & Fire

This studio for ceramics and the arts offers art classes in mosaics, sculpture, painting, and drawing. Ceramics involve picking out a project, decorating it, and having the staff glaze and fire it. There are weekly specials, including Daddy and Me on Sunday and Mommy and Me on Friday in which a child up to age 7 can paint a free tile. There are also classes for kids in ceramics and mosaics from time to time.

LOCATION: 61C Mountain Blvd., Warren (Somerset County).
HOURS: Tue., Thu., 10–9; Wed., 10–6:30; Fri.–Sat., 10–6; Sun., 12–5.
ADMISSION: Varies with project. **PHONE:** 908-222-9993.
WEBSITE: www.earthpaintfire.com. (BP)(SC)

The Ceramic Barn

This paint-your-own-pottery place has more than 2,000 different pieces to choose from, including many children's items, with both spray and fire finishes. Both bisque and greenware pieces are available. There are also 4-week classes with the pottery wheel for kids. Classes are held when there are three students who want classes on the same evening.

LOCATION: 5145 Church Lane, Mount Laurel (Burlington County).
HOURS: Tue., 10–2; Wed.–Fri., 5:30–9; Sat., 10–2.
ADMISSION: Studio fee, $, plus project costs. **PHONE:** 856-234-0455.
WEBSITE: www.theceramicbarn.us. (BP)

The Pottery House

This arts and crafts studio offers painting pottery, beading, mosaics, fused-glass art, and metal art. Children and parent can walk in and paint anytime. There are also classes including Parent & Child Hand-building with Clay (two sessions), in which parent and child learn coil, pinch, and slab hand building, making projects like masks, mugs, and animal rattles. In Handbuilding with Clay, teachers show kids projects involving slabs, coils, and extruded shapes, and they can learn how to glaze (two two-hour classes, one class each week). There's also Fused Glass Jewelry Making, a one-hour class over 2 weeks. Kids make a pendant, a pin, and a set of earrings the first week. In the second session, following an overnight firing, kids learn to apply the wire wrapping.

> **LOCATION:** 251 Main St., Matawan (Monmouth County).
> **HOURS:** Tue.–Wed., 11–6; Thu., 11–7; Fri., 11–8; Sat., 11–9; Sun., 12–5.
> **ADMISSION:** Varies with class. **PHONE:** 732-970-7613.
> **WEBSITE:** www.thepotteryhouse.biz. (BP)

DANCE

Art of Dance

This facility has five large dancing rooms and open areas to watch classes through one-way mirrors. It offers dance classes for kids aged 2½ and up in ballet, pointe, tap, jazz, lyrical, Irish, and hip-hop as well as gymnastics. There can be a number of times or days for the same class. Specific classes include Ballet & Tumbling (ages 2½–3½), Beginner Ballet, Tap & Tumbling (3½–5, 5–7), No-Beginner Ballet, Tap & Acro (4–5, 5–7), Ballet (7 and up) on different experience levels and specialties, Pointe (three levels), and Lyrical (7 and up) on two levels. There are also classes in Musical Theatre (8 and up), Jazz (5–6, 7 and up) on six levels, Hip-Hop (6–9, 7–10, 9–12) on several levels, Tap (6 and up) on different levels, Gymnastics (5–9, 9 and up), Irish (four levels), special Boys Only classes, Special Needs Dancers, and Conditioning for Dancers.

> **LOCATION:** 15 Seminary Ave., Chester (Morris County).
> **HOURS:** Weekdays after school and Sat. Preschoolers weekday mornings and Sat.; see website for specific classes.
> **ADMISSION:** Varies with class. **PHONE:** 908-879-4919.
> **WEBSITE:** www.artofdance.org. (BP) (SC)

Dance Art Creative Center

Dance classes at this center range from ballet, pointe, jazz, and Latin jazz to modern, hip-hop, toddler dance, and baby ballet. Some specific classes include Children's Ballet, Kids Jazz, Children's Freestyle, Hip-Hop, Toddler Fairy Dance, and Baby Ballet. Most classes run for around an hour. In addition to dance, there are also two art classes covering acrylic painting and creative art techniques, one for kids aged 9 and up and the other for ages 4–8. These run for four sessions each. There is also an acting class for ages 10 and up on Friday after school and advanced sessions on Saturday afternoon with Jeff Keller, who starred in *Phantom of the Opera* on Broadway. He also gives private singing lessons.

LOCATION: 519 Cedar Lane, Teaneck (Bergen County).
HOURS: Weekdays after school and evening and Sat. and Sun.
ADMISSION: Class tuition. **PHONE:** 201-801-0278.
WEBSITE: www.danceartcreativecenter.com.

Stories in Motion

This studio offers an innovative approach to teaching dance that links creative movement and storytelling to make stories come alive through dance. Imaginative and age appropriate movement helps nurture a child's innate artistic ability. Classes are available for kids aged 6 months to 12 years. They include Baby Dance Jam (ages 6–12 months, with caregiver) and Ballet Magic (1½–4), which explores the world of fairies, princesses, and magical creatures. There are twenty classes in all. Creative Sparks (3–6) expands kids' range of dance through creative movement play, improvisation, and choreography, with stories a part of each class. Creative Tap (6–9) emphasizes rhythm, style, and sound in studying basic tap steps. Creative Ballet (3–9) explores the magical world of ballet with props, costumes, and stories of great ballets. In Lyrical Choreography (7–9) children express themselves through lyrical dance styles in an introduction to modern dance styles. Most classes run for 16 weeks. There are also 6-week dance workshops for elementary grades.

LOCATION: 1874 Springfield Ave., Maplewood (Essex County).
HOURS: Mon.–Fri., 9:30–6:10; Sat., 9:10–10:45. **ADMISSION:** Course fee.
PHONE: 973-313-1050. **WEBSITE:** www.storiesinmotion.org. Ⓢⓒ

Broadway Bound Dance Center

There are a number of different age and dance categories for kids at this studio. Ballet/Tap for preschoolers (ages 3–4) lasts one hour and teaches kids imaginative ways to develop movement and begin working on balance and body control. Ballet/Jazz dance for kindergarten/first-graders introduces kids to preballet and jazz through song, rhythm, and movement. Kiddie Hip-Hop class for ages 5–6 teaches wave movement and rhythmic perceptions as kids dance. There's also a Tumbling Tots class (5–6) that focuses on developing motor skills through rolling, jumping, and climbing. Classes that focus on one genre, such as ballet, jazz, or tap dancing, introduce kids 6–10 to specific styles and teaches them the vocabulary and techniques of dance as a way of practicing self-expression.

LOCATION: 99 West Madison Ave., Dumont (Bergen County).
HOURS: Vary with class; see website. **ADMISSION:** Course tuition.
PHONE: 201-385-4114. **WEBSITE:** www.bbound.com. (BP)

Broadway Bound Dance Center

This center offers professional instruction in toddler dance, pre-ballet, tap, ballet, pointe, modern, lyrical, jazz, and hip-hop. Workshops are offered throughout the year by top choreographers. Some specific classes include Mini Co. Tap, Ballet, Pre-Pointe Ballet, Pre-teen Hip-Hop, Rhythmic Tap, Jazz, Junior Choreography, and Broadway Babies.

LOCATION: 1245 Rt. 22 East, Lebanon (Hunterdon County).
HOURS: Weekdays after school and Sat. morning.
ADMISSION: Varies with class. **PHONE:** 908-236-8133.
WEBSITE: www.broadwaybounddanceinc.com. (BP)

Broadway Bound Theatrical and Dance Center

There are a number of different programs offered by this center. The Introduction to Dance (ages 3–6) provides a foundation in dance and movement, including how to relate to space, elementary positions, and directions. Pre-ballet/Jazz (6–7) broadens an understanding of classical ballet and provides an introduction to jazz dancing. Jazz classes (8 and up) teach all styles of jazz dancing and the correct turns and leaps as well as dance combinations. Tap Dancing (8 and up) starts with the basics and progresses to more intricate steps. Ballet & Pointe (8 and up) has five levels, emphasizing placement, carriage, and self-discipline. Hip-Hop classes are fast paced and have many techniques to master. There are also voice lessons (5 and up), both private and group, that teach proper breathing, note recognition, working on songs, and correct vocal techniques. Piano classes (6 and up) are also available. Acting classes (8–11, 12–17) teach basic elements and skills, such as cold reading, monologues, improvisation, stage movement, and more. In Musical Comedy (8–11, 12–16) students learn improvisation, basic dance movements, singing, and work on production numbers.

LOCATION: 231 Tontine Ave., Lyndhurst (Bergen County).
HOURS: Weekdays after school and Sat. **ADMISSION:** Varies with class.
PHONE: 201-935-4924. **WEBSITE:** www.broadwayboundnj.com.

Broadway Bound Dance Academy

The center provides quality dance education in a variety of dance styles. Classes include instruction in ballet, pointe, lyrical, and modern dance as well as in tap, jazz, and hip-hop. There are also acro and preschool classes for younger children.

> **LOCATION:** 100 Mckinley Ave., Manahawkin (Ocean County).
> **HOURS:** Vary with class. **ADMISSION:** Class tuition.
> **PHONE:** 609-978-7600. **WEBSITE:** www.njbroadwaybound.com.

West Side Dance Center

Dedicated to teaching the art of dance, this studio offers instruction in ballet, tap, jazz, hip-hop, lyrical, musical theater, and modern dance for students 2½ and up. Classes include Combo Classes (2½–9), which introduce two to three styles of dance; Ballet Techniques, covering the basics of ballet through turns and jumps; Cheer Dance, a combination of hip-hop and jazz; Hip-Hop, teaching basic hip-hop moves (6 and up); Jazz, offers basic jazz dance technique and styles; and Tap, incorporating basic tap skills into floor work. There are also classes in Lyrical, which focuses on ballet-based lyrical style; and Modern, where various styles of modern dance are explored. In addition, the center holds a class in Musical Theatre, which combines singing, acting, and dancing in preparation for performances.

> **LOCATION:** Aspen Business Park, 3 Middlebury Rd., Randolph (Morris County). **HOURS:** Vary with class; call, or see website.
> **ADMISSION:** Class tuition. **PHONE:** 973-927-4444.
> **WEBSITE:** www.westsidedancecenter.com. **(BP)**

Heartbeat Dance Center

This studio with three large dance rooms offers a variety of dance classes. These 9-month courses include Kinderdance (ages 3–4), where kids study ballet, tap, and tumbling and perform one dance in recital. Combo, for kindergarteners, is a combination of ballet and tap, ballet and jazz, or tap and jazz. Mini, for grades 1 and 2, offers a choice of ballet, tap, jazz, or hip-hop. Primary Level (grades 3–5) students choose from ballet, tap, jazz, lyrical, or hip-hop. Junior Level (grades 6–8) students can choose from ballet, tap, jazz, lyrical, hip-hop, ballet technique, modern, or pointe.

> **LOCATION:** 19 Rt. 10 East #2, Succasunna (Morris County).
> **HOURS:** Vary with class. **ADMISSION:** Course tuition.
> **PHONE:** 973-584-3111. **WEBSITE:** www.heartbeatdance.com. **(SC)**

Tricia Sloan Dance Center

Classes in ballet, tap, lyrical, modern, jazz, pointe, creative, and combinations are taught using a level system based on age, experience, and audition. This is used to ensure that a child is in the right level of class. In Creative Movement class (ages 2½–3), kids run, skip, leap, stretch, coordinate, and move to music. In beginner and level I Ballet & Tap (3–4), the basics of barre, center practice, and traveling steps are taught using imagery, games, and songs. In Ballet & Jazz (5–6), the emphasis is similar but with more focus on dance itself. In Tap (8 and up), rhythms and patterns are explored and the emphasis is placed on sounds and technique. At age 7, children begin the formal study of classical forms in ballet and progress from there. Lyrical dance classes (7 and up) emphasize facial expressions and acting to convey the emotions of a song's lyrics in addition to dance movement.

> **LOCATION:** I West Mantua Ave., Wenonah (Gloucester County).
> **HOURS:** See website for schedule. **ADMISSION:** Class tuition.
> **PHONE:** 856-464-0125. **WEBSITE:** www.triciasloandance.com.

Dance Center of New Jersey

Dance classes in a variety of styles are offered for kids aged 2½ and up. Courses last from September to June. For preschoolers, there's Discovery (ages 2½–3½) and Preschool Dance (3–4), in which children learn about expression through different types of movement through a fun approach. Intro to Ballet (5–6) takes the next step and develops an awareness of music and rhythm. Beginner Ballet or Jazz (6–7) teaches basic dance vocabulary and technique and the importance of discipline. Beginner+ Ballet or Jazz (7–9) is for advancing beginners, with more emphasis on dance performance. Beyond that, students advance in classes based on their proficiency. There are also classes in Modern (10 and up), Jazz/Hip-Hop (6 and up), and Contemporary (10 and up), in which students learn these styles of dance from the basics to beyond. Private and semiprivate classes are also available.

> **LOCATION:** St. Bernards's Episcopal Church, 88 Claremont Rd.,
> Bernardsville (Somerset County). **HOURS:** Weekdays after school
> (preschoolers in morning) and Sat. morning. **ADMISSION:** Varies with
> class. **PHONE:** 908-229-4184. **WEBSITE:** www.dcnjdance.com.

DVJC Dance Conservatory

A number of different dance genres are taught at this studio, including four age/experience levels of ballet, jazz, and tap; two levels of modern dance; and two age levels of hip-hop (over and under 12). Students are placed according to their age and ability. There's also a combination dance class for preschoolers (ages 3–5). Each season, students are also offered an opportunity to perform in a theatrical gala.

LOCATION: 2 S. Main St., Woodstown (Salem County).
HOURS: Mon., Wed., Thu. evening and Sat. morning.
ADMISSION: Semester tuition. **PHONE:** 856-769-4004.
WEBSITE: www.dvjcdanceconservatory.com. (SC)

Sharon's Studio of Dance

A wide variety of dance styles are taught at this center. Mommy & Me classes cover singing, ballet, creative movement, and tumbling. Combination Dance Classes include Preschool (ballet, tap, acrobatics), Kindergarten (ballet, tap, and acrobatics), Age 6–7 (ballet, tap, jazz), and Age 8–Adult (ballet, tap, jazz). There are also sessions on Hip-Hop, combining jazz, street, and funk styles; Hip-Hop and Gymnastics Combination, with mat and floor work to walkovers and handsprings; Lyrical, which combines classical ballet, modern, and jazz techniques; Break Dancing, an extension of Hip-Hop; Irish Step, including soft and hard shoe styles; and Ballet, focusing on proper alignment, turnout, and extension. There's also Pointe, an extension of ballet; Jazz, featuring funk and Broadway styles; Tap, developing rhythm and sound coordination skills; and Musical Theatre, combining dance, acting, and drama. Plus there are Cheer Dance Classes, blending dance, tricks, voice projection, squad formations, and pompoms. There are also private piano lessons and group music lessons available.

LOCATION: 622 Rt. 10 West, Unit 25, Whippany (Morris County).
HOURS: Vary with class; see website for schedule.
ADMISSION: Varies with class length. **PHONE:** 973-386-0259.
WEBSITE: www.sharonsdance.com. (SC)

Magnolia Hill Studios

Dance, art, and music classes are offered for preschoolers and older at this center, with the primary emphasis on dance. Some of the offerings are Dancin' Round the Globe, with the dance and music of different countries; Dance with Me, a Mommy and Me class blending music, storytelling, and dance; Hip-Hop, done with child-friendly music; Fairytale Ballet, where kids learn ballet fundamentals through stories from the ballet world; and Steppin' Out, where kids learn to dance to both classic and contemporary show tunes. Art classes include Drawing Dynamics, Drawing Nature, Wet Paint, Mini-Monets, and Petite Picassos. Music sessions include Musical Babies and Twinkle Toddlers, parent-and-me classes that explore songs, books, rhythm, games, and instruments through music.

LOCATION: 1425 Magnolia Rd., Vineland (Cumberland County).
HOURS: Most are on Mon., Wed., Thu., and Fri. after school and on Sat.

ADMISSION: Course tuition. **PHONE:** 856-692-7262.
WEBSITE: www.magnoliahillstudios.com. (BP) (SC)

MUSIC

Calderone School of Music

The school provides private music lessons on every instrument—strings, woodwinds, brasses, percussion, organ, piano, accordion, keyboards, jazz and classical guitar, bass, and harp—as well as voice. All styles of music are available for study, from classical and jazz to Broadway, rock, folk, and pop. There are also Kindermusik classes for kids up to age 7. Students can also take part in ensembles, auditions, and competitions.

> **LOCATION:** 34 Ridgedale Ave., East Hanover (Essex County), and 256 Morris Ave., Springfield (Union County). **HOURS:** Private classes by reservation; Kindermusik, see website for schedule.
> **ADMISSION:** Private classes, $$$$$ per half hour; Kindermusik varies with class. **PHONE:** 973-428-0405 and 973-467-4688.
> **WEBSITE:** www.calderoneschoolofmusic.com. (SC)

Honey Child Music

A variety of fun musical classes are offered for kids. They include Me & Momma Rock, Rhythm Rompers, Keyboard Beginnings, Doors to Music, Jam On, Funky Fusion, Pre-K of Rock, Prince & Princess Academy, Rock On, Tiny Dancers, and Twinkle Toe Tots as well as Sing, Dance, Drum & Prance. Most classes last an hour each and run 14 weeks. There's also a 10-week Red Bank Rockers program. Private lessons are also available for all kinds of instruments as well as voice.

> **LOCATION:** 73 Monmouth St., Red Bank (Monmouth County).
> **HOURS:** Weekdays, day and evening; weekend mornings.
> **ADMISSION:** Class tuition. **PHONE:** 732-530-5884.
> **WEBSITE:** www.honeychildmusic.com. (BP)

Kindermusik

Kindermusik is a classroom learning experience that helps children become better learners. It's about developing skills in the whole child, from newborns to 7 years old. A set of at-home materials comes with each session, which includes a book, CD, age-appropriate instrument, and activity book. The program is designed to assist parents in helping their kids learn outside the classroom and to develop a natural sense of musical appreciation. Classes vary by age and include topics such as Adventures for Baby, Family Time,

Sign and Sing, ABC Music and Me, and others. There are songs and games for the car and storytelling that combines rhythm, movement, singing, and drama. In class, the teacher leads a group of parents and children through activities using music and movement. The program originated in Germany in the 1960s. Today it incorporates the latest research on early childhood development. Children who attend develop an ability to create their own musical compositions, and the courses allow them to explore voice development, and learn musical symbols and pre-keyboard, string, and woodwind instruments.

LOCATION: Bayonne (Hudson County), Flemington (Hunterdon County), Jersey City (Hudson County), Maplewood (Essex County), Spotswood (Middlesex County), Springfield (Union County), and Yardville (Mercer County). **HOURS:** Vary by location and program. **ADMISSION:** Class tuition. **PHONE:** 800-628-5687. **WEBSITE:** www.kindermusik.com. (BP) (SC)

Ridgewood Conservatory

This center offers early childhood music as well as dance classes. The Music Preparatory Program has three parts: Theory and Musicianship Classes, Private Instrument or Vocal Instruction, and Chamber Music and Jazz Ensembles. There are twenty-one lessons per semester for the first two categories and twelve ensemble rehearsals. The Early Childhood Music Program (fourteen classes) includes Family Music for Babies (up to age 1½), which incorporates songs, games, dancing, moving, and singing into musical playtime. Family Music for Toddlers (1½–3) stresses imitation of tonal and rhythmic patterns and develops creativity through singing, moving, dancing, listening, and playing simple instruments. Cycle of Seasons (3–5) teaches rhythmic and tonal patterns in singing, listening, and exploring musical instruments. Music Makers I and II (4–7) is a 2-year preinstrumental program designed to build symbolic music language through singing, creative movement, playing instruments, and ear training.

The vocal music program includes courses like Finding Your Natural Voice, Vocal Performance for Musical Theater, and Discover the Joy of Singing. There are twenty-one lessons per semester. The conservatory's acting program also offers private lessons as well as workshops for vocal students. There's also a 10-week glee workshop with singing and dancing as well as learning how to tell the story, setting a stage, and a Glee at TRC Showcase performance.

For young dancers, there are also ballet, pointe, and hip-hop dance classes, based on age and experience (7 and up) as well as

dance classes for younger students (3–6) with names like Twinkling
Stars, Ballet Bunnies, and Dancing Dolls.

> **LOCATION:** 615 Franklin Tpk., second floor, Ridgewood (Bergen
> County). **HOURS:** Mon.–Sat., morning through evening classes.
> **ADMISSION:** Tuition varies with program. **PHONE:** 201–612–6686.
> **WEBSITE:** www.ridgewoodconservatory.com.

Music Together

Children share songs, instrument play, rhythm chants, and movement in a playful setting. Music is learned according to the learning styles of very young children. Children participate at their own
levels in family-style classes of mixed ages. Parents and caregivers
add to the child's musical environment. A new song collection is
provided for every semester for 3 years, featuring original and traditional songs in a wide range of musical and cultural styles.
There's a new professional CD each semester with new songs,
rhythm chants, play-alongs, and tonal and rhythm patterns for the
car and home. There's also parent education to help adults understand and enhance their child's musical development. The classes
are based on the idea that all children can learn to sing in tune,
keep a beat, and participate in the music of our culture. Actual
music experience rather than music concept is emphasized and
children are introduced to the pleasures of making music instead
of passively listening to CDs or TV. Class locations in many different towns. See website for a list.

> **LOCATION:** Mailing address, P.O. Box 1236, Maplewood (Essex County).
> **HOURS:** Weekly sessions; see website for details.
> **ADMISSION:** Semester tuition. **PHONE:** 800-728-2692.
> **WEBSITE:** www.musictogether.com.

Kids' MusicRound

This organization has fourteen centers throughout the state, with
classes given in more than one location per center. Programs in -
clude mommy-and-me–style music and movement classes designed
to meet the developmental needs of infants, toddlers, and young
children. The focus is on combining music and movement, with
classes designed to promote early childhood music development,
"sparking the inner musician in everyone." Parents and children
sing along to original, traditional, and multicultural music to introduce kids to different tonal and rhythmic meters. They also learn to
follow a beat through drumming, stomping, dancing, and musical
play as well as participate in music activities that help kids develop
their motor skills through such activities as dancing, clapping, and

bouncing. They also get to touch and feel rhythm instruments designed for tiny hands. Home materials are also provided, including a songbook.

LOCATION: Headquarters: 25 Route 31 South, Suite C, Pennington (Mercer County). See website for specific locations.
HOURS: Vary; 10-week semesters. **ADMISSION:** Semester tuition.
PHONE: 609-333-0100. **WEBSITE:** www.kidsmusicround.com.

COMBINATION

Toddlers in Motion

This center is about moving and learning for kids aged 1½–4. The Art Shop offers hands-on experience in discovering the world of color, shape, and texture. Parent and child create art using brushes, rollers, sponges, and fingers. Toddlers in Motion lets parents enjoy their children as they run, jump, gallop, slide, tiptoe, and rock while playing with balls, hoops, and musical instruments. Music, Art & Storytime brings a weekly story to life through creative play as well as with music, dance, and art. Stepping Stones offers kids an opportunity to move toward independence through creative play, music and movement, and art. Fun with French expands kids experience as they sing French songs, listen to French music, and create an art project. Leaps and Bounds is a movement class that uses stories, an imaginative-play obstacle course, music and dancing, and a little art. Artist Portfolio teaches kids about modern art masters, and they create a project of their own. Explorers World combines a curiosity of science with the beauty of art. Kids do simple experiments, play games, listen to stories, and do art projects.

LOCATION: Unitarian Church, 67 Church St., Montclair (Essex County), and 28 Glen Rd., Rutherford (Bergen County).
HOURS: Classes weekday mornings and afternoons and Sat. morning.
ADMISSION: Varies with course. **PHONE:** 973-783-1537.
WEBSITE: www.toddlersinmotion.com. (BP) (SC)

Creative Kids

This center provides kids 3 months and up with programs in art, movement and dance, and creative play drawn from other quality organizations nearby. The Art Studio (ages 1½–10) offers drawing, painting, sculpture, and acrylics, with kids creating a new work each week while learning about famous artists. Little Maestros music class for tots features live musicians and musical story times, songs, imaginative play, puppet shows, and more. Stories in Motion (½–12) combines movement, dance, and storytelling. TADA! Youth Theater lets kids explore and perform musical theater arts. Rahway Music Group teaches music. Preschool of Rock is an energetic musical experience for kids 3 months and up as they discover all types of music and instruments. Future Fashionistas is a series of fashion design classes that focus on fashion illustration, collection design, and runway fun.

> **LOCATIONS:** 1008 South Ave. West, Westfield (Union County), and 615 S. Livingston Ave., Livingston (Essex County).
> **HOURS:** See website for schedule. **ADMISSION:** Varies with class.
> **PHONE:** 908-232-4949 and 973-994-0096.
> **WEBSITE:** www.creativekidsnj.com. (BP)(SC)

FASHION

Sashay School of Fashion & Design

Creative programs for kids aged 7–17 provide a behind-the-scenes fashion experience. Beginners Fashion Design is an 8-week session that teaches the basics of fashion design, including participation in Project Runway–style competitions. Intermediate Fashion Design also lasts 8 weeks and includes perfecting fashion design sketching and draping skills and Project Runway–style competitions as well as putting together a portfolio. Fashion & Creative Design is a 6-week after-school design-and-sew class. There is also a separate Sunday morning Sewing & Design class for ages 12 and up. Fashion Design Workshop is a one-time 90-minute introductory workshop for ages 7–14. Classes are held at Lord & Taylor Fashion Center in Ridgewood, Benjamin Franklin Middle School in Teaneck, and Richard Rodda Center in Teaneck.

> **LOCATION:** 992 Windsor Rd., Teaneck (Bergen County).
> **HOURS:** Vary with location. **ADMISSION:** Class tuition.
> **PHONE:** 201-836-3070. **WEBSITE:** www.sashayllc.com. (SC)

Play Time

At Kids Towne USA in Hamilton Township, children can use their imaginations to explore the world of adult work, with six themed rooms representing different vocations, including driving a school bus. *(Photo courtesy of Kids Towne USA)*

Kids Towne USA

There are a number of different play environments at this facility. Monkey Around is a giant jungle gym, with four levels of soft play fun, with cargo nets, inflatable balls, a forest of foam, wavy and spiral slides, zigzag web elevators, web bridges, and crawling tubes. Kids Towne Village lets kids use their imaginations to explore the adult workplace, with six themed rooms representing different vocations. There are plenty of hands-on activities in Miss Ava Grace's School House, Michael's Tool Towne, Alex Kowals' Market, Marielle's Puppet Theater, Rob's Diner, and Lisa's Animal Hospital.

There's also Mount Kidstowne Climbing Tower, an 18-foot-high rock climbing challenge overlooking the village. In addition, this center also has Space Quest Laser Tag and Laser Frenzy. Laser tag offers the latest tech advances to the sport. Kids wear an LED-lit vest with phasor pistol and two-way radio, with teams "tagging" opposing players and bonus targets. Spectators watch the action on high-definition monitors. Laser Frenzy is an individual sport in which kids negotiate a high-tech maze and laser beams to set the best time. Plus, there's also a game arcade where kids can have fun. Laser games and climbing tower have extra fees.

LOCATION: 3 Nami Lane, Hamilton (Mercer County).
HOURS: Mon.–Sat., 10–8; Sun., 10–6. **ADMISSION:** $$.
PHONE: 609-838-1881. **WEBSITE:** www.kidstowneusa.com. (BP)(SC)

Baby Power & Forever Kids

A structured program designed to help kids 6 months to 10 years old develop self-esteem, skills and friendship through movement, learning, and fun. Baby Power consists of parent and child play classes for kids up to age 3½. These are broken up into three age groups and include warm-up, gym, music, instruments, crafts, and story time. Class activities and songs depend on the age group. Family Power (up to age 5) classes are for siblings of mixed ages. Also offered are drop-in play time for kids aged 1–6 and Mom's Morning Out (daily with reservations). Forever Kids classes are designed for children aged 3½–10 and include art and science. These classes include Singing Chefs (3½–6), a cooking class for preparing simple, fun appetizers, meals, and desserts and also includes crafts and gym play; Sports & Games (3–6), a noncompetitive sports and games class with an emphasis on developing motor skills, strength, and flexibility; the Squirmy Worm (3–6), in which a new book is read every week along with exercise, gym play, games, and crafts; and Art Power (2–3 and 4–6), which gives children an opportunity to explore art and their imaginations, with projects that use a variety of art materials, such as paint, glue, clay, and plaster. There's also Girl Power (5–7), a girlie-girl art class that includes designing bedroom accessories, purses, friendship gifts, jewelry, and more, as well as Labcoat Kids (5–7) for children who enjoy exploring and learning about science.

LOCATION: 18 South St., New Providence (Union County).
HOURS: Class times and open play times vary; see website for schedule. **ADMISSION:** Semester tuition for classes; open play, $$.
PHONE: 908-464-2233. **WEBSITE:** www.babypower.com. (BP)(SC)

Funtime Junction

This facility features a large soft play area with a cloud bounce, web climb, super slide, playhouse, and a baby-only area. There are also small kiddie rides, including a helicopter ride, cars, and other fun vehicles as well as buccaneer blasters and laser tag. Plus there's an area where kids create sand art, a game room, and a room where they can make a Build-a-Buddy stuffed animal. Funtime Junction is also part of a complex that includes Dynamite Falls Miniature Golf, and party packages often combine activities at both facilities.

> **LOCATION:** 400 Fairfield Ave., Fairfield (Essex County).
> **HOURS:** Tue.–Fri. and Sun., 11–6; Sat., 10–6.
> **ADMISSION:** $$. Under age 2, $. **PHONE:** 973-882-9777.
> **WEBSITE:** www.funtimejunction.com. (BP)

Giggles Play Station

Activities at this center include a two-story jungle gym with two tube slides, triple racing slide, and school-bus ball pit; an old-fashioned carousel; a clubhouse featuring puppet shows as well as music, dancing, and interactive games; and a toddler area, with a playhouse, kitchen, slide, and riding toys. Also present are a bounce house, a four-car caterpillar train ride, and a game area.

> **LOCATION:** 350 Rt. 46 East, Rockaway (Morris County).
> **HOURS:** Thu., Sun., 10–6; Fri.–Sat., 10–8.
> **ADMISSION:** $$; weekends $$$. Adults free. **PHONE:** 973-586-PLAY.
> **WEBSITE:** www.gigglesplaystation.com. (BP)

Jellybean Jungle

The activity centers at this fun play facility are designed to encourage social and physical exploration for kids aged 1–5. There's a ball pit room, climbing maze with slides, tunnels, a miniature bounce house, a carnival center with a mini carousel, an ocean center with a pirate ship, and a Jungle Theater. Adults must be present to supervise their kids except for Parents Night Out on Friday evenings.

> **LOCATIONS:** Crispin Square Shopping Center, 230 N. Maple, Marlton (Burlington County). **HOURS:** Mon.–Thu., 9:30–4:30; Fri., 9:30–8, Sat., 9:30–5. **ADMISSION:** $$; under 1, $. **PHONE:** 856-596-8889.
> **WEBSITE:** www.jellybean-junction.com. (BP)

Kid Junction

This center provides open play daily on large soft-play equipment and offers a creative play place for kids 1–9. One of the main features is a kid-sized interactive town, which includes a play grocery store, pizzeria, animal hospital, post office, kids exercise room, theater, and costume shop that are designed to encourage role playing and socializing. For older kids there are also two levels of tubes, slides, obstacles, and bridges with see-through panels and netting that lets parents keep an eye on their little ones. Toddler Town, for kids 1–3, is a miniature play unit with soft flooring and safe discovery toys, slides, and tunnels. There are also sports-oriented arcades that provide a different type of play for the kids. Kid Junction also offers Parents Night Out one Friday a month.

> **LOCATION:** 3322 Rt. 22 West, Bldg. 12, Branchburg Commons, Branchburg (Somerset County), and 16000 Commerce Pky., Suite A, Mount Laurel (Burlington County). **HOURS:** Sun.–Thu., 10–6; Fri. & Sat., 10–8. **ADMISSION:** $$. **PHONE:** 908-252-0055 and 856-273-9500. **WEBSITE:** www.kidjunction.com. (BP)

Kid-netic

This indoor playground includes a large play area with a three-level play structure, a mat-filled floor, and a rock-climbing wall. There are plenty of open play hours during the week and on Sunday morning. A lot of opportunities for playing are available here, with a ball room, punching bag room, alligator pit, island-hopping room, helicopter, and lots of tunnels and bridges and speedy slides. The rock wall is for kids under 10, and is designed for horizontal climbing. There are also enrichment classes for kids 2–4, which includes singing and dancing with movement, exploring the open play area, and creating in an art studio. There is also a Chef-tastic class involving the creation of tasty treats and making a personal cookbook. Kid-netic also offers a Kids Nite Out and a Mom's Morning Out.

> **LOCATION:** 2 Changebridge Rd., Unit E, Montville (Passaic County). **HOURS:** Open play, Mon., Wed., Fri., 10:30–3:30; Tue., Thu., 9–7; Sun., 9–10:30. Hours vary with season. **ADMISSION:** $$. **PHONE:** 973-331-9001. **WEBSITE:** www.kidneticnj.com. (BP)

Wiggles & Giggles

This educational play center offers a structured play program designed to help children from 4 months to 4 years grow and develop. At this weekly program, children can have fun rocking, bouncing, climbing, crawling, jumping, sliding, and running in safety on colorful, age-appropriate equipment. It is designed for fitness, playing with new friends, and developing social skills. There's also learning through play with numbers, letters, colors, songs, and listening. The instructors guide kids in songs, circle games, bubbles,

Wiggles and Giggles in East Hanover is an educational play center that offers a structured play program as well as a chance for kids to have fun with their parents. *(Photo courtesy of Wiggles and Giggles)*

and other kinds of fun. There are weekday sessions for moms and tots, babies only, and drop-offs for ages 2 and up.

LOCATION: 182 Rt. 10 West, East Hanover (Essex County). At the Funplex. **HOURS:** Open play on weekends; times vary. Weekday classes. See website for schedule.
ADMISSION: Single and multipass; prices vary. **PHONE:** 973-428-1788.
WEBSITE: www.wigglesandgiggles.com. (BP)(SC)

Kidz-KaZoom

This center has a fully matted gym room along with a bubble machine, crawl tubes, space station, tunnels, slides, ball pits—a lot of foam-filled, molded plastic, and inflatable equipment for kids 4 months to 9 years. This facility provides open play, with parents supervising their children. Kids can explore a toy room, an indoor playground, an arts-and-crafts/music room, a computer lab, and a toddler room. Open play is available weekday afternoons and evenings and there is unscheduled time between parties on weekends. In addition to being a play center, Kidz-KaZoom is also a daycare facility.

LOCATION: 49 E. Midland Ave., Paramus (Bergen County).
HOURS: Open play, Mon.–Fri., 3:30–5 and 6–8.
ADMISSION: Open gym, $$ for 1 hour, $ afterward.
PHONE: 201-225-1212. **WEBSITE:** www.kidz-kazoom.com. (BP)

Party & Play USA

This center features a wide variety of play features for children ages 1–14 to enjoy. There's a bouncing bridge, net maze, 35-foot zip line, preschool area, ball pit, punching bags, and net tower. When they've done those activities, kids can move on to a rock-climbing wall, a cargo net climb, bouncing tunnels, video games, a bubble machine, a real stone castle, and several slides, including a 42-foot super slide. Parents can watch or join in the play for free.

LOCATION: 351-E Matawan Rd., Town Square Shopping Center, Matawan (Middlesex County). **HOURS:** Daily, 10–6, until 7 on Fri. and Sat. **ADMISSION:** $$. **PHONE:** 732-583-0504. **WEBSITE:** www.partyandplayusa.com. (BP) (SC) (in conjunction with area camps).

Uptown Playaround

This is an open 5,000-square-foot play, party, and enrichment center for infants to 10-year-olds. A town-themed setting encourages play to enhance cognitive and physical skills and socialization. Children can climb and slide on a two-and-a-half-level play system, put on an improv performance on a stage, and explore a large playhouse. There's also a separate area called Toddler Ave., which has mirrors, tunnels, and slides designed to make smaller kids happy.

LOCATION: Rt. 27, Kendall Park (Middlesex County). **HOURS:** Mon.–Thu., 9:30–6; Fri., until 3; weekends, call. **ADMISSION:** $$ for walkers, $ for crawlers. **PHONE:** 732-955-2005. **WEBSITE:** www.uptownplayaround.com. (BP) (SC)

Jump On In

A large indoor gym for kids aged 3 and up with large inflatable bounce houses, obstacle courses, slides, tunnels, trampolines, and more. There's a giant trampoline basketball game and a soft-play batting cage. The facility is primarily devoted to parties, but reserved open play time is available on a regular basis.

LOCATION: 85 Fulton St., Boonton (Morris County). **HOURS:** Open play hours vary; call or visit website to reserve a spot. **ADMISSION:** $$. **PHONE:** 973-588-7733. **WEBSITE:** www.jumponinfun.com. (BP)

JumpNasium

This indoor inflatable center is all about jumping, bouncing, and having fun, as the name suggests. There's plenty to choose from: inflatable climbers, bouncers, obstacle courses, interactive games, toddler activities, slippery rock slide, and more. There's also a basketball trampoline for kids ages 7 and under. Inflatables are for children 2 years and older. There are also Little Tykes ride cars, bowling, hula hoops, kids learning carpets, and bouncy Rhodes castles to try out. Plus, kid-friendly arcade games are available as well as child-sized air hockey.

LOCATION: 204 Passaic Ave., Fairfield (Essex County).
HOURS: Open jump hours vary; reserve a time on the website.
ADMISSION: $$$. **PHONE:** 973-808-1700.
WEBSITE: www.jumpnasiumparty.com. (BP)(SC)

Junglerrrific

A soft play area for kids, featuring an Amazon jungle gym, a toddler area, and children's rides. Kids can have fun exploring a foam forest, a cargo crawl-through, a two-level spiral slide, a web climb, and soft foam climbing toys. And there are also ride-ons, an alpine tunnel slide, baby nuts and bolts, a game cube, and arcade games. All in all, there are plenty of things to keep active kids happy.

LOCATION: Ideal Plaza, 2226 Rt. 9 South, Howell, and 2105 Rt. 35 North, Oakhurst (Monmouth County). **HOURS:** Howell: Mon.–Wed., 10–6; Thu.–Fri., 10–5. Oakhurst: Mon., Wed.–Fri., 10–3; Tue., 10–6.
ADMISSION: Call for prices. **PHONE:** 732-577-1118 and 732-918-1900.
WEBSITE: www.junglerrrific.com. (BP)

Pump It Up

Filled with large inflatable slides, bounce houses, obstacle courses, and more, this center lets kids bounce and play to their heart's content. The primary focus here is on parties, but there's also Pump-Start structured play, with weekly playtime incorporating jumping, bouncing, singing, games, and other activities based on specific age groups. There's also Family Jump and Pop-in Playtime, which is an open bounce, slide, and playtime. A Parent's Night Out is also available on the first Saturday of the month.

LOCATIONS: 10 Middlebury Blvd., Randolph (Morris County); 500 Business Park Dr., Freehold (Monmouth County); 8 Commerce Way, Suite 135, Hamilton (Mercer County); and 8 E. Stow Rd., Suite 160, Marlton (Camden County). **HOURS:** Family jump time varies with location; call or check website. **ADMISSION:** Family jump, $$.
PHONE: 866-977-5867. **WEBSITE:** www.pumpitupparty.com. (BP)

Bounce U

Three kinds of open bounce are offered at these centers. Preschool Playdate provides weekly sessions with bouncing, music, and games for the younger kids. Family Bounce Night is for the entire family.

And there's an All Ages Open Bounce, which is available by reservation and includes inflatables, games, and other fun.

LOCATION: 165 Amboy Rd., Morganville (Monmouth County), and 3E Chimney Rock Rd., Bridgewater (Somerset County).
HOURS: Hours vary; call or check website for schedule.
ADMISSION: $$. **PHONE:** 732-972-6862 and 732-469-2193.
WEBSITE: www.bounceu.com.

Sports for Kids

At Classic Gymnastics and Cheer in Morganville, kids can do gymnastics work on the floor, uneven bars, balance beam, trampoline, and parallel bars. *(Photo by Steve Sarafian/ Fliptography.com. Courtesy of Classic Gymnastics and Cheer)*

GYMNASTICS

Classic Gymnastics and Cheer

This facility offers a variety of gymnastic, trampoline, cheerleading, and dance programs for kids from 1½ to 18 years old. Recreational and competitive gymnastics for boys and girls are held on afternoons during the school year and on Saturdays. The Rising Star cheerleading program provides competitive cheerleading for girls aged 7–18 after school and on Sundays. Trampoline and tumbling offers a high-aerobic, low-impact way to build strength and control.

The youngest kids' classes start with Mommy & Baby and progress to Parent & Tot. Then comes Tumble Tots for 3–5-year-olds, which includes gymnastics, ball handling, and movement to music. There's also overall fitness development on the trampoline and on obstacle courses as well as exercises in basic floor skills and a Tumble Trak leading into a foam pit. For school age children, the classes are more traditional, with gymnastics work on the floor, uneven bars, balance beam, trampoline, and parallel bars as they advance through different levels. Note: Just as this edition went to press, Classic Gymnastics closed. However, it has been replaced by Premier Gymnastics and Cheer Academy, with a similar program.

LOCATION: 202 Commercial Ct., Morganville (Monmouth County).
HOURS: Vary with class; see website for schedule.
ADMISSION: Course tuition. **PHONE:** 732-970-7900.
WEBSITE: www.premiergymnasticsnj.com. (BP)

Atlantic Coast Gymnastics and Cheer

This facility offers a number of options for kids. There's a separate preschool gym and play center, where younger kids can have fun and get started in gymnastics. It features giant inflatables, climbing max, trampoline, and foam jumping pits. There are a large regular gym, where the traditional gym courses are held. And there's tumbling and in-ground pits with a 40-foot trampoline designed for cheer where kids learn to somersault, tumble, and do cartwheels.

LOCATION: 1041 Glassboro Rd. (Rt. 322), Williamstown (Gloucester County). **HOURS:** Class times vary; see website for schedule.
ADMISSION: Semester tuition. **PHONE:** 856-875-1300.
WEBSITE: www.acgymnastics.com. (BP)

CS Gymnastics

Classes are offered at CS for kids aged 1½ and up. The Bunny Tots program offers activities for parent and child together, with rhythmic warm-ups followed by fun exercise circuits that include tumbling, low bars, the trampoline, low beam, and more. In the next level, Bouncin Bunnies, kids gain proficiency in tumbling, low beams, trampoline, spring boards, and low bars. In Rompin Rabbits, they refine and learn entry-level gymnastics skills using fun progressions and circuits. The Gym n Learn Preschool combines gymnastics and education for 3–5-year-olds. From age 7 and up, placement is based on ability and teacher recommendation. There's also a tumbling class for kids 8 and up that emphasizes gymnastics skills for cheerleading. CS also has a Parents' Night Out the second Saturday of the month that features organized fun, activities, and games.

LOCATION: 4 Gold Mine Rd., Flanders (Morris County).
HOURS: Vary with day and class; see website for schedule.
ADMISSION: Semester tuition. **PHONE:** 973-347-2771.
WEBSITE: www.csgymnasticsinc.com. ⓑⓟ

Garden State Gymnastics

Toddler and preschool programs and recreational gymnastics classes at this gym are designed to create overall health and fitness along with confidence and self-respect. Tumble Tots is a 45-minute class for kids aged 1–3, with a parent accompanying the child as the class explores music, movement, activities, games, and free exploration in a special mini gym. Preschool Gymnastics for ages 3–4 includes a warm-up to music and a gymnastics circuit with games and activities to increase attention and build physical abilities. There are also boys' and girls' gymnastics set up by age and abilities; tumbling, where kids focus on floor skills and cheerleading skills; trampoline sessions; and special needs classes. Open gym time is available on Saturdays, 4–6.

LOCATION: Lacey Business Park, 702 Challenger Way, Forked River (Burlington County). **HOURS:** Vary with class; see website for schedule. **ADMISSION:** Semester tuition. **PHONE:** 609-242-1658. **WEBSITE:** www.gsgymnastics.com. ⓑⓟ

Diamond Gymnastics

The preschool program at this facility starts with kids 15 months to 3 years and includes parental assistance classes designed to develop small-motor skills. Activities include climbing, jumping, and balancing, which are enhanced with music, hoops, parachutes, etc. There's also a pre-school class without parents that continues developing movement skills with simple gymnastics through games and obstacle courses that include a foam pit, springboards, ropes, and similar setups. For ages 5 and up, classes are tailored to the age and ability of individual children, helping them develop to more advanced gymnastics skills. There are also cheerleading classes, designed to improve tumbling and jumping skills.

LOCATION: 182 Rt. 10 West, East Hanover (Essex County).
HOURS: Preschool: Mon.–Sat., morning and afternoon; ages 5 and up, weekdays after school and Sat. morning. **ADMISSION:** Course tuition.
PHONE: 973-560-0414. **WEBSITE:** www.diamondgymnastics.com. ⓑⓟ ⓢⓒ

Go for the Gold Gymnastics Center

A number of different classes here are designed to develop kids' gymnastics skills from ages 1½ and up. The Parent and Me class for

18–24-month-olds features colorful obstacle courses with music and movement. Tiny Tots begins physical education by introducing basic gym equipment. The Preschool class also introduces kids to regulation gym equipment but takes the familiarization further with a step by step approach. Kinder Kids is an introduction to gymnastics for kindergartners. The difference in these early childhood classes is that they are designed around the children's abilities and ages. Recreational Gymnastics, the next step, is organized by age and ability for kids 4½ and older and is designed to teach kids strength and skill building with gymnastics equipment. The gym also has Tumbling Classes, which are designed for dancers, cheerleaders, and those who want to focus on this area. Plus, there are Trampoline classes as well as Cheer-Tumbling and Cheerleading sessions. The gym also offers classes for children with special needs.

LOCATION: 40 Leslie Ct., Whippany (Morris County).
HOURS: Vary with class; see website for schedule.
ADMISSION: Semester tuition. **PHONE:** 973-739-9100.
WEBSITE: www.goforthegoldgymnastics.com.

Gymboree

This national franchise has numerous locations throughout the state, all with similar programs in gymnastics, music, and art, with these activities often blended together. There are Play & Learn classes set up for six age groups for kids from ages 0 to 3. These are the most popular classes, and they use sensory stimulation, problem-solving games, and storytelling in conjunction with ramps, slides, and other play environments to develop children's communication, discovery, and coordination. There are also four levels of music-oriented classes that encourage development and love of music through songs, dance, movement games, and instruments. Art classes are offered as well, and these are designed to inspire kids' imaginations and self-expression with hands-on art activities, such as painting, sculpture, drawing, collage, dramatic play. A number of sessions include parent involvement. Each location is individually owned and operated; check with your local center for its specific program.

LOCATIONS: Basking Ridge, Chatham, Cherry Hill, Chester, Hillsborough, Howell, Jersey City, Metuchen, Monroe, Ocean Twp., Old Bridge, Paramus, Pine Brook, Princeton, Red Bank, Tenefly, Toms River, Waldwick, and Westfield. **HOURS:** Vary with location; see individual branch website. **ADMISSION:** Semester tuition. **PHONE:** 877-4-GYMWEB. **WEBSITE:** www.gymboreeclasses.com.

Gymnastics Inc.

Gymnastics are taught at this facility in a graduated series of classes. Preschool classes range from Parent and Me sessions for kids up to age 3. These include Tumble Bears, in which kids learn basic gymnastic positions and skills, and Koala Bears, where kids have fun while learning a wide variety of movement concepts. Black Bears for 3-year-olds starts kids' independent learning of basic gymnastics. In Teddy Bears, kids learn to master specific skills like cartwheels, bridges, and handstands. There's also a full after-school program for children 6 and up that helps kids build their skills progressively, using bars, beam, floor vault, trampoline, and the TumblTrak. Tumbling classes that include cartwheels, roundoffs, back handsprings, and more are also offered for older kids. The gym also has a Parents' Night Out playtime, generally one Saturday evening a month, which is also open to nonmembers.

> **LOCATION:** 80 Dell Ave., Kenvil (Morris County). **HOURS:** Classes run Sep.–June, grouped in three courses. **ADMISSION:** Semester tuition. **PHONE:** 973-252-4300. **WEBSITE:** www.gymnasticsincnj.com. ⒷⓅ Ⓢ©

Jets Gymnastics

Classes for kids aged 2 and up are divided into different skill levels and ages. There are beginner, intermediate, and advanced classes, with different age groups—eight different classes in all. There are also three levels of cheer tumbling classes as well as trampoline classes. Sessions include warm-up, review of previously taught skills, work on new skills, practice time, warm-down, and evaluation. There are exercises at stations, circuit training, individual instruction, group instruction, and time on the equipment. Tasks are set up to be appropriate for each level so students feel challenged but not overwhelmed.

> **LOCATION:** 20-A Roland Ave., Mount Laurel (Burlington County). **HOURS:** Classes are held Mon.–Sat., with individual times varying with each course. **ADMISSION:** Semester tuition. **PHONE:** 856-273-2822. **WEBSITE:** www.jetsgymnastics.com. ⒷⓅ

Kangaroo Kidz Youth Gymnastics

The smallish gym offers noncompetitive gymnastics for children, with nine different types of classes. Classes vary by age and experience for kids aged 2½–12. The youngest preschoolers start by learning to use gym equipment to build their techniques. As they advance in age, kids refine those skills and learn things like doing headstands, cartwheels, and bridges. More advanced techniques follow for kids up to age 12. There's also a class just for developing tumbling skills, with an eye on using those talents for cheerleading, including handsprings. There's also a yoga class for kids.

LOCATION: Kings Shopping Center, Rt. 202, Bernardsville (Somerset County). **HOURS:** Classes start at various times, Mon.–Fri. 9–6, Sat., 9:30 and 10:30, depending on age. See schedule on website. **ADMISSION:** Seasonal tuition. **PHONE:** 908-766-0300. **WEBSITE:** www.kangarookidz.com.

Little Gym

This chain of children's gyms features a noncompetitive class schedule designed to build motor skills while having fun and building socialization. From 4 months to age 12, there are programs filled with movement, music, learning, cooperation, and fun, with age-appropriate activities that help children progress at their own pace. Programs include music, gymnastics, sports, exercise, and games. There are three programs for gymnastics: Parent/Child classes (four levels), in which kids learn balance, body awareness, and coordination; Preschool/Kindergarten (three levels plus two advanced levels), with fun gymnastics and other physical activities; and Grade School (beginning, intermediate, and advanced groups), in which kids advance their physical strength, flexibility, and coordination through gymnastics training and skill proficiency. There are also Sport Skills Development classes that teach fundamental sports skills geared toward kids aged 3–6. They take part in drills and simulated games for popular sports, including soccer, baseball, basketball, football, hockey, and golf. They learn the rules and strategies of each sport and gain an understanding of teamwork and sportsmanship in a fun, noncompetitive environment. Cheerleading classes (four levels, ages 3–12) teach stunts, jumps, chants, and cheers in a setting that emphasizes teamwork. And there's a dance class (four levels, ages 3–12) that combines ballet, tap, creative movement, and gymnastics to improve balance, posture, and grace. Kids learn the basic steps and positions while building flexibility, strength, and coordination and improving their rhythm and poise.

LOCATIONS: Barnegat, Bridgewater, Cherry Hill, Cranford, Englewood, Flemington, Hasbrouck Heights, Jackson, Jersey City, Livingston, Manasquan, Marlton, Millville, Montclair, Morganville, Roxbury, Somerset, Spotswood, Summit, Swedesboro, West Windsor, Waldwick, Washington Twp. (Turnersville), and Wayne. **HOURS:** Vary with location; see individual branch website. **ADMISSION:** Semester tuition. **PHONE:** 480-948-2878. **WEBSITE:** www.thelittlegym.com. (BP) (SC)

My Gym Children's Fitness Center

At this chain of fitness centers, kids attend parent participation classes until the age of 3-plus, then they move into independent gym classes. These are broken up into four sections from 3½ to 13 years. In Mighty Mites they do relays, play complex games, and are introduced to beginning sports skills. In Whiz Kids they master such skills as running, jumping, hopping, skipping, throwing, kicking, and catching to help them prepare for group sports and to build strength and agility. Champions classes focus on mastering sports and gymnastic skills. And the Cardio Kids program for 7–13-year-olds combines cardio workout with strength and flexibility exercises using a four-station circuit course, and kids learn health and fitness as a way of life. These centers also have Mommy & Me free play and Parents' Night Out as well as 2–3-hour Fit & Fun Days, which combine gymnastics, sports, relays, arts and crafts, story time, music, and more.

My Gym art class involves hands-on art exploration, story time, interactive circle time, and more. Each week kids learn about an artist, an art concept, or a foreign country and create art around that theme with brush painting, sponge painting, sculpture, and cutting and pasting.

LOCATIONS: Cherry Hill, Glen Rock, Howell, Manalapan, Parsippany, South Brunswick, Shrewsbury, Westfield, and West Orange.
See website for details. HOURS: Call or see website for schedule.
ADMISSION: Semester tuition. PHONE: 800-4MYGYMS.
WEBSITE: www.my-gym.com. (BP) (SC)

Sunburst Gymnastics

A wide variety of classes are offered at this gym, from beginner to advanced for kids 18 months and up. There are Parent and Tot classes for kids up to age 3½ that teach basic motor movements and awareness. Tiny Tot sessions for kids up to 4½ years introduce the basics of gymnastics, focusing on balance, coordination, and concentration as they learn through obstacle courses, trampoline, tumble track, rope swing, floor exercises, vault, balance beam, and more. Kinder classes for children up to 5½ years develop those skills, and Recreational classes from that age and older develop those skills steadily as kids grow in age. There's also a Kids Night Out one Saturday evening a month, which includes gymnastics, arts and crafts, games, and movie time.

LOCATION: 565 Rahway Ave., Union (Union County).
HOURS: Class times vary; see website for schedule.
ADMISSION: Semester tuition. PHONE: 908-810-1300.
WEBSITE: www.sunburstnj.com. (BP) (SC)

Envision Gymnastics

Ready-2-Learn is a program for kids aged 2 and 3 and combines the Little Tads gymnastics class with a preschool academy with parent participation. Kids get to use a variety of gymnastics equipment, such as pits, trampolines, spring floor, tumbling strip, and a specialized preschool area. Open gym is available on Friday evenings. Cheer tumble classes are also offered, based on skill level.

LOCATION: 6 Lina Lane and Rt. 206, Eastampton (Burlington County). **HOURS:** Class times vary; see website for schedule. **ADMISSION:** Semester tuition. **PHONE:** 609-261-1140. **WEBSITE:** www.envisiongymnastics.net. (BP)

Gymnastics & Cheerleading Academy

Parent and child classes (ages 2–3½) introduce kids to gymnastics fun, with lots of climbing, jumping, and rolling. The next level, taken without a parent, helps kids develop strength, flexibility, and coordination through a number of exercises. Kindergarten classes then introduce basic gymnastic skills through designed circuits along with special fun activities. A special girls' gymnastics program (for ages 6–11) has three levels in which girls use gym apparatus with an emphasis on developing confidence and self-esteem. There are also boys' classes that focus on control, strength, and flexibility. A girls' cheer tumble program (for age 5 and up) covers skill development on the spring floor, trampolines, tumble track, and mats.

LOCATION: 5 Larwin Rd., Cherry Hill, and 476 Centennial Blvd., Voorhees (Camden County). **HOURS:** Class times vary; see website for schedule. **ADMISSION:** Semester tuition. **PHONE:** 856-795-4599 or 856-627-8483. **WEBSITE:** www.thegcacademy.com. (BP) (SC)

TEAM SPORTS

In the Swing

This sports entertainment and teaching facility features baseball and softball batting and instruction. There are six batting cages, with professionally trained instructors helping youngsters from T-ball level through high school to improve their skills in hitting and fielding, including overall coordination, throwing, and base running. There are four types of lessons: Future Stars, a fun introduction to baseball; T-ball Drills, Intermediate Drills, and Advanced Drills. Separate pitching and catching clinics are also available. The facility also has six pitching machines, from 45 to 75 mph plus slow and fast pitch softball, so players can work on their hitting skills outside of clinic time. Besides baseball, there's also a soft-play area that features slides, tunnels, crawl-throughs, an air bounce, and two ball pits for younger kids. The facility also has a video arcade.

LOCATION: 145 Hopper Ave., Waldwick (Bergen County).
HOURS: Mon.–Fri, 10–8; Sat., 9–8; and Sun., 9–6.
ADMISSION: Varies with lesson package. **PHONE:** 201-444-3556.
WEBSITE: www.intheswing.biz. (BP) (SC)

Professional Baseball Instruction

This full-time baseball school offers instruction from age 3 to high school. Training sessions cover hitting, base running, pitching, catching, fielding, and throwing. The Squirts program (ages 3–5) is a noncompetitive, 6-week session that teaches the basics of the sport. School-age classes are broken up into five levels based on age and skill, and there's also a softball training course. The instructors break down the hitting mechanics for kids step by step. There are twelve hitting stations, each emphasizing a different aspect of the swing, helping establish good hitting habits. Batting cages let all students hit live pitching—a program set up by major league managers Clint Hurdle and Felipe Alou. The Building Blocks pitching program, designed with the help of major league pitching coach Leo Mazzone, has kids throwing strikes consistently, with topics including mechanics, pitch grips, fielding, live throwing, and more. The facility uses the latest equipment, including the Rotation Genius, which teaches the proper rotation on basic pitches. There's also an Infield program to help kids learn the secrets of infield play, from fielding to footwork to throwing and double plays. Similar level of instruction also covers catching, outfield, base running, and sliding.

LOCATION: 107 Pleasant Ave. at Rt. 17 North, Upper Saddle River (Bergen County). **HOURS:** Mon.–Fri., 10–10; weekends, 9–6. Somewhat shorter hours in summer. **ADMISSION:** Clinic tuition.
PHONE: 800-282-4638. **WEBSITE:** www.baseballclinics.com. (BP) (SC)

BB Grand Slam

The Better Baseball sporting complex and family entertainment center has six batting cages, with speeds from 25 to 75 mph; four fast-pitch softball cages, from 25 to 65 mph; and two arc-pitch softball cages. There's also a pitching tunnel with mound and radar gun. The complex also offers basketball court rentals, Lazer Tag (with barriers, strobe lights, energizer, and computer-tabulated scoring) for team play as well as Lazer Ball. There's also a soft play area for kids under 12 called Adventure Climb, featuring tunnels and tubes, ropes, a ball pit, a super slide, and air bounces as well as arcade games.

LOCATION: 910 Oak Tree Ave., South Plainfield (Middlesex County).
HOURS: Mon.–Fri., 11–10; Sat.–Sun., 9 A.M.–10 P.M.
ADMISSION: Tokens/token cards for batting cages. Rentals of cages, pitching tunnel, and basketball courts. Laser tag, $$ per person per session. **PHONE:** 908-756-4446. **WEBSITE:** www.bbgrandslam.com.

Langan Baseball

This organization offers individualized, year-round professional baseball and softball instruction in a step-by-step system. There are four hitting cages, two pitching tunnels, three pro batter simulator cages, a 5,500-square-foot turf field, and a baseball strength training area. All this supports an instruction program in baseball and softball for kids of all ages and skill levels. The pitching instruction is designed to improve mechanics and increase velocity and teach body control, stride, release point, and follow-through. The hitting instruction covers mechanics, balance, stance, approach, contact, and follow-through at the plate. Fielding instruction includes fielding stance, footwork, balance, and other proper techniques. There are also programmable pitching machines for baseball and softball. In addition, a limited amount of golf, soccer, and lacrosse instruction is available.

LOCATION: 712 Ginesi Dr., Morganville (Monmouth County).
HOURS: Mon.–Fri., 3:30–10; Sat., 9–7; and Sun., 10–6.
ADMISSION: Half-hour and hour-long lessons; packages available.
PHONE: 732-536-4900. **WEBSITE:** www.langanbaseball.com. (BP) (SC)

CK's Baseball 4U

Small group and individual instruction is provided for half- and full-hour sessions. There are position-specific clinics, including fielding, throwing, and catching as well as hitting, pitching, and sliding. There's also video consultation in a state-of-the-art conference room that compares kids to one of their favorite major league plays with a DVD to take home. Fitness4u is a speed and agility training program related to baseball, especially in developing the ability to push off and drive the ball, along with assistance in nutrition and exercises to maintain a healthy arm. The facility includes batting cages, pitching mounds, radar guns, and electronic baseball machines. The batting cages are also available for rental.

LOCATION: 210 Commercial Ct., Morganville (Monmouth County).
HOURS: Six-week clinics, one hour long each.
ADMISSION: Varies with clinic. **PHONE:** 732-617-8117.
WEBSITE: www.cksbaseball4u.com. (BP) (SC)

Frozen Ropes

Classes are geared to teach baseball and softball skills while improving social interaction and peer learning skills. Kids learn both by watching and through friendly competition. Programs include Rookie Class, School Academy, Minor League Class, Major League Class, Throw Like A Girl, Diamond Strength and Conditioning Classes, End Game Baseball and Softball Pitching Classes, Scope and Ropes Hitting Classes, and Girls Got Game Softball Training Classes. Using age- and skill-appropriate programs, kids can improve their hitting, fielding, and throwing in an indoor, state-of-the-art facility. Designed for ages 6–12. There is also softball instruction for ages 8–14. Certified instructors lead nationally recognized drills.

> **LOCATION:** 120 Kenyon Drive, Lakewood (732-363-8913); 30 Hook Mountain Rd., Unit 202, Pine Brook (973-396-2610); 31 Park Road, Tinton Falls (732-380-0040); and 60 Milltown Road, Union (908-686-9060). **HOURS:** Vary with session.
> **ADMISSION:** Course tuition. **WEBSITE:** www.frozenropes.com. Ⓢ︎Ⓒ︎

Spartans Sports Factory

This indoor training facility offers month-long baseball and softball clinics year-round for kids of preschool age and up. Hour-long T-Ball clinics teach the youngest players the basics of hitting, catching, throwing, base running, and the rules of the game. There's also an Intro to Softball course that covers the same skills. Both introduction courses are held after school. The Mini Sluggers program (for boys and girls aged 1½–3 and 3–5) teach sports skills like running, throwing, catching, hitting, and kicking in a noncompetitive atmosphere, with kids learning at their own pace. Parents can participate with their kids if they want. Classes are held daily in the morning. There are weekend-evening classes in windmill pitching and hitting clinics for girls aged 5–14, with age-specific skills taught to kids at their own pace. There's also an indoor hitting league, in which kids compete in hitting off pitching machines. Videotaping of players' mechanics are also used to help kids understand their own batting mechanics.

In addition to baseball, there's also a fall flag football league for kids aged 7–14 that includes four games and practice prior to each game. The facility also hosts a fall lacrosse program that runs four weeks, with 1½-hour sessions on Saturday mornings.

> **LOCATION:** 90 Herbert Ave., Closter (Bergen County).
> **HOURS:** After school and weekends. **ADMISSION:** Varies with class.
> **PHONE:** 201-286-4723. **WEBSITE:** www.spartanscamp.com. Ⓑ︎Ⓟ︎ Ⓢ︎Ⓒ︎

All Stars Sports 4 Kids

This site offers an all-sports program for "Future Stars" (ages 1½–8 in seven age groups), focusing on one sport a week—soccer, basketball, football, and hockey. Each class starts with a warm-up, then 20 to 30 minutes of instruction followed by team games. Kids then move to a nonsport event, such as a scooter pull, bounce house, ring toss, and other games. Various drills and games are incorporated into sessions to develop coordination as well as balance, strength, and teamwork. For boys and girls from grades 3 through 8, there are also basketball clinics. Next Level clinics evaluate kids before and during training sessions to better evaluate individual progress. For guard and post player classes, players are separated into the two categories, and training emphasizes the skills needed for each type of position. One-day mini classes and one-week mini camps are also held during school breaks. Plus, there are Recreation Nights and a Parents' Night Out on the first Friday of the month.

> **LOCATION:** 209 Commercial Ct., Morganville (Monmouth County).
> **HOURS:** Vary with session. **ADMISSION:** Course tuition.
> **PHONE:** 732-970-5555. **WEBSITE:** www.allstarsports4kids.com. (BP)(SC)

Hoop Heaven Basketball Center

Hoop Heaven offers a wide variety of clinics, from after-school sessions to private instruction for all skill levels of basketball. All facets of offense and defense are covered, including shooting, rebounding, passing, ball handling, man-to-man defense, and game situations. Ten- to twelve-session after-school clinics for pre-K to 8th grade are divided into five divisions. Kids learn a variety of court skills, from ball handling, shooting, and proper footwork to defense, rebounding, setting and using screens, and moving without the ball. Classes typically last an hour.

> **LOCATIONS:** 3E Chimney Rock Rd., Bound Brook (Somerset County).
> **PHONE:** 732-271-4667. 125 Algonquin Pky., Whippany (Morris County).
> **PHONE:** 973-884-4667. 132 Hopper Ave., Waldwick (Bergen County).
> **PHONE:** 201-251-6560. **HOURS:** Vary with session; generally Mon.–Fri.
> after school and Sat. morning. **ADMISSION:** Semester tuition.
> **WEBSITE:** www.hoopheaven.com. (BP)(SC)

Hoop Group

This facility offers a variety of different training classes, clinics, and leagues for improving basketball skills. SpeedZone Conditioning (grades 3–12) improves ball handling skills, footwork, and shooting. Core Skills Training (grades 3–12) provides overall skill development for all levels of players, emphasizing game speed drills and player conditioning to develop the competitiveness necessary to get to the next level. Dead Eye Shot Factory (grades 3–12) is a shooting course that is based on college-level drills and includes statistical analysis to aid improvement. Little Dribblers (K–2) is an introductory course for learning the fun and fundamentals of the game, including dribbling, passing, and shooting the ball while learning the basics of offensive and defensive footwork. Baskets are 8 feet high for this class. Individual Youth League (grades 3–6) sessions include 45 minutes of instructional drills in ball handling, passing, footwork, shooting form, and one-on-one play followed by a regulation game. There's also Hoop Group Elite (grades 3–8), a training class for kids who have handled the basics and are ready to expand their skills. In addition, one-day clinics are also offered on school holidays. There are girls' and boys' classes at all levels, and most classes run 5–7 weeks.

LOCATION: 1930 Heck Ave., Neptune (Monmouth County).
HOURS: Tue.–Thu. evenings and Sat. **ADMISSION:** Varies with class.
PHONE: 732-502-2255. **WEBSITE:** www.hoopgroup.com. (BP) (SC)

Soccer Centers

This large indoor-outdoor facility features year-round training in soccer and field hockey, with classes taught by Dutch soccer professionals. There are classes for kids aged 2–8 that focus on basic athletic skills and the basics of playing soccer. Itty Bitty Ball for ages 2–4 introduces children to basic athletic skills, such as coordination, balance, catching, throwing, and more, with parents taking part. Steppin into Soccer introduces kids 4–6 and their parents to the game of soccer, including learning how to dribble, pass, and score. Soccer instruction starts with DTS Junior Academy 1, which is designed for kids aged 5–6 in after-school and Saturday morning sessions. The next level, DTS Academy 2, is for kids 7–8. Futsal Young Lions introduces 7–8-year-olds to the related game of futsal, an 8-week, after-school course that helps students learn the fundamentals of soccer, including dribbling, passing, and shooting. There are also classes for goalies aged 7–8 as well as a Steppin into Sports program that offers kids a sampling of different sports.

LOCATION: 300 Memorial Dr., Somerset (Somerset County).
HOURS: Vary with session; see website for schedule.
ADMISSION: Course tuition. **PHONE:** 732-748-4625.
WEBSITE: www.soccercenternj.com. (BP)

McLoughlin School of Soccer

Taught by Tom McLoughlin, head soccer coach at Fairleigh Dickinson University, classes are held at almost two dozen locations in

Children receive professional-level instruction in soccer at the United Soccer Academy in Bound Brook. *(Photo courtesy of the United Soccer Academy)*

Morris and Somerset counties. There are Parent-Child classes (ages 3–4), which introduce soccer in a fun way as kids play and learn with their parents. Parents also learn games to play with children at home to reinforce the class instruction. Kiddie Soccer (age 3½) teaches children soccer-related skills through fun games. Soccer Kids (ages 4–5) teaches skills and tricks through fantasy games designed for kids of this age along with a basic version of soccer. Soccer Kids II adds skills, with more emphasis spent on playing soccer games. Soccer Skills (K and 1st grade) teaches kids through progressive games in which they experiment with scrimmages. Soccer Skills II (ages 7 and up) teaches developing skills facing opponents and tactical decision making. Classes are 45–75 minutes long.

> **LOCATION:** Headquarters: 17 Division St., Somerville (Somerset County). **HOURS:** Vary with session; see website for schedule. **ADMISSION:** Course tuition. **PHONE:** 908-393-5811. **WEBSITE:** www.soccer-kids.com. (BP) (SC)

United Soccer Academy

This is an innovative soccer center that teaches kids various aspects of the sport of soccer from age 3 up. Among the different types of courses are an introductory course as well as those focusing on specific skills like footwork, speed and agility, one-on-one, and shooting. There are also sessions just for girls. The academy is also able to tailor a specific program for individual children. All sessions are taught by certified professional coaches. Summer camps are held at dozens of locations throughout the state.

LOCATION: 12 Maiden Ln. Suite 1, Bound Brook (Somerset County).
HOURS: Vary with session; see website for schedule.
ADMISSION: Course tuition. **PHONE:** 732-563-2525.
WEBSITE: www.unitedsocceracademy.com. (SC)

Soccer for Life

The focus here is on soccer and motor skills development for kids aged 3–6 in which they learn the proper ways to kick and dribble and how to share the ball. They play such games as soccer freeze tag and soccer bandits. Classes are held at the Sports Academy in Millburn. This is a fun, noncompetitive environment where players learn the basics of the game while developing ball handling and foot skills and how to behave in a group environment. Each player receives individual attention that helps build confidence and self-esteem while learning the principles of sportsmanship, fair play, and cooperation. Summer soccer camps are also held for preschoolers along with all-sport camps for ages 6–12 in Millburn and Berkeley Heights. Classes are also held in a number of towns in Morris, Essex, and Union counties.

LOCATION: 56 E. Willow St., Millburn (Essex County).
HOURS: Vary with program. **ADMISSION:** Varies; call for rates.
PHONE: 973-912-9002. **WEBSITE:** www.soccerforlife.com. (SC)

The Sports Academy

This multisports academy in a 30,000-square-foot, state-of-the-art facility features three basketball courts, four practice soccer fields, indoor soccer, and a baseball/softball hitting tunnel and machines. Instruction features a graduated basketball hoop height program for ages 4–9 and clinics for grades 1–12. Soccer classes start for nursery-age kids and for ages 4–7, with training on specific skills and positions. Baseball and softball instruction includes hitting, pitching, and position-specific fielding along with mini-ball indoor baseball for ages 4–7.

LOCATION: 56 E. Willow St., Millburn (Essex County).
HOURS: Vary with session; see website for schedule.
ADMISSION: Course tuition. **PHONE:** 973-912-9002.
WEBSITE: www.the-sports-academy.com. (BP)(SC)

Sports and More in Sewell offers clinics where kids can develop their skills in basketball, gymnastics, and soccer and have fun with their teammates. *(Photo courtesy of Sports and More)*

Sports and More

Programs are offered by this facility in basketball, gymnastics, and soccer. The basketball training classes for boys and girls, aged 8–17, work on fundamentals, skill enhancement, and shooting. Basketball skill clinics are set up by age and skill level to help kids improve their ball handling, passing, shooting, and overall basketball IQ. Basketball shooting clinics focus on building a better shot from any-where on the court and work to increase jumping height, range of motion, and more. Private lessons are also available. Classes are held Mon.–Fri. after school and on Saturday.

There are also individual, small group, and large group soccer classes for kids aged 8–17 as well as morning and afternoon Pee Wee Soccer sessions (ages 2–6). These courses offer specialized soccer training from a nationally licensed coach and cover passing and receiving, first touch ball control, dribbling, juggling, and shooting.

Tumble Times are classes designed to help kids at all levels learn balance, coordination, and flexibility on balance beams, gymnastic bars, trampoline, tumbling floor, moon bounce, and more. There are a variety of classes for kids ages 1–10. There's a parent and child class for exploring the gym together while learning the basics of gymnastics. Classes for older kids teach proper stretching tech-niques and demonstrate the dynamics of gymnastics. There are also classes for children with special needs. Open gym time is available

Tuesday evenings. Tumbling and stunting classes are also available for cheerleaders. All ages work on back handsprings, back tucks, layouts, flying, and other skills.

> **LOCATION:** 1855 Hurffville Rd., Sewell (Gloucester County).
> **HOURS:** Mostly after school and Sat.; call or check website for schedule. **ADMISSION:** Varies with class. **PHONE:** 856-401-8111.
> **WEBSITE:** www.sportsandmorefun.com. (BP) (SC)

City Sports

All-sports programs are offered for kids ages 2–8. There's a Mommy & Me class for children aged 2–3 in which the kids warm up for 5–10 minutes and then move to a variety of activities with their parents. The emphasis is on building coordination first before they are introduced to a particular sport and shown the basics of each. All-sports sessions for ages 3–8 delves into one sport a week for kids, including basketball, baseball, football, hockey, and soccer. There is half an hour of instruction and the same amount of time for play. For kids 5–8, there are single-sport classes on basketball, baseball, football, or soccer that introduce different aspects of the sport. Classes run 9 weeks. Mommy and Me classes are held weekday mornings; the others are in late afternoon. There are also instructional basketball classes after school for grades 1 through high school, set up by grade level. These nine-week sessions last an hour for grades 1–3 and 1½ hours for grades 4 and up.

> **LOCATION:** 62 Rt. 4 East, Englewood (Bergen County).
> **HOURS:** Vary with class; see website for schedule.
> **ADMISSION:** Course tuition. **PHONE:** 201-567-1111.
> **WEBSITE:** www.citsportson4.com. (BP)

OTHER SPORTS

Basking Ridge Golf Academy

Junior golf clinics are offered for kids aged 2–17 at the Basking Ridge Country Club. For ages 2–4 there are half-hour parent-and-child sessions covering a variety of activities that help develop basic golf movements. Mobility, hand-eye coordination, spatial awareness, kinesthetic awareness, and visualization are emphasized. This class runs for three sessions. Junior golfers aged 9 and under have three-session one-hour classes available, focusing on improving fundamental movement skills and including golf concepts like grip, posture, alignment, ball position, and weight shift along with rules, safety, and etiquette that are learned through games that simulate golf. The 2-hour classes for kids 9 and up are designed to improve athletic ability, physical strength, and golf aptitude. Students practice movement skills and grip, posture, alignment, and weight shift are taught along with green reading and rules of the game through on-course games and lessons. There are also 1½-hour after-school classes offered for 6 weeks that teach specific skills.

LOCATION: 185 Madisonville Rd., Basking Ridge (Somerset County).
HOURS: Most classes Sat., May–Oct. **ADMISSION:** Course tuition.
PHONE: 908-766-8200, ext. 143. **WEBSITE:** www.baskingridgecc.com.

New Jersey Rock Gym

Youth climbing classes provide instruction in rock climbing techniques, including tying, top roping, bouldering, and climbing safety. After-school and Saturday morning classes are offered in 8-week sessions that help kids learn how to climb in a safe and friendly environment. There's also a separate Kids Climb for ages 6 and up lasting for 1½ hours on Sunday morning.

LOCATION: 373D Rt. 46 West, Fairfield (Essex County).
HOURS: Class times vary. Facility: Mon.–Fri., 2–10:30; Sat.–Sun., 10–8.
ADMISSION: Course tuition. **PHONE:** 973-543-9860.
WEBSITE: www.njrockgym.com. (BP) (SC)

Rockville Climbing Center

This state-of-the-art rock climbing facility provides an after-school climbing program that helps kids develop a sense of body control and balance useful in more traditional sports. Many different aspects of climbing and safety are emphasized. Classes meet once a week for 8 weeks. An Intro to Climbing package is also available.

LOCATION: 200 Whitehead Rd., Hamilton (Mercer County).
HOURS: Classes on Tue. or Wed., 4–5:30. Facility hours are
Mon.–Tue., 3–10; Wed.–Sat., 12–10; Sun., 12–8.
ADMISSION: Course tuition. Day pass, $$$. **PHONE:** 609-631-ROCK.
WEBSITE: www.rockvilleclimbing.com. (BP) (SC)

Garden State Rocks

Ongoing 8-week sessions are offered for kids 6–14 that focus on proper equipment use, basic climbing, and safety techniques. When kids master the basics, more advanced lessons follow. The basics include proper use of hands and feet, how to shift weight and maintain balance, and improving endurance while climbing. All students learn to master specific routes on a variety of wall features. The 6,000-square-foot climbing surface includes overhung terrain with bulges, roofs, arêtes, and slabs with realistic cracks. Special sections of this wall are designed for lessons.

LOCATION: 705 Ginesi Dr., Morganville (Monmouth County).
HOURS: Facility hours, Mon.–Fri., 3–10:30; Sat.–Sun., 12–7.
Call for class hours. **ADMISSION:** Day pass, $$$. Classes: Tuition.
PHONE: 732-972-3003. **WEBSITE:** www.gardenstaterocks.com. (BP)(SC)

Ice House

With four NHL-size rinks, this facility has more than 1,000 hockey players ages 5–16 enrolled in its programs. There is a 10-week Learn to Skate Clinic for hockey on Tuesday and Thursday after school and a Learn to Play Hockey Clinic on Monday and Wednesday evenings and Sunday afternoon, broken into three skill levels. Sessions include 30 minutes of power skating and 30 minutes of stick skills. There are also specialty hockey clinics based on position, including goalie, power skating and stick handling, and travel player programs.

There's also a notable figure skating program, which has sent a number of skaters to the Olympics, and the facility's learn-to-skate program is ranked as one of the ten best by the U.S. Figure Skating Association. Classes are set up by proficiency level, Basic 1 to 8, including a three-level Tot program. Preschool-age Parent/Tot classes are offered weekday afternoons and weekend mornings. Snowplow Sam 1 through 3 introduces preliminary moves to preschool agers not ready for Basic 1. For those 6–14, Basic 1–8 allows a beginner to feel comfortable on the ice while gaining basic skating knowledge to advance. There are weekday afternoon, after-school, and weekend morning sessions. Classes include half an hour of instruction and half an hour of practice.

LOCATION: 111 Midtown Bridge Approach, Hackensack (Passaic County). **HOURS:** Vary with class. **ADMISSION:** Course tuition.
PHONE: 201-487-8444. **WEBSITE:** www.icehousenj.com. (BP)

Floyd Hall Skating Arena

Hockey lessons are offered for a variety of age levels. A Tot Hockey program for beginners ages 3–5 provides 4–5 weeks of one-hour instruction that covers standing on skates, hockey stance, hockey position, forward strides, stick handling, passing, shooting, and turning as well as a 15-minute scrimmage. Held on Monday and Wednesday after school and Saturday morning. The Tykes on Ice program is for kids 4–7 and covers the next level of skills. Held on Monday and Wednesday after school and weekend mornings. The Hockey Development program for ages 7 and up develops skills in both skating and hockey with a similar schedule. This arena also offers a Learn to Skate program that covers a variety of skill levels, with skaters progressing from learning the basics of balance, marching, and gliding to mastering crossovers, backwards skating, and even spins and jumps. Courses generally run 7 or 8 weeks and are held Tuesday and Thursday after school and on Saturday. Classes are grouped according to age and skill level.

LOCATION: Montclair State University Campus, One Hall Dr., Little Falls (Passaic County). **HOURS:** See description. **ADMISSION:** Semester tuition. **PHONE:** 973-746-7744. **WEBSITE:** www.floydhallarena.com. (BP) (SC)

Skylands Ice World

This facility offers four Learn to Skate programs. The main one is the Basic Skills program as developed by the U.S. Figure Skating Association. It covers all ages and abilities and features badges marking certain achievements. The Basic Skills program is also a feeder for USA Hockey and US Speedskating. A second program is Parent and Tot, suited for preschoolers and their caregivers during weekday hours. Lessons last 30 minutes and include free admission to the remainder of the public session that follows. The PreSchool program is for ages 3–6 and provides extra attention for the youngest skaters as they learn the basics of skating. Lessons last 30 minutes and include a 1½-hour free skate afterward. There's also a Learn to Skate program for special needs children that focuses on kids having fun and enjoying being on the ice.

LOCATION: 2765 Rt. 23, Stockholm (Sussex County). **HOURS:** Vary with class. **ADMISSION:** Course tuition. **PHONE:** 973-697-1600. **WEBSITE:** www.skylandsiceworldnj.com. (BP) (SC)

Ice Vault Skating Arena

The Learn to Skate Class features six half-hour group lessons for kids 3–6 on Wednesday afternoons. Parents can join their kids on the ice. There's also a Youth Hockey Skills Learn to Skate program after school, featuring half-hour sessions for 9 weeks for ages 5 and up. The basic skills course is required. A 6-week Bridge Skating Program, held on Saturday mornings or Tuesday after school, introduces kids to competitive recreational skating and helps them advance their skills (teacher recommendation is needed). The Basic Skills Program is endorsed by USFSA and includes 9 weeks of half-hour lessons followed by half an hour of practice time. Classes are held Monday and Friday after school and on Saturdays.

LOCATION: 10 Nevins Dr., Wayne (Passaic County). **HOURS:** Class times vary. **ADMISSION:** Course tuition. **PHONE:** 973-628-1500. **WEBSITE:** www.icevault.com.

Bridgewater Sports Arena

This three-rink facility—two NHL-sized and a smaller skills rink— offers a Learn to Skate program for skaters 2½ to adult. Classes are divided by skill level and age. Private lessons are available as well as group lessons for skaters with special needs. The facility follows the USFSA structure, from Tiny Tots for ages 2½–3; Snowplow Sam for new skaters aged 4–6; Basic 1, for new skaters ages 7–14, with higher levels in each category as kids advance. There are also hockey lessons. After the Basic 4 level is complete, skaters can join the Bridge Training program. Classes are held on Wednesday after school and on Saturday mornings and Sunday afternoons. Classes meet for 30 minutes a week and run 6–10 week sessions. Four free public skating admissions are included. New participants also receive a free 15-minute private lesson and a yearly Basic Skills membership. There are also Learn to Skate open sessions and hockey clinics that focus on certain aspects of the sport.

The arena also features a laser tag facility, called LaserZone. Teams compete for points in black-light, fog-filled areas wearing a special vest and carrying a high-tech laser (phaser) for scoring points. They start with a demo of how to play the game, learning about the phaser, bases, mines, and scoring.

LOCATION: 1425 Frontier Rd., Bridgewater (Somerset County). Off Rt. 22 West at Rt. 287. **HOURS:** See above. **ADMISSION:** Class tuition for skating lessons; $$$$$ for six-pack of laser tag games. **PHONE:** 732-627-0006. **WEBSITE:** www.bsaarena.com. (BP) (SC)

Union Sports Arena

Developmental programs for players ages 5–13 are offered. There's an after-school program that is designed to introduce beginners to hockey (ages 5–8) that runs ten sessions of one hour each. A Learn to Skate program is held on Saturdays and Sundays and after school; it consists of 25 minutes of instruction with additional public skating time afterward. Depending on a skater's level and age, kids can learn to snowplow, glide on one foot, do forward crossovers, and learn a number of other skills.

LOCATION: 2441-A Rt. 22 West, Union (Union County). **HOURS:** Vary. **ADMISSION:** Course tuition. **PHONE:** 908-687-8610. **WEBSITE:** www.unionsportsarena.com. (BP)

Blue Water Divers

Kids as young as 10 can learn to Scuba dive and achieve a junior certification at the store's indoor heated pool. Kids dive with an adult instructor and form the foundation for an education in diving.

Classroom time and diving time are split about evenly. Kids learn how to breathe underwater with apparatus in a warm, clear pool. The course consists of a one-session introductory Discover Scuba session and an Open Water Diving course, which is offered weeknights for three weeks. There's also an Executive Open Water course covering the same ground but done during an intensive weekend, with reading and homework completed prior to the first session. The final activity for the courses is a training dive at a local recreation area during warmer months or an optional travel trip to a warmer location in colder months.

Blue Water also has a swim school with professional instruction. There is typically one 30-minute lesson a week for 12 weeks. Locations are in Saddle Brook and Mahwah, and classes are offered for all ages and levels.

> **LOCATION:** 201 Rt. 17 South, Rochelle Park (Bergen County).
> **HOURS:** Mon., 11–7; Tue.–Fri., 11–9, Sat., 9–5.
> **ADMISSION:** Course tuition. **PHONE:** 201-843-3340.
> **WEBSITES:** www.bluewaterdivers.com and www.bwdswimschool.com.
> (BP) (SC)

The Tennis Farm

Kids who want to learn tennis can develop their skills with the Tennis Farm's lessons. There are two levels for children: Whipper-Snappers (ages 3–6) and Juniors (ages 7–16). The younger class runs one hour a week for 8 weeks and uses fun games and interactive drills to enhance hand-eye coordination along with assisted hitting and developing the strokes of forehand, backhand, volley, and overhead. The Basic program for Juniors concentrates on learning and developing fundamental strokes through specialized drills. Students learn forehand, backhand, serve, volley, grips, scoring, lobs, footwork, court position, singles, and doubles. The Competitive Play Program is designed to help kids play under match conditions and work on secondary shots used during advanced games. The Juniors classes generally last 3 hours.

> **LOCATION:** Moorestown High School, Bridgeboro Rd., Moorestown (Burlington County). **HOURS:** Sundays. **ADMISSION:** Class tuition.
> **PHONE:** 800-7-TENNIS. **WEBSITE:** www.tennisfarm.com.

Exploring Museums

At the Infection Connection exhibit in Liberty Science Center, children and their parents can see how daily choices contribute to the rise and fall of infectious diseases and how science develops technologies to prevent and treat infections. *(Photo by Patrick Sarver)*

ART AND SCIENCE MUSEUMS
Liberty Science Center

Set in the middle of Liberty State Park, Liberty Science Center presents nine permanent exhibition galleries covering subjects that deal with daily life and exploring science in ways designed to appeal to all age groups, but it is especially popular with kids. From time to time throughout the day, there are also live science demonstrations that augment the exhibits (there's a schedule at the welcome desk in the lobby).

The first floor of the center features a large lobby space and a major exhibit on skyscrapers—how they're constructed, their history, and examples from around the world. There are cut-away views of tall building interiors, displaying the design, operation, and ecology of modern high-rise structures.

On the second floor, young kids (2–5) have their own section called I Explore where they can learn about their bodies, their world, and their own talents. In an outdoor exhibit open in warm weather called Wildlife Challenge kids can crawl, climb, and claw through the daily challenges that face urban wildlife. Near this are a number of simulator rides (extra $).

Next floor up includes a gallery called Communication, which covers a wide range of topics, such as electronic graffiti, language karaoke, and other exhibits that explore the various facets of human communication. Other galleries here include Eat and Be Eaten, where you explore the predator-prey life cycle, and Infection Connection, where you get a fascinating look at the world of microbes and their role in the spread of disease. There's also Breakthroughs, which features colorful screens and other displays that offer insights into science in the news.

On the very top level an exhibit gallery called Our Hudson Home explores the relationship between people and nature along the nearby lower Hudson River, including hands-on exhibits. There's also a section on Earth's energy resources, a traveling exhibition gallery, and forty favorite exhibits from the previous science center, such as the Resonance Tube, a rock climbing wall, and brain-teaser stations.

The IMAX Theater, on the second floor, is the largest of its kind in the country, housed in a geodesic dome that features an eight-story curved screen. Movies produced in the IMAX format are twice as large as feature films and use a six-channel sound system (extra fee). Nature films are popular here. Reserve when you come in (or even ahead of time). Two or three different movies may be shown on a single day. The Joseph D. Williams Science Theater features 3-D shows (extra fee) that are usually very good. (*Note:* IMAX is not recommended for children under 6.)

Young Scientist Wednesday Workshops from October to June offer one-hour morning classes for children ages 3–5 with adult caregivers. Activities include an interactive story and hands-on science project on a wide variety of subjects such as trains, snow, shells, healthy eating, and the science of pirates. At the Jennifer A. Chalsty Center for Science Learning and Teaching, groups of students explore interactive science in laboratory workshops led by knowledgeable science educators on such topics as clouds, everyday chemistry, amphibians and reptiles, and bacteria and viruses.

LOCATION: Exit 14B, N.J. Turnpike, turn left, follow Liberty State Park signs, take Burma Road to the Science Center. **HOURS:** Tue.–Fri., 9–4; weekends, 9–5. Open an additional hour and on Mon. in summer. **ADMISSION:** $$$$; children 2–12, $$$. Under 2 free. Combination fee with IMAX & 3-D show available. **PHONE:** 201-200-1000. **WEBSITE:** www.lsc.org.

Newark Museum

Newark Museum is open, airy, and convenient—a truly first-class museum. There is room to show off the collection—American paintings, Tibetan statues, African masks—plus plenty of space for the special exhibits. The American Art Galleries covers two floors on the North Wing, tracing the development of art in the United States from the colonial to the contemporary. Works from major artists are displayed in separate galleries according to period and theme.

The Dynamic Earth, in the Victoria Hall of Science, adds a strong natural science angle to the museum's collections, and is done in a way that appeals to kids. It features seven galleries that cover forces shaping the natural world, an exploration of the world's ecosystems, and a look at New Jersey's natural setting. Hands-on activities are mixed with traditional exhibits for exploring volcanoes, earthquakes, and survival of the fittest. There's a Discover Field Station, where kids can do their own scientific investigations. You'll also find a real mastodon skeleton uncovered in a "dig," ancient insects trapped in amber, fluorescent minerals from New Jersey, and fossils in a re-created New Jersey cave. There's also a Junior Gallery and a Native American Gallery that offers costumes and artifacts.

Drop-in workshops are often held for families on weekend afternoons, focusing on such activities as making stained glass and candles. Special weekend programs are held from time to time, with topics like Circus Science, Bug Day, and Ethno Science Day. Check the website for a schedule of these upcoming events.

In addition, the fifty-seat Dreyfuss Planetarium is near the garden entrance and offers afternoon sky shows to the public (Fee: $). The museum also includes a pleasant garden complete with several modern sculptures. A tiny one-room schoolhouse that dates to 1784 and a Fire Museum are also part of the garden.

LOCATION: 49 Washington St., Newark (facing Washington Park). **HOURS:** Wed.–Sun., 12–5. Oct.–June, open weekends at 10. July–Sep., open weekends at noon. Closed major holidays.

ADMISSION: $$. **PHONE:** 973-596-6550; planetarium, 973-596-6529.
WEBSITE: www.newarkmuseum.org. (SC)

Montclair Art Museum

A true art museum nestled in a town that was once an artists' center, the Montclair Art Museum reflects a high level of community support. This solid, neoclassical museum is dedicated to painting and sculpture, with a permanent collection of more than 12,000 works. The collection consists entirely of American art, covering a period of three centuries. Many familiar names, such as Hopper, Nevelson, Sargent, Peale, Eakins, Copley, O'Keeffe, Warhol, and Currier & Ives, are represented here along with other prominent American artists. One gallery is dedicated to the work of George Inness, the Hudson River School painter who did much of his work in Montclair. The paintings in the permanent collection are often used for changing exhibits, which are themed for a certain point of view. Many traveling exhibits of notable artists are also shown throughout the year, all with an American art-related theme.

Kids are likely to find the permanent Native American collection most interesting. Costumes and artifacts highlight the Plains and Southwest Indians, including interesting displays of Sioux and Navajo dress. The museum also shows works by contemporary Native American artists.

This is an active museum, with classes, children's programs, and gallery tours. Ongoing children's art classes are held at the museum. There are also other programs for kids. MAM Park Bench, held one Wednesday morning a month, introduces young children to the museum and serves as an artistic social outing as the kids work on fun art projects and take a guided tour of the museum. Imagination Station is a drop-in weekend program on Saturdays that focuses on a different artwork or theme each week in which there's active looking, discussion, interactive activities, scavenger hunts, and sketching in the galleries. There are also special programs, such as Come Build Montclair Lego, in which families work with an architect to turn photographs of specific buildings in Montclair into Lego models that are placed on a 30 by 20 foot map of downtown Montclair.

LOCATION: 3 S. Mountain Ave., Montclair (Essex County).
HOURS: Wed.–Sun., 12–5. **ADMISSION:** $$$. Under 12 free.
PHONE: 973-746-5555. **WEBSITE:** www.montclairartmuseum.org. (BP)(SC)

Princeton University Art Museum

One of the leading university art museums in the United States, the Princeton University Art Museum features a collection of 72,000 works ranging from ancient to contemporary, with concentrations on the Mediterranean, Western Europe, China, the U.S., and Latin America. The museum's greatest strengths are its collections of Greek and Roman antiquities from the university's excavations in Antioch, as well as Chinese and pre-Colombian art, most notably Olmec, Maya, and Aztec items. Medieval European works include sculpture, metalwork, and stained glass. Western European paintings encompass important examples from the early Renaissance through the nineteenth century, with a growing collection of twentieth-century and contemporary art. The American Gallery includes works by such artists as Copley, Peale, Eakins, Homer, and Sargent, while the Nineteenth-Century Gallery features works by Impressionist notables like Cezanne, Degas, Gaugin, Van Gogh, and Monet. Special exhibits show portions of these collections on a rotating basis.

The art museum offers self-guided activities for families, with themes such as "I Spy a Masterpiece" and "The Writing Is on the Wall," with activity packets available at the information desk. There are also tours for classes with teachers. And, in mid-June, there's an Americana Barbeque—a special event with kids' activities to kick off the museum's summer program.

LOCATION: Princeton University Campus, Nassau and Witherspoon Sts., Princeton (Mercer County). From Nassau St., walk past the left side of Nassau Hall. Museum is straight ahead.
HOURS: Tue.–Sat., 10–5, Thu. until 10; Sun., 1–5. Closed major holidays.
ADMISSION: Free. **PHONE:** 609-258-3788.
WEBSITE: www.princetonartmuseum.org.

Grounds for Sculpture

Located on the former grounds of the New Jersey State Fair, the 35-acre site includes two large buildings dedicated to indoor exhibitions and an expanse of greenery that serves as a backdrop for large sculptures. Although there are many abstract pieces, you will also find "lifelike" forms by such artists as J. Seward Johnson. Johnson was the founder of this facility, and a number of his works on the grounds interpret well-known Impressionist paintings as sculptures. Overall, dozens of artists' works in all manner of media are displayed at this art park. Special exhibits are offered several times a year, and there are guided tours May to October.

The Domestic Arts Building includes large spaces for rotating exhibits. A formal Water Garden, which features reflecting pools, concrete walkways, plantings, and outdoor "rooms" of sculpture, is next to the building.

There are children's workshops for 6–9-year-olds and 10–14-year-olds. Topics include sand casting, found objects, and papier-mâché. There's also a Tots on Tours program for kids 3–5 offered March through October on the third Saturday morning of the month in which children explore the park and learn about sculpture, make an original work of art, and listen to a story.

LOCATION: 18 Fairgrounds Road, Hamilton Twp. (Mercer County). Rt. 295, Exit 65B. Follow signs.
HOURS: Tue.–Sun., 10–6. May–Oct., tours Sat. at 11, Sun. at 2.
ADMISSION: $$. Discounts: Seniors, students, children.
Under 6 free. **PHONE:** 609-586-0616.
WEBSITE: www.groundsforsculpture.org.

Zimmerli Art Museum

The Jane Voorhees Zimmerli Art Museum, on the Rutgers Campus in New Brunswick, has over 50,000 works (paintings, lithographs, drawings, photographs). The lobby level is home to American Art, a large Russian Art collection, and Soviet nonconformist art. Upstairs, on the mezzanine level, is the home of American prints and an environmental sculpture gallery. A spiral ramp leads to the lower level, where a maze of walls presents ancient art, modernist European and American art, Japonisme, European art, special exhibition galleries, and additional Soviet nonconformist works.

The American Art collection includes paintings and sculpture from the late eighteenth century to today, including nineteenth-century portraits and landscapes and American art influenced by surrealism and abstraction. Other American collections cover women artists, original illustrations for children's literature, and a regional stained-glass design.

The Riabov Collection of Russian Art contains a wide variety of periods and media, including folk prints, sculpture, religious icons, landscapes, and stage designs, as well as Russian émigré art. The Dodge Collection of Non-conformist Art from the Soviet Union is the largest collection of its kind in the world, encompassing more than 17,000 works by dissidents.

The Zimmerli also has a large graphic arts collection from the nineteenth century. European modernism is represented through the graphic arts, displayed in the twentieth-century galleries. There is a small teaching collection of European paintings from the fifteenth to nineteenth centuries.

A Japonisme room also displays a permanent collection of European and American works on paper and ceramics—a selection that reflects the strong influence of Japan on Western art in the late

1800s and early 1900s. Plus, the museum features a number of traveling exhibits throughout the year.

Families can enjoy a fun introduction to the Zimmerli's diverse collections at Studio Z: The Adi Blum Learning Center, which offers self-guided activities for the family, including an interactive computer terminal. Kids will enjoy this center and its interactive learning materials on art. The museum also offers guided tours of the galleries on Sundays at 2 during the school year.

LOCATION: 71 Hamilton St., New Brunswick (Middlesex County). At corner of George St. **HOURS:** Tue.–Fri., 10–4:30; weekends, 12–5. Closed major holidays and Aug. **ADMISSION:** $. Under 18 free. **PHONE:** 732-932-7237. **WEBSITE:** www.zimmerlimuseum.rutgers.edu.

New Jersey State Museum

Down the block from the state capitol and overlooking the Delaware River, the renovated State Museum offers changing exhibits on natural history, archeology, cultural history, and fine art. Set up as a family museum, with exhibits to interest both children and adults, the museum offers a balance between its various sections. The first floor offers a variety of exhibits, usually simultaneous presentations on natural history and art. The second floor tends to focus more on the fine arts although historical exhibits are also presented there, while the third floor offers changing exhibits on natural and cultural history.

The separate Museum Theater building out front, which has a stage for special shows, has two smaller galleries, one on the history of Trenton and the other devoted to changing exhibits such as dinosaurs. There's also a permanent display of Civil War flags and a changing exhibit in the State Archives building at 225 W. State Street.

The adjacent planetarium, the state's largest, seats 150 visitors in reclining seats and features high-definition digital projection and full-dome video. Both traditional sky and laser programs are offered in this state-of-the-art facility. Shows are held at 1, 2, 3, and 4 P.M. on weekends ($).

The museum also offers a number of special events for the family. Sunday Explorers is a series of fun, hands-on workshops for kids, and Free Second Saturday is a series of performances designed for the family. There are also other children-oriented events throughout the year. See the website for upcoming events.

LOCATION: 205 W. State St., Trenton. Use Rt. 29 along Delaware River or Rt. 1 into State St. **HOURS:** Tue.–Sat., 9–5; Sun., 12–5. **ADMISSION:** Free. Planetarium, $.

PHONE: Museum, 609-292-6464; planetarium, 609-292-6303.
WEBSITE: www.newjerseystatemuseum.org.

Morris Museum

The Morris Museum of Arts and Sciences is a dependable bastion of culture housed in a lovely old mansion surrounded by large trees. One popular area is the rock and mineral exhibit (complete with a dark room for viewing fluorescent rocks). Another is the natural science section with its glass-encased exhibits of stuffed mammals and birds in their natural habitats. And since it is called a museum of arts and sciences, there is always at least one art exhibit on display that changes every few months. In recent years, major traveling exhibits have taken over much of the first floor. Sometimes, they are interactive and continue onto the outside terrace.

Permanent exhibits include a collection of vintage toys and dolls, a model railroad, Native American artifacts, and a small dinosaur room. The gracious Dodge Room is kept as a reception room with some excellent paintings, and decorative arts are shown in a domestic atmosphere. The museum is also the home of the Guinness Collection of historic mechanical musical instruments and figures.

Also on site is the comfortable 300-seat Bickford Theater, which is the setting for dramas, musicals, comedies, and children's shows.

The museum offers several series of drop-in workshops, including Open Art Workshops, Vacation Day Family Workshops, Super Science Saturdays, and Tot Tours. See the website for upcoming sessions.

LOCATION: 6 Normandy Heights Rd., Morristown (Morris County). Off Columbia Tpk. HOURS: Wed.–Sat., 10–5; Sun., 1–5; Thu. until 8. ADMISSION: $$. Thu., 5–8, free. Under 3 free. PHONE: 973-971-3700. WEBSITE: www.morrismuseum.org.

Noyes Museum of Art

This striking, beach-style museum overlooks a lily-pad lake on the edge of a national wildlife refuge. Inside, you'll find a dozen or more changing exhibits a year of contemporary paintings, photography, and sculpture by regional and national artists. It also has a growing collection of its own American fine and folk art, including a nice collection of vintage duck decoys. A special gallery for exhibits by students from area schools and community groups adds a nice touch. The museum also offers preschool art classes, story time, and themed art workshops. See website for schedule.

This museum was established by Fred W. Noyes, an academically trained painter and creator of nearby Smithville. A second museum location was recently opened in Hammonton.

LOCATION: 733 Lily Lake Rd., off Rt. 9, Oceanville, and 5 Second St., Hammonton (Atlantic County). **HOURS:** Tue.–Sat., 10–4:30; Sun., 12–5. **ADMISSION:** $. Under 7 free. **PHONE:** 609-652-8848 and 609-561-8006. **WEBSITE:** www.noyesmuseum.org.

CHILDREN'S MUSEUMS

New Jersey Children's Museum

Set in a reconditioned industrial building in Paramus with 15,000 square feet of space, the museum is 100 percent hands-on fun for kids. Children can touch, climb, put on clothes, and play-act to their hearts' content. The walls are brightly painted, the floor is carpeted, and the place may remind you of a giant nursery school. But the exhibits are far more expansive than those at a local preschool. There is a real helicopter, for instance, simplified so that a child can climb inside and pretend to fly. There is a genuine backhoe with a hard hat to match, and a fire engine complete with fire hose and bell. Each of the thirty interactive exhibits is designed around a theme, including a medieval castle, a dinosaur cave where kids can scribble their own "cave paintings" on a blackboard, and a driving and drawing exhibit that you steer to create patterns on a flat-screen TV. At a virtual reality exhibit, kids find themselves playing soccer goalie, petting farm animals, and playing the drums.

The huge space is divided into sections devoted to dance, music, medicine, construction, and so forth. The pizzeria keeps the kids busy for hours. There's also a Baby Park for the smallest children. Parents must supervise children and are welcome to join in the play. There are assistants around to help.

LOCATION: 599 Valley Health Plaza, Paramus (Bergen County). Off Ridgewood Ave. between Rt. 17 and Garden State Parkway, Exit 165. Call for directions. **HOURS:** Tue.–Sun., 10–5. **ADMISSION:** $$. Under 1 free. **PHONE:** 201-262-5151. **WEBSITE:** www.njcm.com. ⓑⓟ

Garden State Discovery Museum

This interactive children's museum is a 15,000-square-foot center with painted murals on the walls and twenty large interactive exhibit areas. The theme is New Jersey, so there's a diner complete with chrome and red vinyl seats and a kitchen where kids can whip up plastic hamburgers. They can explore the Storybook Castle, which has regular storytelling sessions, as well as climb a tree house or create their own art using completely recycled art materials. They can also learn about health and human anatomy at a doctor's office or learn all about nocturnal animals and stars at Into the Night.

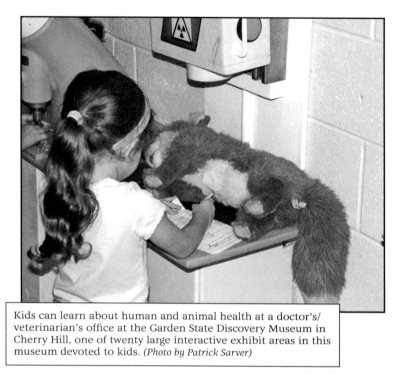

Kids can learn about human and animal health at a doctor's/veterinarian's office at the Garden State Discovery Museum in Cherry Hill, one of twenty large interactive exhibit areas in this museum devoted to kids. *(Photo by Patrick Sarver)*

Other areas include a rock-climbing wall and a hundred-seat theater where the kids can put on costumes and act. There's a Subaru science shop and service station and a house construction complete with gravel pit and junk. Musical instruments are also on hand. Kids can get a workout at the new Get Fit area, which features scaled-down basketball, a hockey rink, and miniature golf. There's also a special Little Discoverers Barnyard section just for toddlers. The museum is designed for children up to 10 years old—and parents must accompany them.

The museum also offers classes for kids. Early Explorers (ages 1½–3) is a weekly hands-on fun class that offers activities including music, dance, stories, and crafts. Mini Masters (4–6) is a first class where a child is exposed to art exploration using different materials and techniques. And in Artlab (6–9) kids explore the science of art with fun experiments and exploratory hands-on craft projects. Other classes are offered through outside organizations that specialize in language, music, theater, and sports. There are also a number of special events, including storytelling, entertainment, singing and dancing, and ethnic celebrations.

LOCATION: 2040 Springdale Rd., Cherry Hill (Camden County). Not far from N.J. Turnpike, Exit 4, or Rt. 295. Call or see website for directions. **HOURS:** Oct.–Apr., daily, 9:30–5:30; Sat. until 8:30. **ADMISSION:** $$. Under 1 free. **PHONE:** 856-424-1233. **WEBSITE:** www.discoverymuseum.com. (BP)

Monmouth Museum

This is a three-part museum. One section is a museum for adults and two sections are devoted to exhibits for children. The Main Gallery features changing exhibits in art, history, science, and nature. The Becker Children's Wing is geared toward kids ages 6–12 and mounts major exhibits on school subjects related to science and cultural history (such as the Western frontier, Changing Climate, or Space) that run for 2 years. The third section, the WonderWing, is designed for the 6-and-under set. It contains interactive play areas, including a tree house, pirate ship, whale slide, and kelp forest in an under-the-sea setting. There's also Tiki Theater, a tree house, and a lighthouse. A lot of activities are packed into a small setting.

LOCATION: Brookdale Community College campus, Lincroft (Monmouth County). Garden State Parkway, Exit 109, then west on Newman Springs Rd. (Rt. 520). **HOURS:** Main Gallery: Tue.–Sat., 10–4:30; Sun., 1–5. Becker Children's Wing: Tue.–Fri., 2–4:30; Sat., 10–4:30; Sun., 1–5. WonderWing: Fri., Sat., 10–4:30; Sun., 1–5; Tue.–Thu., call for hours. **ADMISSION:** $$. Under 2 free. **PHONE:** 732-747-2266. **WEBSITE:** www.monmouthmuseum.org. (BP)

Imagine That!!!

A discovery center with fifty hands-on activities in 16,000 square feet, it includes a ballet/tap area, art and music rooms, shadow play, VW Bug, and a real Piper plane. There's also a TV newsroom, a real fire truck, a grocery store, train exhibit, a post office, computer room, simulated space shuttle, science area, and a Dr./Dentist office. There are lots of crafts here, too, as well as special events, such as a Princess Breakfast, making pirate maps, and arts enrichment classes.

LOCATION: 4 Vreeland Rd., Florham Park (Morris County). **HOURS:** Daily, 10–5:30. **ADMISSION:** $$; under 1 free. **PHONE:** 973-966-8000. **WEBSITE:** www.imaginethatmuseum.com. (BP)

Jersey Explorer Children's Museum

Inside an East Orange Library, this noncommercial museum is dedicated to bringing the Afro-American heritage alive for children, including older kids. It includes a Time-Traveler Theater, arts and crafts, interactive storytelling, and some exhibits.

LOCATION: 192 Dodd St., East Orange (Essex County).
HOURS: Open to groups only, by reservation: Tue.–Fri.
Open to the public: Sat., 10–3. **ADMISSION:** $$. Under 3 free.
PHONE: 973-673-6900. **WEBSITE:** www.jerseyexplorer.org.

Community Children's Museum

This smaller museum features such exhibits as exploring Nancy's
Lake House and John Glenn's Space Capsule. There's also a portrait
studio, an electricity exhibit, art studio, homes around the world,
theater area, and more.

LOCATION: 77 E. Blackwell St., Dover (Morris County).
HOURS: Thu.–Sat., 10–5. **ADMISSION:** $. **PHONE:** 973-366-9060.
WEBSITE: www.communitychildrensmuseum.org. (BP)

Jersey Shore Children's Museum

This smaller museum has sixteen exhibits, such as a TV newsroom,
hospital ER, construction zone, car factory, post office, puppet cor-
ner, country store, and more. For children ages 1–8. Summer and
family memberships available.

LOCATION: Shore Mall, 6725 Black Horse Pike (Rt. 40/322), Egg Harbor
Twp. (Atlantic County). Garden State Parkway, Exit 36 N or 37 S.
HOURS: Mon.–Sat., 10–5; Sun., 12–5. **ADMISSION:** $$. Under 1 free.
PHONE: 609-645-7741. **WEBSITE:** www.eht.com/childrensmuseum. (BP)

AVIATION MUSEUMS

New Jersey Aviation Hall of Fame

Located on the southern edge of Teterboro Airport, this museum is
filled with aviation memorabilia with a focus on the Garden State.
There are loads of model airplanes, a section devoted to women
pilots, and photos of all sorts of early air machines. Hanging from
the ceiling are models of satellites and astronaut uniforms. There
is also a small helicopter you can try out, and a balloon basket that
children can climb into. At the sixty-seat theater you watch a film
on the history of aviation in New Jersey. In the tower room you can
listen in on pilot-control tower conversations. There's also an X-1
rocket engine, the aircraft used by Chuck Yeager to break the
sound barrier; an X-15 engine, a rocket plane that was the first aircraft in space; a 48-cylinder reciprocal engine built by Curtis
Wright; and a Hindenburg display with a piece of the ill-fated air-
ship's frame.

Outside, you can climb aboard an old-fashioned propeller plane
and see how people in the 1940s and 1950s used to ride. And behind

the building, a Bell helicopter and a M.A.S.H. unit with jeeps and a truck re-create a Korean War scene. There is even a mess tent for lunch. This is a fun place for kids.

LOCATION: 400 Fred Wehran Dr., Teterboro Airport, Teterboro (Bergen County). Off Rt. 46 at the eastern edge of the airport. **HOURS:** Tue.–Sun., 10–4. Closed major holidays. **ADMISSION:** $$. Discounts: Children. Under 5 free. **PHONE:** 201-288-6344. **WEBSITE:** www.njahof.org.

Air Victory Museum

Set within a hangar in the South Jersey Regional Airport, this museum celebrates American air power and the technology and engineering behind it. The large collection of major aircraft on display includes an F-14A Tomcat, F-4A Phantom II, F104G Starfighter, F-86 Sabrejet, A-4 Skyhawk, and A-7B Corsair II. There are also a number of small helicopters in the hangar, such as the Bell helicopter. Small replicas of famous planes (such as the Wright Brothers Flyer) as well as wooden and plastic models of a large variety of aircraft can be found throughout the museum. There is also a full display of flight suits, bombardier jackets, and other memorabilia.

Kids can try the Flight Trainer 150 and other interactive exhibits and visit a special area devoted to astronauts and space flight. Outside, you can inspect a full-sized helicopter, capable of carrying fifty-five soldiers.

LOCATION: South Jersey Regional Airport, 68 Stacy Haines Rd., Lumberton (Burlington County). Rt. 38, south on Ark Rd., then left on Stacy Haines Rd. **HOURS:** Wed.–Sat., 10–4; Sun., 11–4. Closed Sun., Nov.–Mar. Check winter hours. **ADMISSION:** $. Under 4 free. **PHONE:** 609-267-4488. **WEBSITE:** www.airvictorymuseum.org.

Naval Air Station Wildwood Aviation Museum

There are lots of planes here, honoring the WW II naval air training facility. Planes include an F-14 Tomcat, A-4 Skyhawk, MiG-15, Vietnam-era Huey helicopter, 1940s biplane, TBM Avenger torpedo bomber, V2 rocket, and many others inside Hanger #1. There's also an exhibit room, orientation room with a video, and an interactive aviation technology exhibit.

LOCATION: Cape May County Airport, Rio Grande. Garden State Parkway, Exit 4, onto Rt. 47 West, left on Seashore Rd., then right on Breakwater to airport. **HOURS:** Apr.–Sep., daily, 9–5; Oct.–Nov., 9–4; Dec.–Mar., Mon.–Fri., 9–4. **ADMISSION:** $. Under 3 free. **PHONE:** 609-886-8787. **WEBSITE:** www.usnasw.org.

SPECIALTY MUSEUMS
Yogi Berra Museum & Learning Center

Yogi Berra was not only a famous catcher for the New York Yankees and a famous manager for the New York Mets, he is just as famous for his funny sayings. This is an interesting, well-done museum that adjoins the Yogi Berra Stadium on the campus of Montclair State University. The Berra family lives in Montclair, which is a major reason that this New York baseball star is honored in New Jersey.

The museum not only has loads of memorabilia about Yogi but also lots of general baseball lore. Exhibits on the evolution of the catcher's glove or the qualities of wood and aluminum bats are typical. Plus, there are cases of trophies, World Series rings, and newspaper clippings about the Yankees and other teams as well as a permanent exhibit on the history of the Negro Leagues.

In the 125-seat auditorium you can watch a movie about the glory days of the Yankees. The museum is open late on days when a baseball game is played. From a special "group" area you can overlook the outdoor stadium where both the Montclair State baseball team and the minor-league New Jersey Jackals play. If you have a kid who memorizes baseball statistics or a relative who remembers the 1961 World Series—take them here! Special programs for school and scout groups.

LOCATION: 8 Quarry Road, Little Falls (Passaic County). North end of Montclair State campus. HOURS: Wed.–Sun., 12–5. Closed holidays. ADMISSION: $$. Discount: Students. PHONE: 973-655-2378. WEBSITE: www.yogiberramuseum.org.

Vietnam Era Museum and Educational Center

The New Jersey Vietnam Veterans Memorial is set on a green hillock a short distance from the PNC Arts Center and features a circular black wall engraved with the names of the fallen. A hundred feet or so behind it stands the Vietnam Era Educational Center, a beautifully constructed building that is dedicated to the whole Vietnam era—not just the war. It was designed by the same firm that created the Holocaust Museum in Washington, D.C., and refurbished Ellis Island. The museum captures the tempo of the 1960s and early 1970s without taking sides in the debate of those times. It is an evenhanded presentation of the events behind the war. The history of Vietnam, the history of communism, the French colonization of Indochina, and the Japanese occupation in World War II are all covered.

Given the themes of this museum, it's not for smaller children. But since it is recent history—one that kids' parents and grandparents experienced—those from around 8 or 9 and up can relate to it.

A double timeline runs along the walls of the circular building. On top, there is a montage of photos of the era's culture. Scenes from 1950s and 1960s television shows, pictures of Marilyn Monroe and JFK, Elvis and the Beatles, the 1970s disco era, presidential conventions, and moonshots are featured. Below that, there are pictures and text on America's growing involvement in the war: the French defeat at Dien Bien Phu, the Red scare in this country, and the Domino Theory.

For a personal touch, there are handwritten letters to mothers, wives, and sweethearts back home—many from soldiers who never returned. Interactive TV sets allow you to call up a scene from a specific year—the murder of a Vietnamese official or a college anti-war rally. The tone of the TV narration changes over time from brisk reports to "up close and personal" views of battle scenes and burning villages. In the central theater a continuous movie shows "testaments" from various viewpoints—dog soldiers, officers, commanders. From the museum you can walk directly to the Vietnam Veterans' Memorial through a row of stately trees.

LOCATION: Holmdel (Monmouth County). Exit 116 on Garden State Parkway to PNC Arts Center. Follow signs.
HOURS: Tue.–Sat., 10–4. **ADMISSION:** $. Under 10 free.
PHONE: 732-335-0033.
WEBSITE: www.njvvmf.org.

Ripley's Believe It or Not! Museum

A hologram-like Robert Ripley at his desk welcomes you to such displays as a Chinese unicorn man, a bottle cap suit, a dog with false teeth, a shrunken head, a model of the Sydney Harbor Bridge made out of matchsticks, and a section of the Berlin Wall. In all, there are thirteen galleries displaying odd relics and true stories collected by Ripley in his travels to over two hundred countries. You'll even walk on a swaying bridge through an Old Mine Tunnel as the wall spins around you! Kids can have a great time here.

LOCATION: 1441 Boardwalk, at New York Ave., Atlantic City (Atlantic County). **HOURS:** Open daily; call for hours.
ADMISSION: $$$$. Ages 5–12, $$. Under 5 free. **PHONE:** 609-347-2001.
WEBSITE: www.ripleys.com.

Franklin Mineral Museum

New Jersey is both the zinc mining and fluorescent rock capital of the world. Sussex County provides lots of fun for budding rock hounds. Here, you will find both the Franklin Mineral Museum and the Sterling Hill Mining Museum.

Children seem to have a fascination with rocks—as any mother can attest—and they can find plenty here. The museum itself is divided into several sections: a fluorescent rock display, a general exhibit on zinc and other local minerals, exhibits of 6,000 worldwide mineral specimens, and a replica of an actual mine.

As part of the tour you are ushered into a long, narrow room where you face a row of gray, ordinary rocks behind a glass case. The guide flicks off the lights, and—lo and behold—the rocks turn into an extraordinary array of shining colors. Green, purple, red, and blue luminous rocks glow behind the glass. Next is a tour of the mine replica, which is a plaster labyrinth filled with mock-ups of miners and ore carts. You can also check out the annex, dedicated to dinosaur footprints and Indian artifacts. At the gift shop you'll find a good selection of rocks, gemstones, and necklaces.

For many, the highlight of the trip is the chance to go prospecting in the rock dump at the back of the museum, although the possibility of finding a real specimen is slim. Check with the museum about equipment and age requirements.

LOCATION: 32 Evans St., Franklin (Sussex County). Rt. 80 to Rt. 15 to Sparta, then Rt. 517 North to Franklin and a mile north on Rt. 23. **HOURS:** Apr.–Nov., Mon.–Fri., 10–4; Sat., 10–5; Sun., 11–5. Weekends only in March. **ADMISSION:** $$. Discount: Children. Same rate for mineral dump. Combination tickets: $$$. **PHONE:** 973-827-3481. **WEBSITE:** www.franklinmineralmuseum.com.

PLANETARIUMS

Aside from the planetariums in major museums, there are other places star-seeking New Jersey kids can visit for sky programs. Children under six are sometimes not admitted to programs for good reason—once those doors shut in darkness, there is no escape. Luckily, many planetariums feature special "Stars for Tots" shows on Saturdays. The staff uses both the "canned" slide shows and its own give-and-take lecture. These county college planetariums may close down when school is not in session. Here's what is available.

Ocean County College

The Robert J. Novins Planetarium is located in Toms River on a large campus. The planetarium not only schedules public shows year-round but also has a special astronomy curriculum for school grades 1–6 during the school year. Weekend shows (Friday nights and several Saturday and Sunday viewings) are well attended. They do shut down every once in a while to prepare a new show, so call first. The 117-seat planetarium has recently been upgraded with the latest projection technology that turns the planetarium dome into a virtual 3-D video space.

LOCATION: College Drive, Toms River.
ADMISSION: $$. Discounts: Children. **PHONE:** 732-255-0342.
WEBSITE: www.ocean.edu/campus/planetarium/index.htm.

Raritan Valley College

This state-of-the-art planetarium has six high-definition digital projectors and seats one hundred people. It hosts many school shows plus has an adult-style sky show. Changing laser light shows are also popular. There is a nice little astronomy museum before you go in. Reservations are required. It is at the top of a long set of stairs, but you can use the elevator in the adjoining building.

LOCATION: Lamington Rd. & Rt. 28, North Branch (Somerset County).
ADMISSION: $$. **PHONE:** 908-231-8805.
WEBSITE: www.raritanval.edu/rvcc/frameset/planetarium.html.

Morris County College

This automated eighty-seat planetarium with a new digital projection system offers not only several programs to the public but also courses for those who really want to delve into the subject. Shows for school and other groups are scheduled during the week and early Saturday. Public showings take place one Saturday per month, usually while the college is in session. Since they fill up, reserve beforehand.

LOCATION: Rt. 10 & Center Grove Rd., Randolph. **ADMISSION:** $$.
PHONE: 973-328-5755. **WEBSITE:** www.ccm.edu/planetarium.

Also see the Newark Museum and the State Museum in this chapter for more planetarium listings.

History Made Fun

Kids can help with shucking corn along with other traditional farming chores at Howell Living History Farm in rural Mercer County. *(Photo by Jeff Kelly; courtesy of Howell Farm)*

Howell Living History Farm

This active farm in Mercer County preserves the turn-of-the-century lifestyle. Various stages of mechanization are shown: the reaper reaps and binds mechanically, but it does not thresh. The wheat is bound by machine, but the machine is pulled by a plodding draft horse. The wagon that picks up the bound sheaves is also available for hayrides.

There's plenty of acreage, and you feel the farm's bucolic atmosphere from the moment you walk down the dirt road to the farmhouse. You pass sheep, pigs, and goats—all safely behind fences. A renovated barn serves as the visitor center. The early 1800s farmhouse itself is a simple one, with a furnished parlor, antique kitchen, and gift shop. School groups are welcome here to take part in seasonal activities. On Saturdays, a real farmer is on hand to guide the draft horse in plowing, sowing, and reaping. Several Saturdays are devoted to such things as hayrides, tree planting, and a fall festival. Special events, such as a 4-acre maze in a cornfield, are held in season. Visitors are invited to help plant, cultivate, and harvest crops, care for animals, or make soap, butter, and ice cream.

LOCATION: Valley Rd., Howell Twp. (Mercer County). **HOURS:** Apr.–Nov.: Tue.–Sat., 10–4; Sun., 12–4. Dec.–Jan.: Sat., 10–4. Feb.–Mar.: Tue.–Sat., 10–4. Programs, Sat., 11–3. **ADMISSION:** Free. Fee for children's crafts and maze. **PHONE:** 609-737-3299. **WEBSITE:** www.howellfarm.org. (SC)

Historic Allaire Village

Set in Allaire State Park, this complex was an active workers' community during the nineteenth century. There's a huge brick blast furnace left over from the bog iron days when James P. Allaire bought the ironworks in 1822 to supply iron to his marine steam engine works in New York City, the largest in the country. He sought to establish a self-contained community because of its isolation. After 25 years, competition from high-grade iron ore brought economic ruin, and in 1850 Allaire moved to the village and retired. A well-documented display on the ironworks can be found in the Visitor Center.

What interests kids is that during warm-weather weekends (including Fridays), docents dressed in 1830s costumes are in the various buildings talking about village life. Perhaps a blacksmith, pattern maker, or woodworker, tinsmith, or wheelwright will also be about. There's a pond, a bakery with fresh bread, plus several other houses. During the week, when docents may or may not be around, you can still walk around the grounds.

Weekends feature lots of activities and historic demonstrations, themed around the 1830s, the heyday of the village. These include St. Patrick's Day in the 1830s, Bee Hive oven baking, a spring festival, 1830s school days, Independence Day celebration, and a harvest festival. There are also hayrides in October and lantern tours and holiday events in late November and December.

While at Allaire, be sure to ride the Pine Creek Railroad, a narrow-gauge rail line that runs a short trip on both diesel and steam locomotives. For information call 732-938-5524. The park also offers a nature center and trails, bicycle trails, and picnic areas.

LOCATION: Allaire State Park, Rt. 524, Wall Twp. (Monmouth County). Garden State Parkway to Exit 98; go 2 miles west. **HOURS:** Park: dawn–dusk. Buildings: summer, Wed.–Sun., 12–4; May, Sep.–Nov., weekends, 12–4. Visitor Center and store: Mar.–mid-Dec., Wed.–Sun., 12–4; daily in summer, 10–5. **ADMISSION:** $ on weekends May–Nov. Under 5 free. $ for parking on summer weekends. **PHONE:** 732-938-2371 (park); 732-919-3500 (village). **WEBSITE:** www.allairevillage.org.

The Hermitage

This historic home built in 1750 was owned by Lt. Colonel Prevost and his wife, Theodosia, and was host to George Washington, James Monroe, Alexander Hamilton, Marquis de Lafayette, and Aaron Burr, among others. When Colonel Prevost died, Burr wooed his widow and married her in 1782 in the parlor of the Hermitage. Twenty-five years later Dr. Elijah Rosencrantz bought the house (which his family retained for 163 years). In 1847 the structure was remodeled into a picturesque Gothic Revival home. Steep gabled roofs trimmed with carpenter's lace and diamond-paned windows give it the Victorian look often associated with Charles Dickens. In fact, one of the several programs given at the house is a performance of *A Christmas Carol.* The Hermitage portrays the upper middle class life of the late Victorian period, including furnishings, personal items, and papers of the Rosencrantz family. There are also changing exhibits based on the museum's large collection of antique clothing. One-hour after-school classes are offered that explore the everyday life of a middle-class Victorian family, architectural secrets of Gothic Revival houses, New Jersey in the Revolution and Civil War, life ways of the Lenape before and after European settlement, and women from colonial to modern times. Plus, there are four special Family Weekend programs throughout the year.

LOCATION: 335 N. Franklin Tpk., Ho-Ho-Kus (Bergen County). Rt. 17 to Hollywood Ave. exit, then west to Franklin Tpk. **HOURS:** Wed.–Sun., 1–4. Last tour, 3:15. **ADMISSION:** $. Under 6 free. **PHONE:** 201-445-8311. **WEBSITE:** www.thehermitage.org. (BP) (SC)

Emlen Physick Estate

The Physick House hosts a popular, year-round tour (hours and days vary throughout the year). This sprawling 1881 stick-style home is typical of the late Victorian era, both in its multiangled red roof and its charming period furnishings, and is said to have been designed by noted architect Frank Furness. The interior is very well done, from the ornate fireplaces to the stained glass windows in Dr. Physick's bathroom door. Tours may include costumed docents, and on certain days there is even an actor playing the part of Dr. Physick. The Mid-Atlantic Center for the Arts operates an extensive list of activities out of this estate. Throughout the summer there are special family-oriented activities, including a Cape May Family Treasure Hunt, Children's Storytelling Lunch, Children's Trolley Ride, Emlen Physick Estate Children's Tour, Kids Day at the Physick Estate, Lighthouse Story Time, Pirates and Plunder Children's Trolley Tour, Storytelling at the Physick Estate, and Teddy Bear Tea Parties.

LOCATION: 1048 Washington St., Cape May (Cape May County). **HOURS:** House tours, generally four times a day in summer, less often the rest of the year. **ADMISSION:** $$$$; children 3–12, $$. See website for event and tour prices. **PHONE:** 800-275-4278. **WEBSITE:** www. capemaymac.org.

Longstreet Farm

A visit to Longstreet Farm presents kids with the sights and smells of farm life a century ago. Although the farm is kept to the 1890s era, the machinery here was used well into the 1920s. Old-fashioned combines and tractors, an apple corer, and other antique farm machines are kept in a series of barns and sheds. There are pigs lying in the mud as well as horses, cows, sheep, and chickens. The milking shed is fitted out with slots for the cow's head and buckets for hand milking. The carriage house contains a variety of buckboards.

Since Longstreet is a living historical farm, the workers dress in casual 1890s clothes as they go about their farm chores. During summer there is a historical camp for children in which the kids help out. Other hands-on programs are held for all ages, are festivals, old-time crafts and farm demonstrations, and classes. The main farmhouse, which dates to the late 1700s, offers tours on weekends and holidays. It contains a number of rooms in late Victorian style, with most of the furnishings belonging to the family that lived here for generations.

LOCATION: 44 Longstreet Road, Holmdel (Monmouth County). **HOURS:** Daily, 10–4. Farmhouse, weekends and holidays, 12–3:30. **ADMISSION:** Free. **PHONE:** 732-946-3758. **WEBSITE:** www.monmouthcountyparks.com/page.asp?agency=130&id=2530.

Fosterfields

A living history farm that dates from the turn of the century, Fosterfields has many agricultural implements on display and a variety of farm animals, including horses, pigs, chickens, and cows. As you walk along the road from the Visitor Center toward the house on the hill, you will also see a large plowing field and outbuildings.

The main house, the Willows, is a Gothic Revival farmhouse built in 1854 (for a grandson of Paul Revere) and has many original furnishings intact. The farm was later owned by the Fosters, and tours of the house reflect the life of the young Caroline Foster, growing up in the early twentieth century.

On weekends from spring to fall, staff in period clothes demonstrate such farm tasks as plowing, sowing seed, or threshing. Kids can wash and dry clothes, churn butter, collect eggs, pump water, crush corn to feed chickens, and milk "Woody" the artificial cow. There is a barn to visit as well as a 1920s farmhouse. There's a horse-drawn wagon that tours the farm. Many special interest programs highlight various aspects of farming life, largely oriented toward children, such as learning the role of toads in a garden, threshing oats, washing a lamb, making bird seed mix, digging potatoes, and making cider.

The Visitor Center has changing exhibits and also offers a short film on the history of Fosterfields. Downstairs, Foster's early twentieth-century cars are preserved.

LOCATION: 73 Kahdena Rd., Morris Twp. (Morris County). Just off Rt. 510/124. **HOURS:** Apr.–Oct.: Sat., 10–5; Sun., 12–5. House: Thu.–Sun., 1–3:30. **ADMISSION:** $$; children, 2–16, $. Under 2 free. **PHONE:** 973-326-7645. **WEBSITE:** http://morrisparks.net/aspparks/ffmain.asp. ⓈⒸ

Thomas Edison National Historical Park

This National Park site preserves both the research and personal sides of the famous inventor's life. The Edison Laboratory Complex stands in downtown West Orange, and Glenmont, Thomas Edison's home, is half a mile away in the private enclave of Llewellyn Park.

The laboratory section, which encompasses fourteen historic structures, has been recently renovated and reopened. It includes 20,000 square feet of added exhibit space, including two floors of the main laboratory building never before open. The original music recording studio, Edison's private lab, and photography studio are open for the first time. The original furnishings have been moved back into many rooms, and the vast museum collections are now available to the public. A new elevator and stair tower adjacent to the main laboratory building allow new public access to the upper floors of the laboratory that feature new exhibits, including the drafting room, precision machine shop, and Edison's private lab on the second floor, and the music room, new phonograph gallery, and new artifact exhibit on the third floor.

A visit starts at Building 1, the Physics Laboratory, which is now the Visitor Center. There you can see a 20-minute orientation film called "The Invention Factory" and shop at the museum store. The entire complex is designed for self-guided tours, with new exhibit panels with plasma display screens throughout the main lab building. An optional self-guided audio tour and a special children's audio tour are also available (extra fee). Throughout the day, there are also ranger-led programs, including an early phonograph demonstration, a tour of the chemistry building, and a talk and closer look at the Black Maria, the world's first motion picture studio. Times are posted in the Visitor Center. A Junior Ranger Day takes place in April.

LOCATION: 211 Main St., West Orange (Essex County).
HOURS: Laboratory, Wed.–Sun., 9–5; house, Wed.–Sun. Tours start on the hour, 12–4. **ADMISSION:** $; under 16 free. **PHONE:** 973-324-9973.
WEBSITE: www.nps.gov/edis.

Morristown National Historical Park

The winter of 1779–1780 was the coldest in a century. On December 1, 1779, General George Washington entered Morristown and took up residence at the house of Mrs. Jacob Ford, Jr. Meanwhile, 4 miles south, soldiers cut trees to build more than 1,000 log huts along the slopes of Jockey Hollow. Severe snowstorms hindered their work and delayed the supply of food needed for survival. Starvation confronted the army, which also suffered from inadequate clothing, disease, and low morale.

At Washington's Headquarters (the Ford Mansion), you enter at a separate museum, where displays emphasize the role of the citizens of Morristown and how they reacted to the soldiers in their town. The museum includes two exhibit galleries, a 20-minute video, a PowerPoint presentation of the house, and a free booklet of the Ford Mansion's interior. The film was shot on location both here and in Jockey Hollow, south of town.

A park ranger takes you on a tour of the mansion. As you enter the long central hallway, you notice how well such halls were suited for line dances, such as the Virginia reel. The Ford family lived in two rooms while the general and his staff occupied the rest of the house. The furnishings are authentic to the period and many are true Ford family pieces. Beds include the canopied master bed used by Washington. Highboys, chest-on-chests, wall maps, and lots of straw mattresses are all on display.

At Jockey Hollow, a tour starts at the Visitor Center, which provides plenty of information about the encampment. There's a mini theater where a 10-minute video begins at the touch of a button. The story is told by typical foot soldiers huddled in a simple hut waiting for rations and money that take forever in coming. After the film, you can move on to a mock-up of a soldiers' hut and see the straw beds, muskets, and clothing used at the time.

From the Visitor Center, you head out the back door to the Wick Farm. The farmhouse was occupied by both the Wick family (owners of a farm that included Jockey Hollow) and General Arthur St. Clair and his aide. A vegetable/herb garden, a well, and a horse barn surround the wooden cottage. Inside, you will often find a guide dressed in colonial garb cooking, melting down candles, or just answering questions. A tour shows the little bedroom of Tempe Wick, the family bedroom, the general's office/bedroom, and the kitchen. A short drive from the Wick House leads to the simple soldiers' log huts on a hill and the various brigade lines. On special weekends there are often demonstrations, musters, or other events both at the Wick Farm and the huts.

LOCATION: Jockey Hollow: Rt. 287 to Rt. 202 to Tempe Wick Rd. (south of Morristown). Follow signs. Mansion: Rt. 287 to exit 36 or 36A to Morris Ave. East, Morristown (Morris County). Follow signs to Washington's Headquarters. **HOURS:** Visitor Center: Daily, 9–5. Museum: Daily, 9–5; Mansion tours: Daily, 10–4. Buildings closed major winter holidays. Grounds: Spring and summer, 8–8; fall and winter, 8–5. **ADMISSION:** $. Under 16 free. **PHONE:** 973-539-2016. **WEBSITE:** www.nps.gov/morr.

Batsto Village

This self-contained community in the heart of the Pinelands is part of Wharton State Forest, the largest parkland in the state. Pine, oak, and cedar woods; open lowlands; and a sparkling lake provide a scenic backdrop for a place that preserves the lifestyle of bygone days in the South Jersey pines. Founded in 1766, Batsto was once the center of the bog iron industry in New Jersey, and its iron provided armaments for the Revolution. Later, in the 1800s, glass was manufactured here, then lumbering and cranberry farming were tried. Today Batsto is a handsome farm surrounded by split-rail fences with a worker village beside a scenic lake.

William Richards bought the iron works in 1784, and it remained in his family's hands for 92 years. The Richards Mansion has an eight-story mansard-roofed tower rising from its center. The rooms inside are filled with the furniture of the well-to-do families who lived there, and the wall-to-wall library of Joseph Wharton, the financier who bought the complex in 1876, is most impressive. So is the dining room, with a table that could seat thirty-six. And from the third floor, there's a narrow, twisting stairway up to the tower, which offers a 360-degree panorama of the village and surrounding Pinelands.

The first stop at Batsto is the Visitor Center. If you want the mansion tour, buy your tickets immediately, for only fifteen people are admitted at a time. The tour takes 45 minutes and is very comprehensive. A walk-through museum at the Visitor Center features local history, with tools and other artifacts accompanied by colorful display panels.

Except for the mansion tour, you can stroll the village on your own. Among the structures are the general store, a post office, a barn with farm animals, and a few workers' houses. During the summer, the houses usually have some craftsmen inside—a weaver or a potter at work. The working sawmill is usually open only Sunday afternoons in summer.

A nature center, nature trail, picnic area, and a large lake where fishing is allowed are all part of the grounds. Special events are held throughout the year, including a country-living fair, guided hikes, and canoeing.

LOCATION: Rt. 542, Wharton State Forest (Burlington County). Rt. 9 to Rt. 542 west. Garden State Parkway to New Gretna exit to Rt. 9 South to Rt. 542. **HOURS:** Grounds, daily, dawn to dusk. Village, daily, 9–4:30. Mansion tours Fri.–Sun. starting at 11:30. Call first. **ADMISSION:** Mansion, $. Under 6 free. Parking fee on summer weekends. **PHONE:** 609-561-0024. **WEBSITE:** www.batstovillage.org.

Monmouth Battlefield State Park

The Battle of Monmouth on June 28, 1778, proved that American troops, honed by Von Steuben's training at Valley Forge, could hold their own against British regulars in open field fighting. Today's park covers the scene of that hot day's artillery battle in which General Charles Lee ordered a retreat (later reprimanded by Washington), and a legendary lady named "Molly Pitcher" (whose real name was Mary Hays) became a heroine.

The rolling fields, woodlands, and orchards at Monmouth Battlefield are now peaceful, with several miles of nature trails. A large Visitor Center provides information and displays, including relief maps of the battle and videos of a reenactment of the fight as well as battle artifacts recovered from the area. The site of Molly Pitcher's well was near the Continental Army's artillery line on Perrine Ridge.

Monmouth Battlefield State Park in Manalapan preserves
the site of the Battle of Monmouth during the Revolution,
which is reenacted every June. *(Photo by Patrick Sarver)*

The highlight of the year is on the last weekend in June with a
two-day annual reenactment of the battle, complete with dozens of
troops firing muskets and cannons booming on the hillside below
the Visitor Center. There are also military marches, a colonial troop
encampment, and an opportunity before the main battle reenactment for kids to chase down and capture a squad of British troops.

> **LOCATION:** Rt. 9 or Rt. 33 to Bus. Rt. 33 (Freehold Rd.), Manalapan
> (Monmouth County). **HOURS:** Park: Daily, winter, 8–4:30;
> spring & fall, 8–6; Memorial–Labor Day, 8–8. Visitor Center:
> Daily, 9–4. **ADMISSION:** Free. **PHONE:** 732-462-9616.
> **WEBSITE:** www.state.nj.us/dep/parksandforests/parks/monbat.html.

Miller-Cory House

Every Sunday during the school season, volunteers cook, spin, or
perform seasonal tasks in and around this 1740 farmhouse. The
everyday, humdrum tasks of colonial life—from soap making to herb
drying—are emphasized here. The house, the adjacent Visitors Center, and a separate kitchen and kitchen garden comprise this small
enclave of colonial life. In pleasant weather, wool spinners and
other workers may be found outside. The separate kitchen is the
scene of soup and bread making by volunteers who use an open
hearth and beehive oven.

Guided tours of the house proper take about half an hour. The
tour is thorough and includes everything from how to tighten the
rope on a colonial bed to how to make utensils from a cow's horn.

Schoolchildren and adults will find the house tour highly educational, while preschoolers may be content to explore the grounds. They can tour the herb garden, visit the museum shop, or watch the outdoor volunteers at work. There is a full schedule of events throughout the year, many especially suitable for children, that are designed to show the lifestyles of the past. The museum also puts on demonstrations of historic crafts at local schools.

LOCATION: 614 Mountain Ave., Westfield (Union County). Rt. 22 to Mountain Ave. **HOURS:** Mid-Sep.–mid-June, Sun., 2–4. **ADMISSION:** $. Discount: Students. Under 4 free. **PHONE:** 908-232-1776. **WEBSITE:** http://millercoryhouse.org.

Red Mill Museum Village

The old red mill with a churning waterwheel sits by a 200-foot-wide waterfall, and it is one of the most photographed structures in New Jersey. It is also the hub of a village that includes smaller buildings scattered along the banks of the South Branch of the Raritan River. There's a log cabin, little red schoolhouse, general store/post office, blacksmith shop, tenant house, carriage shed, and quarry with stone crusher.

The 1810 mill offers several floors of exhibits. The agricultural development of the region is followed with a series of displays of tools and country life. Everything from barrels to baskets is shown, with the sound of the water from the wheel always within earshot. The museum also offers special events. These include Revolutionary and Civil War encampments, spring and fall antiques shows, summer concerts, the New Jersey Renaissance Festival, and the Haunted Mill for Halloween weekend. (Extra fee for events.)

LOCATION: 56 Main St., Clinton (Hunterdon County). **HOURS:** Apr.–Sep., Tue.–Sat., 10–4; Nov.–Mar., Tue.–Sat., 12–4; also open Nov.–Dec., Sun., 12–4. **ADMISSION:** $$. Under 12 free. **PHONE:** 908-735-4101. **WEBSITE:** www.theredmill.org.

Historic Speedwell

Historic Speedwell in Morristown was the scene of one of the most important American achievements. Here, Samuel Morse and Alfred Vail spent years perfecting the electromagnetic telegraph, which later gave rise to radio and television. One thing you learn at this old-fashioned village compound: you don't have to be a scientist to be an inventor. Morse was a portrait painter by profession. At the Vail House (the main building of the complex), you can see the portraits he painted of the senior Mr. and Mrs. Vail. The carriage house is devoted to an exhibit concerning the making and molding of iron machinery and to the ironworkers themselves. The foundry was best known for its early steam engines. In fact, the first transatlantic steamship engine was built here in 1819.

The factory building, originally built as a grist mill (there's a covered water wheel) and then used for cotton weaving, now features an exhibit about the telegraph. Vail and Morse held the first public demonstration of their new wonder here in 1838. A hands-on, interactive exhibit illustrates the invention and development of the telegraph. L'Hommedieu House, which is now the renovated visitor center, includes changing historical exhibits and classroom. There are lots of special events and classes on weekends and in summer. Kids can learn about such subjects as electricity, Victorian games, the telegraph during the Civil War, magnetism, tin punching, open-hearth cooking, and archeology.

LOCATION: 333 Speedwell Ave. (Rt. 202) at Cory Rd., 1 mile north of Morristown. **HOURS:** Apr.–June: Wed.–Sat., 10–4; July–Oct.: Wed.–Sat., 10–5; Sun., 12–5. Last tour at 3:30. **ADMISSION:** $. Under 4 free. **PHONE:** 973-285-6550. **WEBSITE:** www.speedwell.org. (SC)

Washington Crossing State Park

On Christmas Night 1776, General Washington crossed the icy Delaware from Pennsylvania with 2,400 men, plus artillery and supplies. The crossing took nine hours, and the men and officers converged on this spot. The ensuing surprise attack on Trenton gave a first taste of victory to the discouraged American forces.

Today, the Visitor Center is filled with information on this and other early battles of the Revolutionary War, plus the uniforms and muskets of the time. There are a variety of exhibits and two videos on the crossing and events over the following 10 days. New Jersey's role in the Revolution is presented by the extensive Swan collection of eighteenth-century armaments and other artifacts.

Near the Delaware River sits a monument marking the spot where the troops disembarked. Also here is the Johnson Ferry House, a refurbished 1740 farmhouse and inn furnished with period furniture, with a colonial herb garden outside. The house also hosts special events and demonstrations of Revolutionary-era cooking, crafts, and home life.

LOCATION: Rts. 29 & 546, Titusville (Mercer County).
HOURS: Visitor Center, daily, 9–4. Johnson Ferry House: Guided tours, Wed.–Sat., 10–12 & 1–4; Sun., 1–4. Park open dawn to dusk.
ADMISSION: Free, but there is a parking fee ($) on summer weekends.
PHONE: Visitor Center, 609-737-9303, Ferry House, 609-737-2515.
WEBSITE: www.state.nj.us/dep/parksandforests/parks/washcros.html.

Liberty Hall Museum

Liberty Hall, an estate on the Essex/Union County border, was the home of two illustrious New Jersey families—the Livingstons and the Keans. Today it is a living history museum tucked behind corporate buildings across from Kean University.

William Livingston built the original homestead in 1772. A member of the Constitutional Convention, Livingston was the first elected governor of New Jersey. When one of his daughters married John Kean, the two families became entwined. The house is full of history. John Jay, the first Chief Justice of the Supreme Court, married Livingston's daughter Sarah in the front hall. When he was a teenager, Alexander Hamilton lived in one of the upstairs bedrooms for a year. And in 1780, during the Revolutionary War, British soldiers invaded the home—the hatch marks of their sabers are still evident on the banisters. They fled when they thought they saw the ghost of Hannah Caldwell, a minister's wife who had been killed in the nearby Battle of Springfield, on the staircase.

Since the Kean family lived in Liberty Hall until the 1970s, the furnishings are original to the house and represent all the eras it encompasses: Colonial, Victorian, Edwardian, art deco, and modern. Many people still remember the elegant lifestyle of the last of the family, Mary Alice Kean, to inhabit the house. Regular tours include the Visitor Center (where there's a ten-minute video on the house narrated by former governor Tom Kean), outbuildings, and the surrounding gardens. A separate gardens and grounds tour is also available. Special events, such as an 1890s baseball game, pick your own apples, and a reenacted Revolutionary War battle, are also featured on particular weekends.

LOCATION: 1003 Morris Ave., Union (Union County).
HOURS: Wed.–Sat., 10–4; Sun., 12–4. Closed Jan.–Mar.
ADMISSION: $$. Under 3 free. **PHONE:** 908-527-0400.
WEBSITE: www.kean.edu/libertyhall.

Historic Cold Spring Village

This interesting restored village among the pine trees sits on a quiet stretch of road not far from Wildwood and Cape May. Historic Cold Spring Village has a lot of charm. The twenty-five historic build - ings are set along two country lanes that have a mid-nineteenth-century look. Most all have been moved here from elsewhere. They range from the Colonial to the large Grange Hall, which dates back to 1897.

There are many costumed docents here demonstrating life in the 1800s. Inside the various structures, you'll find a printer in his

Demonstrations of nineteenth-century crafts like pottery making are an important part of the historical lifestyles on display at Cold Spring Village, just north of Cape May. *(Photo by Patrick Sarver)*

shop working at an 1890 press, an 1820s schoolhouse complete with resident schoolmistress, a spinning and weaving demonstration, a tinsmith punching holes in tin, a blacksmith working at his forge, a potter, and many other village crafters of the past. These are docents and craftspeople who explain what they are doing while they work. There's also a barn where you can see rag rugs being woven.

There are bits of country nostalgia here, such as an old-fashioned water pump, a farm enclosure with sheep and other animals, and walkways made of crushed clamshells. A horse-drawn carriage is a big hit with children.

The Welcome Center in Grange Hall offers displays on local history and an orientation video. There's also a large country store. Weekends feature a lot of special events, including crafts and antiques shows, military encampments, concerts, and cultural festivals.

LOCATION: 720 Rt. 9, Cold Spring (Cape May County).
HOURS: Father's Day–Labor Day, Tue.–Sun., 10–4:30; Memorial Day, early June, and Sep., weekends. **ADMISSION:** $$. Under 3 free.
PHONE: 609-898-2300. **WEBSITE:** www.hcsv.org.

Tuckerton Seaport

Kids can learn about the duck hunters, clammers, and fishermen who worked the bays and tidal creeks along the Jersey Shore at this seaport village. Hunting for waterfowl, dredging for oysters, building boats, and carving decoys was a way of life that has just about disappeared. The cornerstone of the village is the replicated Tucker's Island Lighthouse (the original washed way along with its island in the 1920s). Inside is a museum, with exhibits on lighthouses, pirates (Captain Kidd and others), and buried treasure along with examples of duck decoys and lifesaving and other local lore. Outside, about fifteen wooden buildings (some no larger than shacks) line the edge of Tuckerton Creek. Wooden walkways take you from one structure to the next. These include a decoy carving shop, the Perrine Boat Works, a sawmill, an instructional clam house, and the Hotel de Crab. At the boat works a docent describes sneakboxes and the role of these small hunting craft in the local economy. In another house, a decoy maker explains how he hollows out the inside of the ducks and places the head in various positions. And the New Jersey Folklife Center is housed in Kelly's Oyster House. Audio tours are available via cell phone and iPod.

The Visitor Center emphasizes marine ecology and offers several interactive exhibits for the kids, along with a Lenni-Lenape exhibit. Upstairs are exhibits on local environments, maritime history, and research done at the nearby Jacques Cousteau National Estuarine Research Reserve. Lots of special events take place here, including a boat parade and a big decoy show in September. There are also adult and children's classes throughout the year, with children's basket and quilting classes in summer. Boat rides are offered down Tuckerton Creek, and there's a sailing school here as well.

LOCATION: 120 W. Main St. (Rt. 9), Tuckerton.
HOURS: Daily, 10–5. **ADMISSION:** $$. Under 6 free.
PHONE: 609-296-8868.
WEBSITE: www.tuckertonseaport.org.

Wheaton Arts and Cultural Center

Set around a green, with buildings styled in 1888 gingerbread, this village on the outskirts of Millville is dedicated to the glass industry that still flourishes in this corner of New Jersey. One of its main attractions is the Museum of American Glass, which has the most comprehensive collection of American historical glass in the country. It's housed in an elegant Victorian building and includes glass items that go back to colonial times. There are exhibits on Colonial glassmaking, Victorian glass, the local glass industry, and art glass.

Another attraction is the glassworks, where visitors can watch from a gallery above while gaffers plunge their rods into the blazing furnaces and then shape the glass into bowls, wine glasses, bottles, and paperweights. At these "shows" an announcer with a mike explains what the gaffer is doing. This is hot work, and even from the gallery you can feel the intense heat of the furnace. The village has also become a center for glass "sculptors" who specialize in glass art. Other buildings include a craft studio where you can see woodcarvers, potters, and others going about their work.

The Down Jersey Folklife Center offers changing exhibits on the diverse ethnic crafts of the region, such as Japanese origami, Puerto Rican music, or Ukrainian embroidery. There's a small play area for kids, an 1876 schoolhouse to peek in, and an 1897 train station with a 10-minute miniature train ride. On Sundays, throughout the year there are Family Fun Days featuring exhibits, performances, demonstrations, and hands-on arts and crafts activities designed for kids. Plus there are special-event weekends that feature everything from marbles and fire engine musters to fine craft festivals, antiques shows, and Civil War reenactments.

LOCATION: 1501 Glasstown Rd., Millville (Cumberland County). Exit 26 off Rt. 55. HOURS: Tue.–Sun., 10–5; Jan.–Mar., Fri.–Sun. only. ADMISSION: $$. Under 6 free. Free in winter. PHONE: 800-998-4552. WEBSITE: www.wheatonarts.org.

Rockingham

Washington lived in this house when it was in Rocky Hill in 1783 while Congress met in nearby Princeton, awaiting the signing of the treaty to end the Revolution. Both George and Martha stayed here and entertained extensively for about three months. Guests included Thomas Jefferson, James Madison, and Thomas Paine. It is best known as the house where Washington's "Farewell Address to the Armies" was composed.

This two-story colonial was once part of an estate of 350 acres with barns, coach house, and granary. It has been moved three times, the latest in 2001 to a Kingston Township location. Tours by costumed docents lead through two floors of Rockingham's furnishings, which include such period pieces as Chippendale sets, burnished bureaus, canopied beds, and an antique tea service. The study where the Farewell Address was composed is shown with the ink stand and green cloth on the table. There's even a life-sized replica of Washington. Outside, a sizable kitchen garden displays colonial herbs and vegetables in front of the house. Open hearth cooking is also demonstrated during special events. There's a children's museum in an adjacent former eighteenth-century wash house that features games, activities, and costumes for kids. And in May, there's an annual Children's Day, featuring fun activities and demonstrations of eighteenth-century life.

LOCATION: Laurel Ave. (Rte. 603), Kingston (Somerset County).
HOURS: Tours: Wed.–Sat., 10, 11, 1, 2, & 3; Sun., 1, 2, & 3.
ADMISSION: Free. **PHONE:** 609-683-7132.
WEBSITE: www.rockingham.net.

American Indian Heritage Museum

The Powhatan Renape Nation's museum provides an inside look at Native American culture. Visitors will learn about history, culture, and traditions from guides who gear group tours to visitors' ages. The American Indian staff interprets displays that contain tools, musical instruments, clothing, weapons, and decorative arts. You'll find large dioramas, a gallery of contemporary artwork by American Indian artists, and a Native American gift shop. Outdoors, you can explore a re-creation of a traditional woodland village, walk down nature trails, or see the live bison. There are also three-day Native American arts festivals on this small reservation in May and October featuring musicians, artists, and more than 150 vendors from tribal groups ranging from the Navajo and Cherokee to the Nanticoke and Aztec.

LOCATION: Rankokus Indian Reservation, Rancocas Rd., Westampton (Burlington County). **HOURS:** First and third Sat. of the month, 10–3. Call first. **ADMISSION:** $$; children, $. **PHONE:** 609-261-4747.
WEBSITE: www.powhatan.org/museum.html.

New Jersey Museum of Agriculture

Part of Rutgers University's Cook College, this large museum features early farming equipment, a seventeenth-century trading post, tractors, milk carts, plows, buggies, kitchen utensils, and displays of land-clearing in its surrounding research farm. You'll find every-thing from egg sorters to apple pickers, plus the history of New Jersey chicken and produce farms. There are also early crafts shops, such as those of a tinker, blacksmith, and carpenter. Weekend family specials once a month may include live farm animals. Lots of elementary school programs are offered during the week.

LOCATION: Off Rt. 1 on College Farm Rd., Cook College, New Brunswick (Middlesex County). **HOURS:** Tue.–Sat., 10–3. **ADMISSION:** $. Under 4 free. **PHONE:** 732-249-2077. **WEBSITE:** www.agriculturemuseum.org.

Museum of Early Trades and Crafts

Housed in a Richardson Revival building that once was the Madison Public Library, this museum serves two purposes. The refurbished building, brought back to its circa 1900 glory, with brilliant stained glass windows, bronze chandeliers, and wrought iron balcony, is an architect's delight. And it houses a major collection, on revolving display, of tools for the thirty-four trades that existed in New Jersey in 1776. Some of these reflect the more common trades like coopering (barrel making) and printing from the colonial period onward, while others include the more specialized ones, such as making musical instruments.

Downstairs, the development of local craft businesses from their early origins is traced. For instance, the town funeral home is still owned by a family whose patriarch was a cabinetmaker. He made coffins as a sideline, but when funeral parlors came into vogue, he expanded his business. In similar fashion, a shoemaker, distiller, and cooper are also presented. Docents are on hand, and children can play in an activity room here. The museum also offers a variety of afternoon and summer programs for kids. There are Family Fun Days throughout the year, numerous Smart Start family arts and crafts events, and other events such as a Colonial Cooking Contest (with a kids' division). Also offered are a variety of historical, educational, and fun sessions for school groups.

LOCATION: Main Street (Rt. 124) and Green Village Rd., Madison (Morris County). **HOURS:** Tue.–Sat., 10–4; Sun., 12–5. Closed major holidays. **ADMISSION:** $. **PHONE:** 973-377-2982. **WEBSITE:** www.metc.org. (sc)

Israel Crane House

Built in the Federal period and then remodeled in the Greek Revival style, the Crane House was moved from its original site to the present location by the Montclair Historical Society. The tour starts in the basement exhibit room with a video on the history of the house. Costumed docents give guided tours throughout the three-story building with its furnishings in the Federal and Empire styles. Behind the main house is a two-story kitchen building reconstructed to resemble the 1840 kitchen that once stood there. Open-hearth cooking demonstrations are held most Sundays, Oct.–May. There are also special tours of the house for school classes.

LOCATION: 110 Orange Rd., Montclair (Essex County).
HOURS: Tours, Mar.–Dec., Sun., 1 & 2. Closed holiday weekends.
ADMISSION: $. Under 11 free. **PHONE:** 973-744-1796.
WEBSITE: www.montclairhistorical.org.

Cape May County Museum

This museum in the 1704 Robert Morris Holmes House is operated by the Cape May County Historical and Genealogical Society. The museum includes the 1704 kitchen, a pre-1820 dining room all set up, a children's room with antique toys, and much glassware and china. The Victorian Room includes a unique organ with an inlaid clock. There's a military collection dating from the Revolution to today, including the flag from the Civil War ironclad, the *Merrimac*. The Doctor's Room shows changes in surgical instruments from the Revolution to 1900. Across the yard, the barn features maritime and whaling exhibits; a Native American Room with an extensive arrowhead collection and other Lenni-Lenape artifacts; and a room containing a stagecoach, peddler's wagon, and a restored doctor's sulky. The barn is also home of the original Fresnel lens from the 1847 Cape May Point Lighthouse.

LOCATION: 504 Rt. 9 North, Cape May Courthouse (Cape May County).
HOURS: June-Sep., Tue.–Sat., 10–3; Oct.–May, Fri.–Sat. only.
ADMISSION: Free. **PHONE:** 609-465-3535.
WEBSITE: www.cmcmuseum.org.

New Jersey Historical Society

The society's home across from Newark's Military Park is a handsome townhouse that contains three floors of exhibits about the Garden State. Permanent holdings include furniture, paintings, sculpture, and an incredible number of items covering 300 years of history. Changing exhibits emphasize different periods or themes based on New Jersey history. The opening exhibit in the building was called "From Sinatra to Springsteen" and traced the evolution of teenagers in the Garden State from the 1940s to the 1980s. Another exhibit followed the life of Paul Robeson, and later ones on the popular Jersey diner and on New Jersey rivers. A variety of interactive exhibits are geared for school-age children. The society also has special interactive programs designed for families, including weekly Saturday art/history programs, self-guided games, and twice-yearly family festivals.

LOCATION: 52 Park Place, Newark. **HOURS:** Tue.–Sat., 10–5. **ADMISSION:** Free. **PHONE:** 973-596-8500. **WEBSITE:** www.jerseyhistory.org.

Meadowlands Museum

This small museum in a 200-year-old Dutch farmhouse focuses on local history and fine arts. Permanent exhibits include the Homespun Kitchen and Pre-Electric Kitchen on the first floor. Upstairs you'll find an Antique Toy and Game Room plus a Fluorescent Mineral Room containing fossils and minerals, including fluorescents from the Franklin Mine. Changing exhibits range from quilts to art to history. An annual historic crafts program in August includes weeklong sessions. Kids aged 6–7 learn to sew their own placemats, weave, dip candles, make flowers from buttons, and create homemade books about their hometowns. Children aged 8–9 make homemade books about food they like to eat, create a beginner's hand-woven basket, dip candles, develop sewing skills, and make a button person. Kids 10 and up make a homemade book in the shape of a music CD, make an advanced hand-woven basket, dip candles, sew a cat-shaped pillow, and make a button-framed mirror. There are also once-a-week classes in beginning woodworking and quilting for children aged 8 and up.

LOCATION: 91 Crane Ave., Rutherford (Bergen County). **HOURS:** Mon.–Thu., 10–3; Sat., 1–4; Sun., 2–4. **ADMISSION:** Donation. **PHONE:** 201-935-1175. **WEBSITE:** www.meadowlandsmuseum.com.

Middlesex County Museum

Set in a restored 1741 Georgian mansion (also known as the Cornelius Low House), the museum offers changing exhibits. A one-theme exhibit (about some aspect of the Raritan Valley, its history or population, or on a larger aspect of New Jersey) takes up the entire house and usually lasts a few months.

LOCATION: 1225 River Rd., Piscataway (Middlesex County). Entrance most easily attained through the Busch Campus of Rutgers University. An interpretive path from the parking lot offers a history of the local area. **HOURS:** Tue.–Fri. and Sun., 1–4. **ADMISSION:** Free. **PHONE:** 732-745-4177. **WEBSITE:** www.co.middlesex.nj.us/culturalheritage/museum.asp.

Animals, Animals

Llamas are among the wide variety of animals that kids can see and enjoy at the Turtle Back Zoo in West Orange. *(Photo by Patrick Sarver)*

ZOOS

Wild Safari at Six Flags

The largest safari park in the region takes about an hour to drive through and covers 4.5 miles and nine theme areas and features more than 1,200 animals of fifty-two species. Some, such as camels, elk in heat, giraffes, and rhinos can get almost too close for comfort. Car windows should be closed at all times, so take an air-conditioned vehicle if you're visiting on a hot day. The road through the safari is three lanes wide, and you can travel at your own speed. Each area is separated from the other by wire fences, so you must wait for guards to open the gates between one habitat and another.

In the African Plains section, which has more types of animals than any other section, you can watch herds of elephants eat and socialize. There are enough gazelles, zebras, gnus, elands, water-bucks, and other creatures from the African grasslands to make you think you've wandered off to somewhere in the Serengeti. The ostriches are very surly and would just as soon peck at your fingers as they do your windshield wipers. And nothing can make you feel smaller than sitting knee-high to a giraffe as he nudges up against your car.

The Australian section has kangaroos, and the flightless emu strut, waddle, and bound across the hilly terrain. The Asian section features animals from Central Asia like the yak, Asian water buffalo, and exotic antelope. And the Americas area is populated by deer, elk, bison, and llamas.

As you drive slowly from one section to the next, you will see a Bengal tiger in its own Indian pavilion and, later on, brown bears that are usually up a tree or staying cool in a stream. And there are dozens of baboons safely kept inside a fenced-in area but still close enough to the road to be seen very well.

Near the entrance gate is Exploration Station, which features baby animals, exotic birds, reptiles, and other small animals as well as trainers presenting a capuchin monkey and a kinkajou to the kids. There are also interactive science exhibits at Doc's Discoveries and other hands-on exhibits.

Wild Safari also offers education programs from April to November. Journeys in Learning takes students into Wild Safari for hands-on exhibits at the Exploration Station, then on a private safari bus for a behind-the-scenes guided tour with a focus on animal science.

LOCATION: Jackson Twp. (Ocean County). N.J. Turnpike, Exit 7A, then Rt. 195 east to Exit 16. **HOURS:** Mid-May–Aug., daily, 9–4; Apr.–mid-May, Sep.–Oct., open weekends. **ADMISSION:** Safari, $$$$. Under 3 free. Combo: $$ with Six Flags/Great Adventure admission. **PHONE:** 732-928-1821. **WEBSITE:** www.sixflags.com/greatAdventure/nearbyParks/WildSafari.aspx.

Turtle Back Zoo

Every year there is more construction, and new exhibits and animals come to this zoo. The zoo recently added a walk-through reptile house, as well as renovated river otter and alligator exhibits. Wolf Woods is a naturalistic exhibit where you can watch a family of wolves from behind a see-through shield. Penguins have taken over the old seal pond, and peacocks strut freely around. There's a new Australian aviary where you walk among flying parakeets and feed them. The Essex Farm petting zoo area, which is always popular with kids, is open April to November with goats, pigs, and lambs and also offers pony rides. You'll see a few large cats, such as cougars, an Amur leopard, and bobcats, in cages. There are also black bears, bison, llamas, bald eagles, wallabies, and monkeys. And, of course, birds, turtles, and deer are always there.

There's also a new playground and continuous entertainment and animal programs are presented at the amphitheater. Also featured are an endangered species-themed carousel and a miniature train that travels through surrounding South Mountain Reservation. Special events include World Environment Day, open house, Independence Day, guided night tours, and wildlife workshops for preschool and kindergarten students.

LOCATION: 560 Northfield Ave., West Orange (Essex County). Behind Richard J. Codey Arena at South Mountain.
HOURS: Apr.–Oct.: Mon.–Sat., 10–4:30 (until 6 on Wed); Sun., 11–5:30. Winter: daily, 10–4. **ADMISSION:** \$\$; children 2–12, \$. Under 2 free. Lower rates in winter. **PHONE:** 973-731-5800.
WEBSITE: www.turtlebackzoo.com.

Cape May County Zoo

Various animal enclosures are arranged along meandering paths with pleasant foliage all about. Some of the enclosures simulate the natural terrain of the animals, while others are traditional cages. But the zoo is in a park filled with tall scrub pine and sandy soil, so the general effect is of seeing animals in their natural environments.

Among the many species here you will find alpacas, tigers, cheetahs, alligators, bears, spider monkeys, a lion, bison, and even white-maned and other tamarins. Quite a variety of birds are on hand also, including cockatoos, toucans, flamingos, peacocks, eagles, hawks, and barnyard fowl. The World of Birds Aviary is a two-story atrium filled with numerous species of tropical birds. There's also a reptile and amphibian house. In all, there are 250 species in this fun zoo.

This zoo offers a complete African savannah where giraffes, zebras, and bongo roam and visitors can watch from a shaded gazebo. Outside the zoo there's a children's playground and a picnic area. There's also a new wildlife carousel as well as the Hummingbird Express Train.

LOCATION: Rt. 9 & Crest Haven Rd., Cape May Court House.
HOURS: Daily, 10–4:45; winter, 10–3:45, weather permitting.
ADMISSION: Donation. **PHONE:** 609-465-5271.
WEBSITE: www.co.cape-may.nj.us. Click on the zoo icon. ⓢⓒ

Space Farms Zoo

This private zoo lies amid the farms and hills of northern Sussex County in a rural area that approximates the natural surroundings of many of the animals housed here. The family name here is Space, and it was a farm before it became a zoo. The entrance building includes a Museum of Americana (everything from Indian arrowheads to old clocks) and the stuffed Goliath, a 12-foot-high grizzly that was the world's largest and once the main attraction here. You buy your entrance tickets here (and perhaps some munchies for the animals).

Space Farms is set up for family outings, with many picnic tables, swing sets, and other attractions available for youngsters. A hundred hilly acres are devoted to rather simple cages containing bears, lions, tigers, hyenas, monkeys, and such. A large pond at the center of the acreage allows ducks and geese to paddle about while pens of yak, llamas, buffalo, and goats dot the surrounding hills—500 animals and 100 species altogether. There is a separate den for snakes and a special enclosure for otters.

On the hills to the left of the zoo are the museums: several buildings filled with antique cars, sleighs, old buggies, tractors, dolls, farm machinery, and toys. The antique car collection is surprisingly large. Between the animals, the museums, the swings, and the slides you can make a day of it.

LOCATION: 218 Rt. 519, Beemerville (Sussex County), 7 miles north of Rt. 206 or 5 miles south of Rt. 23. **HOURS:** Mid-Apr.–Oct., daily, 9–5. **ADMISSION:** $$$. Discounts: Seniors, children. Under 3 free. **PHONE:** 973-875-5800. **WEBSITE:** www.spacefarms.com.

Bergen County Zoological Park

This popular small zoo in Van Saun Park exhibits animals from North and South America, so you won't see any tigers, giraffes, or elephants here. There is a North American Great Plains exhibit plus Central and South American animals and a North American Wetlands Aviary. Some large cats, including mountain lions, are on display. The 200 animals here include elk, bison, alligators, bobcats, tapirs, eagles, and more exotic species like the golden lion tamarin and spider monkeys. In the Discovery and Education Center, there's a touch tank with starfish, a tropical aquarium, and a fifty-minute nature film.

Favorites with young children are the miniature train ride and an1890s farmyard with sheep, goats, and chickens as well as pony rides and a carousel across the park road from the zoo entrance. The zoo is part of a 140-acre park that features picnic tables, a fishing pond, and biking and hiking trails.

LOCATION: 216 Forest Ave., Paramus (Bergen County). Off Rt. 4.
HOURS: Daily, 10–4:30. **ADMISSION:** $. May–Oct., Fri.–Sun. and holidays. Discounts: Seniors, children. Under 3 free. Free, Nov.–Apr.
PHONE: 201-262-3771.
WEBSITE: www.co.bergen.nj.us/parks/Parks/Zoo.htm.

Lakota Wolf Preserve

This preserve at Camp Taylor near the Delaware Water Gap is home to more than twenty-four tundra, timber, and arctic wolves as well as some foxes and bobcats. Co-owner and handler Jim Stein presents wolves in their natural surroundings. The preserve is a scenic walk from the campground (rides are also available). The observation area is in the center of four packs of wolves. You'll talk with people who raised the wolves and will learn about the social structure of wolf packs, their eating habits, interaction with humans, and many other aspects of the animals' lives. You'll also learn that wolves respond to their names and be able to see them interact with each other, play, and perhaps howl.

LOCATION: 89 Mt. Pleasant Rd., Columbia (Warren County). Rt. 80, Exit 4 to Rt. 94 North, 2.5 miles to Mt. Pleasant turnoff.
HOURS: Open Tue.–Sun. Admission only at guided tour times, 10:30 and 4 during daylight savings time; 10:30 and 3 rest of year. Weekday tours by appointment. **ADMISSION:** $$$. Discount: Children.
PHONE: 908-496-9244 or 877-733-9653. **WEBSITE:** www.lakotawolf.com.

Cohanzick Zoo

New Jersey's first zoo, founded in 1934, is set in an 1,100-acre park that borders the Cohansey River in Bridgeton. The more than 200 animals include Asiatic bear, leopard, monkeys, white tiger, llama, alligator, reindeer, eagle, falcon, owls, and many others. You can find some unusual species—many in modern, naturalistic settings— as well as a walk-through aviary. The surrounding park contains plenty of picnic areas, nature trails, and lots more.

LOCATION: City Park, Bridgeton (Cumberland County). Rt. 49 to Atlantic St. Follow to Mayor Aitken Dr.
HOURS: Spring/summer, daily, 9–5; fall/winter, daily, 8–4.
ADMISSION: Free. **PHONE:** 856-455-3230, ext. 242.
WEBSITE: www.cityofbridgeton.com/zoo.html.

Popcorn Park Zoo

This is a 7-acre licensed zoo that caters strictly to injured, abandoned, and unwanted fauna, ranging from goats to lions, tigers, and llamas. (There are also kennels of abandoned pets waiting for adoption.) There's a small reptile house; domestic animals like pot-bellied pigs, sheep, and draft horses; and a monkey house as well as a Bactrian camel, bears, emus, and deer. Most animals are given cute names like Cindy Lou Cougar, Boo-Boo the Bear, and Holly the Sicilian Donkey. The facility is run by the Associated Humane Society.

LOCATION: Humane Way at Lacey Rd., Forked River (Ocean County). **HOURS:** Daily, 11–5. **ADMISSION:** $. **PHONE:** 609-693-1900. **WEBSITE:** www.ahcares.org.

Animal Kingdom Zoo

This private zoo hidden behind a pet store in the middle of Burlington County farmland has a surprising number and variety of animals. The cages may not be up to the latest standards of public zoos, but there are at least three dozen species. Kids can enjoy such creatures as giraffes, a leopard, half a dozen monkey species, kangaroos, llama, camel, arctic fox, antelope, baboons, and gibbon. And after looking at the exotic animals, kids might even want to take home a puppy from the pet shop.

LOCATION: 1800 Jacksonville-Jobstown Rd., Bordentown (Burlington County). Route 206 South to Rt. 670 West for 2 miles. **HOURS:** Mon.–Sat., 10–6; Sun., 10–5. **ADMISSION:** $$; children under 13, $. Under 3 free. **PHONE:** 609-267-3111. **WEBSITE:** www.animalkingdomnj.net.

AQUARIUMS

Adventure Aquarium

The New Jersey State Aquarium on the Camden Riverfront has become a major attraction in southern New Jersey. The huge 760,000-gallon Ocean Realm tank houses over 2,000 fish, including tuna, stingrays, and sea turtles. From a theater you can watch volunteer scuba divers go into the big tank and answer questions or wave to a turtle.

Altogether there are eighty freshwater and saltwater exhibits, including a special exhibit on South American fish and birds upstairs. The aquarium also features a mangrove lagoon, a Caribbean beach, and the replica of an ironclad mail ship that sank in 1867. At the touch tanks, children can feel the surface of sharks, sting rays, sea stars, and crabs. There's also a 4-D Theater, which features a twenty-minute special effects program on extreme habitats, with 3-D video and chairs that move (extra fee).

At the West African River Experience you'll encounter hippos, crocodiles, fish in the water, and birds flying above. A presentation at an underwater observation area and a video explain the life of African rivers. There's also a Jules Verne Gallery that has moon jellyfish, giant spider crabs, and octopi. Another main attraction is the 550,000-gallon Shark Realm tank, which has more than twenty sharks as well as stingrays that you can see from underwater observation points but more impressively when you walk through the Shark Tunnel. This clear passageway through the center of the tank makes the toothy predators appear to be "flying" just over your head.

Outside, at the Seal Shores section, a daily "training session" allows visitors to watch as gray seals take on such audience-pleasing chores as catching Frisbees and leaping to touch a suspended ball. Meanwhile, over at Penguin Island, a colony of African black-footed penguins waddle around. This exhibit includes a beach, rocks, and a pool with an underwater viewing area so you can also watch the birds swim. The aquarium also has an outdoor deck with a nice view of Philadelphia across the river.

LOCATION: 1 Riverside Dr., Camden (Camden County). Parking lot across street (fee). **HOURS:** Daily, 9:30–5. **ADMISSION:** $$$$. Under 2 free. **PHONE:** 856-365-3300. **WEBSITE:** www.adventureaquarium.com.

Atlantic City Aquarium

The Atlantic City Aquarium is at Historic Gardner's Basin on the inlet. This multimillion-dollar marine learning center, which anchors the small maritime park, features seventeen large tanks of fish, both tropical and local, including giant moray eels, and a diorama showing local species. A 25,000-gallon aquarium tank displays fish of the Jersey coast, such as nurse sharks, sea bass, and a 100-pound loggerhead sea turtle. There's also a touch tank with horseshoe crabs and other sea creatures as well as exhibits of moon jellyfish, clownfish, and bearded dragons from the Australian Outback. A maritime section upstairs includes diving helmets, a captain's wheel, and lots of explanations about barrier reefs and life along the sea. Kids will like the many computer learning stations here. There's also an open deck on the upper floor where you can walk outside and watch the many boats that pass nearby. The Atlantic City jitney also stops at Gardner's Basin, so it's easy to visit from the boardwalk area.

LOCATION: 800 N. New Hampshire Ave., Atlantic City (Atlantic County). **HOURS:** Daily, 10–5. **ADMISSION:** Adults, $$; children 12 and under, $. Under 3 free. **PHONE:** 609-348-2880. **WEBSITE:** www.oceanlifecenter.com. ⓑⓟ

Jenkinson's Aquarium

This popular spot on the Point Pleasant Beach boardwalk is about a block north of the amusement rides. It is roomier inside than you would expect, and it includes tanks of small sharks and rays, a penguin area, an alligator pit, a Pacific Coast tank with a mini kelp forest, and some hard-working seals. The centerpiece is the sunken ship, the *Bounty*, with freshwater tropicals flitting in and around it. Coral reef fish and colorful parrots are here as well, and you can walk around the center to get a view from all sides. Upstairs is a tropical forest exhibit, with the world's smallest monkeys plus parrots, touch tanks, and numerous other exhibits on fossils and shark teeth.

LOCATION: Boardwalk near Ocean Ave., Point Pleasant Beach (Ocean County). **HOURS:** July–Aug.: daily, 10–10; winter: weekdays, 9:30–5, weekends, 11–5. **ADMISSION:** $$. Under 3 free. **PHONE:** 732-892-0600. **WEBSITE:** www.jenkinsons.com/aquarium.

WHALE AND DOLPHIN WATCHES

Another way to visit fish and other sea creatures is to go out to meet them in their own environment. There are a number of boats at the Jersey Shore that run excursions for whale and dolphin watches or skim through the interior canals to view birds and swamp life. Here are a few. Please note that sailing times, dates, and schedules may change due to weather or other circumstances. Always check ahead.

Cape May Whale Watch and Research Center

The M/V *Whale Watcher* is a 110-foot catamaran designed for whale and dolphin watching, complete with food service. An on-board naturalist instructs passengers on spotting techniques. Whale watches last 3 hours, dolphin watches 2.

LOCATION: 1243 Wilson Dr., Cape May. Rt. 109 to 3rd Ave. to Wilson Dr. **HOURS:** Trips at 10, 1, and 6:30 in summer; May, Sep., Oct., 9:30 and 1. **FARE:** Whale watch, $$$$$; dolphin watch, $$$$$. Under 7 free. **PHONE:** 609-884-5445. **WEBSITE:** www.capemaywhalewatcher.com.

Silver Bullet

This ocean-going 70-foot speedboat offers dolphin watching trips.

LOCATION: Docked at Wildwood Marina, Rio Grande & Susquehanna Aves., Wildwood (Cape May County). **HOURS:** Daily at 9:30, 12, & 2:30;

added trip Tue.–Thu. at 4:30. **FARE:** $$$$$. Under 2 free.
PHONE: 609-522-6060. **WEBSITE:** www.silverbullettours.com.

Thunder Cat

This catamaran speedboat offers a variety of dolphin watching trips.

> **LOCATION:** Docked at Dolphin Cove Marina, 1001 Ocean Dr.,
> Wildwood Crest (Cape May County). **HOURS:** Summer: Daily at 10, 12,
> & 2; added trip Tue.–Thu. at 4:30. Spring and fall trips vary.
> **FARE:** $$$$$. Under 3 free. **PHONE:** 609-523-2628.
> **WEBSITE:** www.thundercatdolphinwatch.com.

Starlight Fleet

Whale and dolphin watching cruises are offered daily around the
Cape May area. There are touch tanks onboard for the kids during
the 9:30 and 1 o'clock cruises.

> **LOCATION:** Starlight Fleet dock at 6200 Park Blvd., Wildwood Crest
> (Cape May County). **HOURS:** May–Sep., daily at 9:30, 1, and a 6:30
> dinner cruise. **FARE:** Whale watch, $$$$$; dolphin watch, $$$$$.
> Under 7 free. **PHONE:** 609-729-3400 also 7776.
> **WEBSITE:** www.jjcboats.com.

Salt Marsh Safari

An enclosed 40-foot pontoon, the *Skimmer,* takes you on 2-hour
back bay and river wildlife trips. These salt-marsh safaris include
birdwatching and talks on marsh life. A limited supply of binoculars
is also available. N.J. Audubon sponsors some of the marsh trips.

> **LOCATION:** Docked at Dolphin Cove Marina, Ocean Dr. (between
> Cape May and Wildwood). **HOURS:** Apr.–Nov., daily, 10, 1:30, & 6.
> Mid-June–Labor Day, Wed. & Thu., sails from Wetlands Institute in
> Stone Harbor (except at 6 on Thu.). **FARE:** $$$$$; children, $$$.
> Under 3 free. **PHONE:** 609-884-3100. **WEBSITE:** www.skimmer.com.

WILDLIFE REFUGES AND NATURE CENTERS

Great Swamp National Wildlife Refuge

The remains of a glacial pocket, the swamp serves as both a refuge
for animals and as a 7,700-acre barrier to suburban development. It
was saved in 1960 by local conservationists from being turned into
an airport and donated to the federal government. The area is a
combination of marshes, grassland, swamp, woodland, and hard-
wood ridges.

Wooden boardwalks at the Wildlife Observation Center on Long
Hill Road let visitors traverse the wetlands and observe whatever

wildlife is around. Mostly it's small—woodchucks, muskrats, frogs, geese, ducks, herons. There are deer, wild turkeys, and foxes, too, though they tend to stay in the interior. There are blinds for picture taking. Swamp officials recommend visits in the early morning or late afternoon. There's also a bird-watching overlook on Pleasant Plains Road not far from the headquarters. About half the swamp is a wilderness area, and almost 10 miles of hiking trails cross this part of the refuge. Old sneakers or waterproof shoes are recommended. Insect repellent is especially advisable.

> **LOCATION:** Helen C. Fenske Visitor Center, 32 Pleasant Plains Rd., Basking Ridge (Somerset County).
> **HOURS:** Park, daily, dawn to dusk. Center, Thu.–Fri., 12–4; weekends, 10–4. **PHONE:** 973-425-1222.
> **WEBSITE:** www.fws.gov/northeast/greatswamp.

While headquarters facilities in the Great Swamp are limited, the following three nature centers bordering the refuge are of interest.

Somerset County Park Environmental Education Center

Located in Lord Stirling Park on the western edge of the Great Swamp, this modern building features classrooms, exhibits about the swamp, a book and gift shop, library, and photography and art shows. More than 8 miles of trails and wooden walkways pass ponds and cross woods and wetlands in the park's 425 acres of natural lands. Bird-watching, guided hikes, cross-country skiing, school programs, and trips are offered each year.

> **LOCATION:** 190 Lord Stirling Rd., Basking Ridge (Somerset County).
> **HOURS:** Park, daily, dawn–dusk. Center, daily, 9–5.
> **PHONE:** 908-766-2489.
> **WEBSITE:** www.somersetcountyparks.org/programs/eec/eec_main.htm.

Great Swamp Outdoor Education Center

Adjacent to the eastern edge of the Great Swamp, this forty-acre facility contains natural history exhibits on animals, a library, and classrooms. There is also an exhibit of art with a nature theme that changes monthly. Nature trails, guided walks, and wooden boardwalks lead into the swamp. Special programs such as maple sugaring are offered, as are scout and family programs.

> **LOCATION:** 247 Southern Blvd., Chatham Twp. (Morris County).
> **HOURS:** Daily, 9–4:30.
> **ADMISSION:** Trails are free; fees for classes.
> **PHONE:** 973-635-6629.
> **WEBSITE:** www.morrisparks.net/parks/gswampmain.htm.

The Raptor Trust

This is a wildlife rehabilitation center for wounded birds, primarily birds of prey. There are several different kinds of owls, hawks, eagles, falcons, and vultures. Those that cannot be released are kept onsite in large cages for public display, for breeding purposes, and for education. It is run by a nonprofit organization that also offers educational programs for school, scout, and adult groups.

LOCATION: 1390 White Bridge Rd., Millington (Morris County).
HOURS: Daily, dawn–dusk (call first). **ADMISSION:** Donation.
PHONE: 908-647-2353. **WEBSITE:** www.theraptortrust.org.

Wetlands Institute

Set in the middle of 6,000 acres of publicly owned salt marsh, not far from the beach at Stone Harbor, this attractive cedar shake education center includes classrooms, an exhibit hall, and six research laboratories. Secrets of the Salt Marsh has more than a dozen aquarium exhibits and hands-on interactive exhibits. Terrapin Station is devoted to diamondback turtles. A book and gift shop is also on hand. There is also an observation deck that provides a view of the surrounding wetlands (and an osprey nest). The building is surrounded by native plant gardens. Periodic guided tours of the marsh, plus a number of lectures and ecology classes, are available. There's also a salt marsh trail open during visiting hours, with guided talks during the summer. A 120-foot pier at the end extends over a tidal creek and offers views of the world's largest colony of laughing gulls. Once a year, the institute hosts the "Wings 'n Water Festival," a popular wildlife art event on the third weekend in September that includes wooden duck carving, seafood dinners, boat rides, and open houses.

LOCATION: 1075 Stone Harbor Blvd. (Rt. 657), Stone Harbor (Cape May County). Off Garden State Parkway, Exit 10B. **HOURS:** May 15–Oct. 15, Mon.–Sat., 9:30–4:30; Sun., 10–4. Closed Sun. and Mon. rest of year. **ADMISSION:** $$. Under 2 free. **PHONE:** 609-368-1211. **WEBSITE:** www.wetlandsinstitute.org.

Meadowlands Environment Center

The Hackensack Meadowlands Development Commission's Environmental Center is a modern circular building that sits in the center of an urban salt marsh. A wide, enclosed observation room offers panoramas of the surrounding marshland, with the turnpike and Manhattan skyline visible in the distance. An outside deck and elevated boardwalk allow closer inspection. It is part of the larger

Richard W. DeKorte Park, which includes several trails. The Marsh Discovery Trail leads across a pontoon walkway through the reeds and marshlands, where you can spot ducks, egrets, sandpipers, gulls, and ospreys. There's also a shorter trail through the adjacent Lyndhurst Nature Preserve as well as a butterfly garden next to the center.

There are some interesting displays inside. The main lobby showcases a 30-foot diorama of a salt marsh and its inhabitants. Discovery Station is an interactive center that includes computer touch-screen learning, microscopes for viewing close-ups of natural specimens, and walk-through mock-ups of a cedar forest and salt marsh. The Flyway Gallery displays changing exhibits of photos, paintings, and graphics. A gift shop offers stuffed animal toys and environmentally related merchandise. The center runs regular public educational programs, guided nature walks, and pontoon boat tours.

There are also a regular schedule of events for kids on Saturdays, including such topics as Bugs in the Garden, a paper marbleizing workshop; Drawing Nature; Billy B the Science Man; and Animals in Winter.

LOCATION: 2 DeKorte Park Plaza, Lyndhurst (Bergen County). From Rt. 3, take Rt. 17 South, exit onto Polito Ave., then left on Valley Brook Ave., 2 miles to end. **HOURS:** Weekdays, 9–5; weekends, 10–3. **ADMISSION:** Free. **PHONE:** 201-460-8300. **WEBSITE:** www.njmeadowlands.gov/ec.

James A. McFaul Environmental Center

An 81-acre center run by Bergen County, this facility includes snakes, turtles, and other small animals as well as aquariums, natural history displays, and a large room overlooking a hummingbird garden and waterfowl pond. Outside, you'll find a nature trail, picnic area, and gardens. There are also outdoor wildlife pens with deer, an eagle, and other animals. The Wildlife Exhibit Hall shows films and slide shows plus museum programs.

LOCATION: Crescent Ave., Wyckoff (Bergen County). Rt. 208 to Goffle Rd. North to Goodwin Ave., then one quarter mile to Crescent. **HOURS:** Exhibit hall, daily, 8–4:45; weekends, 1–4:45. **ADMISSION:** Free. **PHONE:** 201-891-5571. **WEBSITE:** www.co.bergen.nj.us/parks/Parks/McFaul.htm.

Woodford Cedar Run Wildlife Refuge

This lodge-like Education Center on a 184-acre preserve offers workshops, field trips, and hands-on exhibits about wildlife and the

Pinelands. There are some live animals, especially in the snake room, plus a puppet theater and play room. The refuge also has a wildlife rehabilitation hospital that treats 2,000 animals a year and includes an outdoor live-animal compound with foxes, hawks, owls, and deer. Weekend programs (Sat., 10–4, and Sun., 1–4) focus on specific species. Outdoor adventures include Pinelands canoe trips, off-road biking, guided hikes, tracking by compass, and outdoor skills.

LOCATION: 4 Sawmill Rd., Medford (Burlington County). Rt. 73 to Marlton Pky., right on Hopewell Rd. to W. Centennial, then to Borton Rd. Make a right, then a left onto Sawmill. **HOURS:** Mon.–Sat., 10–4; Sun., 1–4. **ADMISSION:** $. Under 4 free. **PHONE:** 856-983-3329. **WEBSITE:** www.cedarrun.org.

Trailside Nature and Science Center

A part of Watchung Reservation, this recently expanded three-level modern building includes an auditorium and a natural history museum. A beech tree rises through the atrium, with running water and live fish and other wildlife specimens at its base. It features a fluorescent mineral room, children's discovery room, and Lenape Indian exhibit. There are also natural history exhibits on forest ecology, conservation, meadow habitats, and the geology of the surrounding reservation. And the Night Theater is a multimedia presentation on nocturnal creatures. The center offers a full schedule of weekend programs, nature walks, and numerous children's programs. Thirteen miles of hiking trails surround the center.

LOCATION: Coles Ave. & New Providence Rd., Mountainside (Union County). **HOURS:** Daily, 12–5. **ADMISSION:** Free. **PHONE:** 908-789-3670. **WEBSITE:** www.unioncountynj.org/trailside/index.htm.

Paws Farm Nature Center

A variety of animal fun awaits kids here. The welcome center features an education room with live animals, stuffed birds, a play area, and a gift shop. Outside, there's a dairy farm with farm animals and a barn with activities and exhibits. A historic farmhouse includes a room with small animals, a reading room, a play vet room, and a blacksmith shop. A short nature trail leads past more animals. There are also a butterfly garden and play areas.

LOCATION: 1105 Hainesport Rd., Mount Laurel (Burlington County). **HOURS:** Wed.–Sun., 10–4. **ADMISSION:** $$. Under 1 free. **PHONE:** 856-778-8795. **WEBSITE:** www.pawsfarm.com.

At Insectropolis in Toms River, kids can learn about common and exotic insects in a small, child-friendly museum setting. *(Photo by Patrick Sarver)*

Insectropolis

This interesting little educational center, which calls itself "the bugseum of New Jersey," was created by a pest control company and exhibits thousands of pinned specimens, including many colorful display cases of colorful butterflies, beetles, and other insects. There are also hundreds of live bugs from all over the world, including a bee hive, tarantulas, Madagascar hissing cockroaches, an ant colony, roaches, and bird-eating spiders. Interactive exhibits include computerized bug games, WBUG communications center, and informational videos. At the Insectropolis zoo (a large room with seats for classes), you can touch live bugs.

LOCATION: 1761 Rt. 9 North, Toms River. Behind Ozane Pest Control. **HOURS:** Tue.–Sat., 10–3; Mon.–Sat. in summer. **ADMISSION:** $$. Under 3 free. **PHONE:** 732-349-7090. **WEBSITE:** www.insectropolis.com. (BP)

Cooper Environmental Center

This center exhibits live reptiles, turtles, and fish and has hands-on seasonally oriented displays about the local environment, including shells, stuffed mammals and birds, and fossils. There are guided hikes on Cattus Island Park's 5 miles of trails through 500 acres of fresh- and saltwater marshes and upland forest as well as bird-watching lessons, slide shows, and a junior naturalist program.

LOCATION: Cattus Island County Park, 1170 Cattus Island Blvd., Toms River (Ocean County). **HOURS:** Park: Daily, dawn–dusk. Center: Daily, 8–4:30. **ADMISSION:** Free. **PHONE:** 732-270-6960. **WEBSITE:** www.co.ocean.nj.us/parks/cattus.html.

Flat Rock Brook Nature Center

One hundred fifty acres of forest with trails and a brook surround a Visitor Center that offers animal and nature exhibits. Various weekend activities, such as tree identification and other classes are held for schoolchildren. A short Backyard Habitat for Wildlife Trail is among 3.2 miles of natural pathways.

LOCATION: 443 Van Nostrand Ave., Englewood (Bergen County). **HOURS:** Park, open daily, dawn to dusk. Building, Mon.–Fri., 9–5; weekends, 1–5. **ADMISSION:** Free. **PHONE:** 201-567-1265. **WEBSITE:** www.flatrockbrook.org.

Buttinger Nature Center

This popular center, located in the Stony Brook Reserve, features a Discovery Room with changing nature exhibits and numerous educational programs. There's also a Demonstration Organic Farm, a butterfly house, a bird-watching area, plus 14 miles of trails through the 860 acres surrounding the center.

LOCATION: 31 Titus Mill Rd., Pennington (Mercer County). Off Rt. 31, 2.5 miles north of Pennington Circle. **BUILDING HOURS:** Tue.–Fri., 10–5, Sat., 10–4. **ADMISSION:** Free. **PHONE:** 609-737-3735. **WEBSITE:** www.thewatershed.org/edu_nature_center.php.

Poricy Park Nature Center

This 250-acre township park offers trails, a nature center, fossil bed, and a colonial farmhouse. A modern building houses nature and fossil displays, art programs, and an extensive list of school programs. Poricy Brook Fossil Beds, where you can explore for fossils, are just a short drive away. Guided tours are available for groups.

LOCATION: Oak Hill Rd., Middletown (Monmouth County). Just west of Rt. 35. **HOURS:** Trails, dawn to dusk. Nature Center, Mon.–Fri., 9–4; weekends, per program schedule. **ADMISSION:** Free. **PHONE:** 732-842-5966. **WEBSITE:** http://poricypark.org.

Tenafly Nature Center

The Nature Center Building on this 52-acre site next to 330-acre Lost Brook Preserve offers interpretive displays as well as a variety of nature and wildlife education programs. There's also an outdoor exhibition of backyard habitats for butterflies.

LOCATION: 313 Hudson Ave., Tenafly (Bergen County). Right off Engle, just north of Clinton Ave. **HOURS:** Trails, daily, dawn–dusk; building, daily, 9–5. **ADMISSION:** Free. **PHONE:** 201-568-6093. **WEBSITE:** www.tenaflynaturecenter.org.

Reeves-Reed Arboretum

A full schedule of events for children includes such sessions as Environmental Explorers, which is a multiweek after-school course that lets kids explore many aspects of the natural world through games, experiments, hikes, and crafts. Discovery Center Saturdays offer a hands-on exploration of nature topics like fall migrations, with stories, crafts, and experiments. There are backpacks with binoculars, field guides, magnifying glasses, and other things needed for exploring the arboretum. Other sessions include Fur, Scales, and Animal Tales and Decorate a Tree for Wildlife.

LOCATION: 165 Hobart Ave., Summit (Union County). **HOURS:** Weekdays, after school, and Sat., 9–1. **ADMISSION:** Free. **PHONE:** 908-273-8787. **WEBSITE:** www.reeves-reedarboretum.org. (BP) (SC)

Essex County Environmental Center

Set at the edge of West Essex Park, this relatively new nature center offers indoor exhibits, a full schedule of environmentally oriented classes, including fun looks at nature. There are also woodland trails, a butterfly garden, paddling on the Passaic River, and a gardening education center. Many events are presented through partnering organizations, such as the New Jersey Audubon Society, which offers sessions on such topics as amphibians and field trips to other locations. Many sessions are designed for kids aged 4 to 12, including a series of gardening classes. There are day sessions for preschoolers and after-school classes for grade-school students.

LOCATION: 621 B Eagle Rock Ave., Roseland (Essex County). **HOURS:** Center, Mon.–Fri., 9–5; Sat., 10–2. Park, daily, dawn–dusk. **ADMISSION:** Free. **PHONE:** 973-228-8776. **WEBSITE:** www.essexcountynj.org.

Liberty State Park Interpretive Center

The interpretive center features exhibits on the natural history and ecology of the Hudson River Estuary. It offers programs for all ages. Children 12 and under must be accompanied by an adult. There are kid-oriented classes such as Tiny Trails, about small creatures all around us; a session on having a suitable variety of habitats for wildlife; classes about trees and birds of prey in NJ; and Estuary Explorers for exploring life by combing beaches.

LOCATION: Morris Pesin Dr., Jersey City (Hudson County).
HOURS: Mon.–Sat, 9–4, and Sun. in summer. Reservations required.
ADMISSION: Free. **PHONE:** 201-915-3409.
WEBSITE: www.state.nj.us/dep/parksandforests/parks/liberty_state_
park/liberty_education.html.

New Jersey Audubon Society

The society operates a number of centers, wildlife sanctuaries, and bird observatories throughout the state (908-204-8998; www.njaudubon.org). You might find art shows, gift shops full of books and binoculars, libraries, sample backyards with lots of bird-houses, and trail maps for the surrounding fields or forests. The centers include the following.

Scherman-Hoffman Sanctuary. Headquarters for the society, the site is a combination of two former estates. The 276-acre sanctuary runs such programs as nighttime or morning rambles, slide programs, art shows, school programs, canoe trips, birding weekends, and more. Free nature walks Fri. and Sat., 8–9 A.M. There are 3.2 miles of upland and streamside trails. There is also a nice nature center with a nature- and birding-oriented gift shop, a bird observation window, classrooms, and a bird display room.

> **LOCATION:** 11 Hardscrabble Rd., Bernardsville (Somerset County). Exit 30B from Rt. 287. Cross 202 onto Childs Rd., then bear right on Hardscrabble. **HOURS:** Tue.–Sat., 9–5; Sun., 12–5. **ADMISSION:** Free. **PHONE:** 908-766-5787. ⓢⓒ

Lorrimer Sanctuary. This center, in a late 1700s house, has an exhibit and lecture room, interpretive and hands-on displays, gift shop, bird observation window, and nature trails on fourteen surrounding acres. Activities include nature programs and workshops plus numerous programs for school kids. Lots of bird-watching.

> **LOCATION:** 790 Ewing Ave., Franklin Lakes (Bergen County). One mile south of Rt. 208. **HOURS:** Wed.–Fri., 9–5; Sat., 10–5; Sun., 1–5. **ADMISSION:** Free. **PHONE:** 201-891-2185. ⓢⓒ

Sandy Hook Bird Observatory. This site has a Visitor Center, a nearby observation deck overlooking New York Harbor, and hiking trails. The observatory offers field trips, morning bird and butterfly walks, bird migration watch mid-March to mid-May, workshops, and many school group programs.

> **LOCATION:** 20 Hartshorne Dr., Fort Hancock, Gateway National Recreation Area (Monmouth County). **HOURS:** Tue.–Sat., 10–5; Sun., 10–3. **ADMISSION:** Free. **PHONE:** 732-872-2500. ⓢⓒ

Weis Ecology Center. Nestled on a 160-acre preserve adjacent to Norvin Green State Forest, this center offers numerous on-site programs covering wildlife, outdoor skills, and interpretive hikes. Campsites and cabins are available, as is a dormitory for school and scout groups. Special residential programs include meals. There's also a small wildlife display area in the center.

> **LOCATION:** 150 Snake Den Rd., Ringwood (Passaic County). Take Rt. 287 to Exit 55 to Rt. 511 North for 4 miles. Left on Westbrook Rd. Left again at fork, then second left onto Snake Den. Take left fork on Snake Den. **HOURS:** Wed.–Sun., 9–4. **ADMISSION:** Free. **PHONE:** 973-835-2160. ⓢⓒ

Plainsboro Preserve. This 631-acre preserve features an environmental education center with interactive displays, a nature bookstore, an observation deck overlooking McCormack Lake, and more than 5 miles of trails. There are natural history programs, interpretive hikes, and slide programs for groups.

> **LOCATION:** 80 Scotts Corner Rd., Plainsboro (Middlesex County). Rt. 1 to Scudders Mill Rd., then left on Dey Rd. to Scotts Corner. **HOURS:** Tue.–Sat., 9–5; Sun., 12–5. **ADMISSION:** Free. **PHONE:** 609-897-9400. ⓢⓒ

Rancocas Nature Center. This is a favorite for bird-watchers. It covers about 120 acres on the edge of Rancocas State Park and has nature displays, a book and gift shop, and a classroom inside and nature trails beyond.

> **LOCATION:** 794 Rancocas Rd., Mt. Holly (Burlington County). **HOURS:** Tue.–Sat., 9–5; Sun., 12–5. Closes at 4 in winter. **ADMISSION:** Free. **PHONE:** 609-261-2495. ⓢⓒ

Nature Center of Cape May. The nature center on the harbor has exhibit aquariums, classrooms, a gift shop, and display and children's gardens. A full schedule of natural history programs runs throughout the year. Extensive program for schools and other groups, from Mommy & Me preschool sessions to kayak eco-tours to a Kids Can! series. Two programs of note are Beachcombing at the Cove and Nighttime on the Beach. The first meets at Cove Beach at 2nd Street and participants seine the shallows to see what's in the water, comb the shoreline for the sea's treasures, and walk along the dunes in search of wildlife. The second meets at Mt. Vernon Ave. off Broadway and involves a search for the elusive ghost crab and other nocturnal creatures from 8:30 P.M. to 9:30 P.M. in July. (Fee for each: Adults, $$; 3–12, $).

LOCATION: 1600 Delaware Ave., Cape May (Cape May County).
HOURS: Vary by season; opens around 10 A.M.
PHONE: 609–898–8848. ⓢⓒ

Cape May Bird Observatory. The Northwood Center is the prime bird-watching area in the state. It is famous for its World Series of Birding weekend in early to mid-May, when millions of birds can be tracked, but there is birding activity year-round. There are birding workshops and daily walks and programs.

LOCATION: 701 East Lake Dr., Cape May Point (Cape May County).
HOURS: Tue.–Sat., 9–4:30. **ADMISSION:** Free. Fees for workshops.
PHONE: 609-884-2736. ⓢⓒ

The Center for Research and Education. This is an 8,600-square-foot building surrounded by 26 acres of marsh and upland that offers lecture rooms, a large gift shop, observation deck, wildlife art gallery, a model backyard habitat and displays, and many educational activities.

LOCATION: 600 Rt. 47, Goshen (Cape May County).
HOURS: Tue.–Sat., 9:30–4:30. **ADMISSION:** Free.
PHONE: 609-861-0700. ⓢⓒ

RIDING STABLES

Essex Equestrian Center

This center offers private and group lessons on horses and on ponies for beginners for riders 6 years and older. More than thirty-five horses and ponies, year-round riding in an Olympic-sized indoor arena, outdoor riding from spring to fall are offered. Quality instruction is provided for all levels of hunter, jumper, dressage, and western riding.

LOCATION: 12–22 Woodland Ave., West Orange (Essex County). Off Prospect near Eagle Rock Reservation.
HOURS: Mon.–Fri., 9–9; weekends until 6.
ADMISSION: Individual private and group lessons and 11 lesson packages.
PHONE: 973-731-4182. **WEBSITE:** www.essexequestrian.com. ⓢⓒ

Washington Riding Stables

A full range of recreational horseback riding programs is offered here, including riding lessons for all levels. Classes include such topics as horse care, safety, handling, grooming, saddling, mounting, reining, posture, commands, exercises, and more. Hand-led pony rides are also available on the weekends for kids age 2 and up.

Parents can walk with their children. The ponies are calm and quiet and are very suitable for younger kids. There are also guided trail rides for families on 8 miles of trails.

> **LOCATION:** 3701 Bordentown Ave., Sayreville (Middlesex County).
> **HOURS:** Call. **ADMISSION:** Individual hourly lesson ($$$$$$)
> and four- and ten-lesson packages. Pony rides, $$ and $$$$,
> depending on number of laps.
> **PHONE:** 732-249-2471. **WEBSITE:** www.washingtonstables.com. ⓈⒸ

Lord Stirling Stable

This stable offers a full complement of riding activities for most ages and abilities, starting at age 9. Introductory rides are offered on select weekends. Each ride begins with a mini lesson and a one-hour trail ride. Lead Line pony rides are great to introduce children to riding. Parents can rent a pony or a small, gentle horse for half an hour and lead their children around the outdoor pony ring or the covered pony pavilion. A stable worker demonstrates the proper way to lead the pony. Children must be old enough to sit up and hold onto the saddle without assistance. There are also one-hour English-saddle riding lessons from beginner up for ten weeks, and beginner trail rides.

> **LOCATION:** 256 S. Maple Ave., Basking Ridge (Somerset County).
> **HOURS:** Weekdays after school and Sat. afternoons.
> **ADMISSION:** Varies with activity. Lower prices for Somerset residents.
> **PHONE:** 908-766-5955. **WEBSITES:** www.new-jersey.com/lord.htm and
> http://somersetcountyparks.org/parksfacilities/stable/lss.html. ⒷⓅ

Legends Riding Stable

Quiet horses are provided for kids so they can have fun. Pony rides for the youngest riders are given on Chocolate Chip, a very friendly pony, which offers a great way to introduce kids to horseback riding. There's also a petting zoo on the grounds as well as scenic trail rides once kids learn to handle their mounts.

> **LOCATION:** Rt. 94, Vernon (Sussex County), ½ mile south of Mountain
> Creek. **HOURS:** Vary with season. Fri.–Wed., 9–5.
> **ADMISSION:** Varies with activity. **PHONE:** 973-827-8332.
> **WEBSITE:** www.legendsridingstable.com.

Silver Bit & Spur Farm

A 60-acre family farm that offers group and private lessons in western and English riding. The trail rides are unguided. There are also pony rides for younger kids age 7 and under, and a playground is on the grounds.

LOCATION: 631 Rt. 523, Whitehouse Station (Somerset County).
HOURS: Daily. Call for reservations same day for trail rides, which start on the hour, weekdays, 10–2; weekends, 9–3.
ADMISSION: $$$$$. Discount with package of four lessons. Less for pony rides.
PHONE: 908-534-4010. **WEBSITE:** www.silverbitandspur.com. (BP)(SC)

Echo Lake Stables

This country farm offers trail rides, lessons, hayrides, and pony rides. There are forty-minute lessons for beginners and novice riders; private lessons only in a ring with an instructor. Trail rides travel through 100 acres of scenic hills and along streams. Children must be at least 7 years old. Group hayrides are available, lasting an hour.

LOCATION: 55 Blakely Lane, Newfoundland (Sussex County). Rt. 23 to Echo Lake Rd.
HOURS: Fri.–Tue., 9–5; call to reserve lessons.
ADMISSION: $$$$$. Less for trail rides and pony rides.
PHONE: 973-697-1257. **WEBSITE:** www.echolakestables.com. (BP)(SC)

Fox Ridge Farm

This is a family-run farm that specializes in teaching children and beginning riders with personalized instruction from age 6 up. They teach English and western riding year round in indoor and outdoor arenas. The emphasis is on fun and developing a harmonious relationship between horse and rider. The goal is to help students improve their skills in a friendly, fun environment. Private lessons only for new riders, which are one-half and one hour long.

LOCATION: 511 Rt. 515, Vernon (Sussex County).
HOURS: Lessons: Weekdays, 4 P.M. until evening; Sat., early morning to noon. Reservations requested. **ADMISSION:** $$$$$ and up.
PHONE: 973-764-2445. **WEBSITE:** www.foxridgefarm.net. (SC)

FARM TOURS AND FUN

Heritage Station Farm

This farm has a petting zoo, hayrides, and corn mazes. At the petting zoo, kids can feed the animals, which include goats, rabbits, a peacock, and roosters. In September and October, a hayride leads to a 5-acre corn maze where kids look for clues to complete a maze puzzle. It takes about an hour and a half to complete. There's also a smaller, one-acre corn maze more suited to younger kids. This farm also has pick-your-own orchards and pumpkins.

At the Terhune Orchards in Princeton, activities include tour of the farm and interacting with goats and other farm animals. *(Photo courtesy of Terhune Orchards)*

LOCATION: 480 Mullica Hill Rd., Richwood (Gloucester County). **HOURS:** Sep.–Oct., Sat.–Sun., 10–5. **ADMISSION:** Free. Hayrides and maze, $. **PHONE:** 856-589-4474. **WEBSITE:** www.heritagestation.com. ⓑⓟ

Terhune Orchards

Fall family weekends here feature wagon rides, pony rides, a corn maze, an adventure barn, pumpkin picking, and more. The top attraction is the barnyard, with sheep, goats, a donkey, horse, ducks, geese, and chickens. There are also pedal tractors available and a farm trail for exploring. Starting the third weekend in September, there's also a corn stalk maze, theme story barn, weekend wagon rides, and a pumpkin patch. Pony rides (small fee) are available at the farm's festivals. The farm also has a Read & Pick program on select Tuesday mornings throughout the growing season that combines listening to a story about a fruit or farm area combined with picking fruit.

LOCATION: 330 Cold Soil Rd., Princeton (Mercer County). **HOURS:** Family weekends, late Sep.–late Oct., Sat.–Sun., 10–5. For other events, see website for calendar. **ADMISSION:** Free. **PHONE:** 609-924-2310. **WEBSITE:** www.terhuneorchards.com. ⓑⓟ Ⓢⓒ

Green Meadows Farm

This farm offers a country learning atmosphere designed to educate kids and grownups about farm animals. There are guided tours geared to age level. Kids will find hundreds of animals, including pigs, cows, goats, sheep, chickens, turkeys, geese, donkeys, horses, mules, and llamas. Everyone on a tour can squeeze milk from a cow. There is also a tractor-drawn hayride, and everyone gets a pumpkin in October.

LOCATION: 10 Green Acres Dr., Hazlet (Monmouth County), off Rt. 36 and Middle Rd. **HOURS:** Spring, Oct. Tours are at 9:30–2 weekdays, until 3 on weekends. **ADMISSION:** $$$. Under 2 free.
PHONE: 732-335-5589. **WEBSITE:** www.greenmeadowsfarmnj.com.

Doyle's Unami Farms

Kids can enjoy a fun, educational taste of farm life here. They learn the history of early settlers and Indians who once roamed these hills. They can also take part in planting or harvesting crops and see hands-on demonstrations of farm machinery and the care of farm animals. Kids can watch goats and cows being milked. There are goats, sheep, chickens, turkeys, horses, ponies, and cows. There's also a hayride to the pumpkin patch. And, for a fee, kids can also build their own scarecrow.

LOCATION: 771 Mill Lane, Hillsborough (Somerset County).
HOURS: Weekends, by reservation only.
ADMISSION: Call for reservations and rates.
PHONE: 908-369-3187. **WEBSITE:** www.doyles-farm.com.

Roesch Farm

This farm has a 4-acre corn maze to explore, and kids can also enjoy rides on ponies (including toddlers, who are strapped into the saddle). There's also a half-hour hayride that passes through a tree farm on the way to a pumpkin patch (the wagon is covered for inclement weather).

LOCATION: 237 S. Cologne Ave., Egg Harbor City (Atlantic County).
HOURS: Call for hours.
ADMISSION: Free. Fees for hayrides, corn maze, and pony rides.
PHONE: 609-965-6652. **WEBSITE:** www.roeschfarm.com. (BP)

Johnson's Corner Farm

The Discovery Barnyard at this farm features rock climbing, a space net, and two pedal go-car tracks, one for small children. There are also a Pretend Farm and Tee-Pee Town as well as three different play areas, including one for toddlers. There are sheep, pigs, and chickens at the Animal Farm. This area has an obstacle course that includes pipe slides, tire climbs, a rope maze, and a Wacky Bridge. There are also hayrides that coincide with various fruit and vegetable picking seasons from May through October, as well as other theme events, such as a Mom's and Tot's hayride ($).

LOCATION: Medford (Burlington County).
HOURS: Apr.–mid-Dec., daily, 9–6 (for barnyard); farm usually closes later. **ADMISSION:** Barnyard, $$. **PHONE:** 609-654-8643.
WEBSITE: www.johnsonsfarm.com. ⓑⓟ

Norz Hill Farm

A 1,200-acre working farm with a Fall Festival that features farm tours, a corn maze, hayrides to a pumpkin patch, pony rides, and a Creepy Hollow haunted corn trail. The farm tours take you on a hay wagon around the farm, with explanations of farming practices. You can get off to see the animals, which include calves, miniature donkeys, horses, llamas, sheep, chickens, goats, bunnies, and a water buffalo.

LOCATION: 116 South Branch Rd., Hillsborough (Somerset County).
HOURS: Mid-Sep.–Oct., weekends, 10–6. **ADMISSION:** $$; under 6 $.
PHONE: 908-371-COWS. **WEBSITE:** www.norzhillfarm.com. ⓑⓟ

Lee Turkey Farm

Guided walking tours of this farm take about 50 minutes and cover a variety of topics, including farm history, fruits, vegetables, honeybees, and turkeys. There's also a 30-minute wagon ride through the fields and orchard that includes a shorter walking tour. Plus, a 50-minute Harvest Tour includes the regular walking tour along with picking a bag of various fruits and vegetables.

LOCATION: 201 Hickory Corner Rd., East Windsor (Middlesex County).
HOURS: Mon.–Sat., 9–5; Sun., 2–5. **ADMISSION:** $–$$, depending on tour. **PHONE:** 609-448-0629 **WEBSITE:** www.leeturkeyfarm.com.

Outdoor Adventures

There are many places to enjoy canoeing in state parklands, including the Delaware & Raritan Canal State Park.
(Photo by Patrick Sarver)

Delaware River Tubing

This outfitter has 3- to 4-hour tubing, rafting, kayaking, and canoeing trips on the Delaware River. Trips start at Frenchtown and head downriver. Each trip includes a barbecue meal along the way at "The Famous River Hot Dog Man" halfway downriver. Tubing trips last 3 to 4 hours, based upon wind conditions and water level, and cover six miles. The river averages 2 to 4 feet deep, although some spots can be as deep as 10 feet. The water current is generally calm, and the water is warmer than the ocean.

Tubing along this stretch is ideal for families. Tubes are available that fit different sized people, as well as double and triple tubes. The river is calm and relaxing in most areas, but there are some fun rapids along the way. You can enjoy seeing wildlife and plenty of scenery as you glide downriver. Families should consider renting a river raft, which can carry up to six people (although four is preferable). Rafting offers the added benefits of letting you keep the kids close and bringing your tackle along for fishing. In addition to tubing and rafts, canoeing and kayaking trips are available on the Delaware River as well as on the Delaware & Raritan Canal, which runs alongside the river.

LOCATION: 2998 Rt. 29, 1mile south of Frenchtown (Hunterdon County). **HOURS:** Mid-May–early Oct. See website for schedule. **ADMISSION:** $$$$–$$$$$$; varies with day and rental type. **PHONE:** 908-996-5386. **WEBSITE:** www.delawarerivertubing.com.

Kittatinny Canoes

This river outfitter headquartered in Dingman's Ferry, PA, is one of the biggest canoe rental companies along the Delaware River, offering a variety of different rafting, kayaking, and tubing trips. Trips are available from north of Port Jervis, NY, south to the Bushkill area, and they range from 2½-mile tubing trips to overnight canoe camping. Special guided learn-to-kayak trips are also available.

LOCATION: Bushkill, PA. **HOURS:** Apr.–Oct. **ADMISSION:** Varies with rental. **PHONE:** 800-FLOAT-KC. **WEBSITE:** www.kittatinny.com.

Bucks County River Country

This company offers canoeing, leisure and white-water rafting, kayaking, and river tubing from upriver on the Delaware River to Point Pleasant, PA. A variety of trip lengths are offered, from 2 hours to overnight. Picnic facilities are also available at the base.

LOCATION: Byram Rd., Point Pleasant, PA. **HOURS:** Mid-May–Oct. **ADMISSION:** Varies with rental. **PHONE:** 215–297–5000. **WEBSITE:** www.rivercountry.net.

Island Surf & Sail

A variety of activities are offered at this Long Beach Island outfitter. There are half- and full-day group windsurfing lessons. There are also one- and two-person sit-on-top kayak rentals for the bay or ocean, as well as 1½-hour surfing lessons and kite-boarding lessons.

LOCATION: 3304 Long Beach Blvd., Brant Beach (Ocean County). **HOURS:** Times vary; call for reservation. **ADMISSION:** Varies per class. **PHONE:** 609-494-5553. **WEBSITE:** www.islandsurf-sail.com/lessons.aspx.

New Jersey Kayak

Kayak rentals, guided tours, and instruction for all levels are provided on the wetlands and open waters of Barnegat Bay. There are guided tours of the Edwin B. Forsythe National Wildlife Refuge as well as escorted kayak rentals that take you to the wildlife refuge boundaries (from there, you're on your own). Family kayak clinics are held on weekends at 10 and 1:30; kids should be 9–15, and an appointment is necessary. There are also special 2-hour introductory kayaking clinics throughout the summer in which participants learn the difference between a recreational and a sea-touring kayak, make safety and navigational chart reviews, learn paddling strokes, and learn how to use the rudder.

LOCATION: 100 East Bay Ave., Barnegat (Ocean County). **HOURS:** May–Oct. **ADMISSION:** $$$$$. **PHONE:** 609-698-4440. **WEBSITE:** www.njkayak.com.

First Bridge Marina & Kayaks

This outfitter offers ecological kayak tours and rentals in the Great Bay Wildlife Management Area, home of thousands of species of fish and birds. Lessons are given prior to every kayak rental and tour, and the experienced guides make casual stops along the tour to explain the finer points of the natural surroundings. There are water trails through a salt marsh estuary, including sheltered back creeks as well as on the open bay. Both guided and self-guided kayak nature tours are available. Also available are recreational, stable kayaks for those who want to go fishing or crabbing. For groups, marine science, ecology, and history programs are also available.

LOCATION: 500 Great Bay Blvd., Tuckerton (Ocean County). **HOURS:** Tours, May-Sep., Wed.–Sun. **ADMISSION:** Varies with type of tour and rental. **PHONE:** 609-296-1888. **WEBSITE:** www.ilove2kayak.com.

Sierra Club Outings

The Sierra Club's local hikes and other outings are led by responsible guides who are very knowledgeable about New Jersey and nearby trails. Numerous hiking and other outings are described on the N.J. chapter's website. There are usually one to two dozen outings a month, some more suitable for children than others. Activities include hiking, kayaking, park cleanups, camping, and canoeing. Most outings are held on weekends, but there are also Thursday and Friday events. Hikes range from relatively easy to more rigorous, and the terrain varies from flat marshland to forested hills. There's enough variety to find something that appeals to kids.

LOCATION: 145 W. Hanover St., Trenton (Mercer County).
HOURS: Vary with individual trips. See website for schedule.
ADMISSION: Generally free, but fees for canoe/kayak rentals.
PHONE: 609-656-7612.
WEBSITE: http://newjersey.sierraclub.org/outings.asp.

Appalachian Mountain Club

The AMC offers a variety of outdoor activities, including hiking, biking, canoeing, kayaking, and more throughout the year in New Jersey and surrounding states. Some activities are for members only, and others take place in areas near New Jersey.

LOCATION (New York/North Jersey chapter): 381 Park Ave. South, Suite 809, New York City.
HOURS: Vary with activity; see websites for upcoming trips.
ADMISSION: Most local activities are free or have a nominal fee.
PHONE: 212-986-1430 (North Jersey–New York chapter).
WEBSITES: www.amc-ny.org. (North Jersey–New York chapter) and www.amcdv.org (Delaware Valley chapter).

Mohican Outdoor Center

This southernmost Appalachian Mountain Club facility stands near Catfish Pond and the Appalachian Trail in the Delaware Water Gap National Recreation Area. An extensive program of outdoor-skills activities is offered here year-round. Kids and their families can hike the Appalachian Trail and trails to Coppermine Falls and the Delaware River; canoe, kayak, or fish on Catfish Pond; see hawks, snakes, turtles, lizards, salamanders, and other wildlife in wetlands; cross-country ski at Blue Mountain Lakes; take a wilderness first aid or rock climbing workshop; and volunteer for a trail work weekend. There are cabins and campsites along with a dining hall with meals available in summer.

LOCATION: 50 Camp Rd., Blairstown (Warren County).
Rt. 94, west of Blairstown to Mohican Rd. Left on Gaisler Rd., then right on Camp Rd.
ADMISSION: Self-guided hiking, free. Fees vary for organized activities.
PHONE: 908-362-5670.
WEBSITE: www.outdoors.org/lodging/lodges/mohican/index.cfm.

Diablo FreeRide Park

This is a separate area for mountain biking at Mountain Creek, with forty downhill trails. You take the gondola to the top of the mountain like skiers, but you go down on a bike. The trails are found mostly in the wooded areas between the ski runs and range from novice to expert. Greenhorn is designed for the less experienced riders. This popular 1¼-mile trail follows a moderately sloped path through the woods about halfway down the mountain. Lower Greenhorn, another novice trail, takes you the rest of the way down. IndyCross is an intermediate slalom course with sculpted terrain. Besides free riding, lessons and rentals are also available.

LOCATION: Rt. 94, Vernon (Sussex County). **HOURS:** July–Labor Day, daily; mid-May–June and Sep.–Oct., weekends. **ADMISSION:** $$$$$. **PHONE:** 973-864-8420. **WEBSITE:** diablofreeridepark.com.

STATE PARKS AND FORESTS

State parks and forests are open daily, sunrise to sunset for the grounds. Historic villages, beaches, and other special attractions in the parks have their own hours. Most are free, although a number charge parking fees on summer weekends. Here are some of the more notable parks that kids will like. For more details on these and other parks, visit www.state.nj.us/dep/parksandforests/parks/parkindex.html.

Allaire State Park

Its 3,068 acres include restored Allaire Village, a narrow-gauge railroad, picnicking, canoeing, hiking and horse trails, camping, fishing, a nature center, and a lively calendar of events at the village.

LOCATION: Rt. 524, Allaire (Monmouth County). **PHONE:** 732-938-2371.

Cheesequake State Park

This is a 1,509-acre park consisting of wetlands and upland forest. Several miles of hiking trails lead through a variety of terrain, including a boardwalk through a cedar swamp. There's also camping, a swimming beach, fishing, canoeing, picnicking, and a nature center.

LOCATION: Off Garden State Parkway, Exit 120, Matawan (Middlesex County). **PHONE:** 732-566-2161.

Delaware & Raritan Canal State Park

This park comprises a long, narrow strip of land between the old canal and the Millstone River, with many canal structures along the way. It also extends along the Delaware River north to Frenchtown. It's a great spot for canoeing, fishing, bicycling, and hiking.

LOCATION: Somerset, Hunterdon, Mercer Counties. **PHONE:** 609-924-5705.

Hacklebarney State Park

The Black River cascades through a scenic, boulder-lined gorge. There's trout fishing in the river and in Trout Brook, streamside and upland hiking, a picnic area, and a playground. This is a small but scenic park.

> **LOCATION:** 119 Hacklebarney Rd., Long Valley (Morris County). Off Rt. 124, west of Chester. **PHONE:** 908-638-8572.

High Point State Park

The highest point in the state is marked by the recently restored 220-foot High Point Monument. There's a swimming beach at Lake Marcia. The Appalachian Trail passes through this park, part of more than 50 miles of trails at High Point. Kuser Natural Area includes a cedar swamp. Three lakes and a pond offer fishing and boating. Also offered are camping, nature tours, bicycling, and a cross-country ski center. A parking fee is charged in summer.

> **LOCATION:** Rt. 23, Sussex (Sussex County). **PHONE:** 973-875-4800.

Liberty State Park

This Hudson River-front park is known as the home of the Liberty Science Center (q.v.) and for the ferry to the Statue of Liberty and Ellis Island. There is also a 1.3-mile Liberty Walk along the Hudson, which offers great views of Lower Manhattan, Ellis Island, and the Statue of Liberty. Other points include the restored Central Railroad of New Jersey terminal, a salt marsh natural area and interpretive center, a marina, boat ramps, playground, picnicking, New York ferry, and special events throughout the year.

> **LOCATION:** Jersey City (Hudson County), Exit 14B of N.J. Turnpike. **PHONE:** 201-915-3440. **WEBSITE:** www.libertystatepark.com.

Ramapo Mountain State Forest

A streamside trail climbs from the lower parking area off I-287 to scenic Ramapo Lake, which is circled by a level path. A semipaved, private road from an upper parking area is much more level and great for biking. A lot of people also seem to bring their dogs here. A side trail leads to Castle Point and the ruins of a 1910 stone mansion. A nice place for hiking, bicycling, fishing, and picnicking.

> **LOCATION:** Skyline Dr., Oakland (Bergen/Passaic Counties). **PHONE:** 973-962-7031.

Round Valley Recreation Area

You can enjoy boating, fishing, hiking, beach swimming, and picnicking at the second largest lake in the state. A summer parking fee

Kids can enjoy an afternoon of fishing at Round Valley Reservoir in Lebanon. *(Photo by Patrick Sarver)*

is charged at the main entrance to the park and beach, but there is also a separate free sportsman's parking area (so long as you have a fishing license).

LOCATION: Rt. 629, Lebanon Twp. (Hunterdon County)
PHONE: 908-236-6355.

Stokes State Forest

The forest includes Tillman Ravine, a 10,000-year-old hemlock-lined gorge; great views from atop 1,653-foot-high Sunrise Mountain; a swimming beach at Stony Lake; beaver meadows along Big Flat Brook; and more than 45 miles of marked trails. There's plenty of swimming, picnicking, hiking, camping, and fishing throughout the forest.

LOCATION: Rt. 206, north of Branchville (Sussex County).
PHONE: 973-948-3820.

Wharton State Forest

At 115,000 acres, this largest parkland in the state lies deep in the heart of the Pinelands. At Batsto, there is a historic village and a scenic lake and stream. Atsion Recreation Area on Route 206 offers a swimming beach, bathhouse, and nearby camping and cabins. There's a boat ramp on the Mullica River at Crowley's Landing east of Batsto on Route 542. There are canoe launch areas off Route 542 near Batsto, at Atsion, and on the Wading River south of Jenkins and

At Stokes State Forest, hiking the Appalachian Trail on Sunrise Mountain includes panoramic views of northwestern New Jersey and the Poconos. *(Photo by Patrick Sarver)*

at Speedwell on Route 563. Plenty of camping, canoeing, hiking, and picnicking are available throughout the forest, including the Batona Trail.

LOCATION: Rt. 542, Hammonton (Burlington, Atlantic, and Camden Counties). **PHONE:** 609-561-0024.

Worthington State Forest

Because of its location, a lot of people think it's part of the Delaware Water Gap National Recreation Area, but it's actually state land. Among the attractions are the Dunnfield Creek hiking area, where the Appalachian Trail leads to Sunfish Pond atop the Kittatinny Ridge, and other trails lead to the top of Mount Tammany, overlooking the Water Gap from 1,500 feet. Along the Delaware north of the Water Gap you'll find the historic Copper Mine Inn and campgrounds. Alternate trails lead from this area to Sunfish Pond. Plenty of fishing, hiking, picnicking, backpacking, and camping in this area.

LOCATION: Off Rt. 80 at the Delaware Water Gap (Warren County). **PHONE:** 908-841-9575.

COUNTY PARKS

Like state parks, county parks are generally free and are open daily, sunrise to sunset. Here is a sampling of some of the more notable ones.

Cattus Island County Park

A nature center and hiking trails through marshland and woods can be found on this 497-acre peninsula in Barnegat Bay.

LOCATION: 1170 Cattus Is. Blvd., Toms River (Ocean County).
PHONE: 732-270-6960.

Garret Mountain Reservation

This hilltop park includes Lambert Castle, a scenic overlook of Paterson and the Manhattan skyline, hiking, and fishing.

LOCATION: Valley Road, Paterson (Passaic County).
PHONE: 973-881-4832.

Holmdel Park

Holmdel Park is filled with attractive landscapes and trails through wooded settings. A sheltered picnic area offers tables and a snack bar. In a pond below the shelter, ducks swim gracefully by. And beyond, you'll find a cultivated arboretum and historic Longstreet Farm.

LOCATION: Longstreet Rd., Holmdel (Monmouth County).
PHONE: 732-946-9562.

Lord Stirling Park

Home of the Environmental Center adjacent to the Great Swamp, this 900-acre park has 8.5 miles of trails and boardwalks that cross forests and wetlands.

LOCATION: White Bridge Rd., Basking Ridge (Somerset County).
PHONE: 908-722-1200.

Watchung Reservation

Part of the Watchung Mountains, the 2,065-acre wooded park includes 50 miles of hiking trails, picnic areas, stables, a playground, a deserted village, nature center, wildlife observation points, and fishing.

LOCATION: Between Rts. 22 and 78, Mountainside (Union County).
PHONE: 908-789-3670.

NATIONAL PARKLANDS

Delaware Water Gap National Recreation Area

This scenic parkland encompasses forests, Appalachian ridges, historic villages, and 40 miles of the Delaware River along the northwestern edge of the state. The **Appalachian Trail** cuts 25 miles through the New Jersey side of this park on its way from Maine to Georgia. There are lots of other hiking trails as well as picnicking, canoeing, swimming, fishing, bicycling, and historic sites. You'll find some real back roads here, where you can travel miles without seeing a house. You might, however, see a bear or two if you're lucky. The 1,500-foot-high Kittatinny Ridge is dramatically cut by the Delaware River, giving the area its name. From a parking lot alongside Route 80 is the Dunnfield Creek hiking area, with trails that lead to Sunfish Pond and the Water Gap overlook. The Mohican Outdoor Center, accessible from Blairstown on the eastern side of the park, is set in a scenic nature area on Catfish Pond.

A number of scenic spots lie north of the Water Gap along the scenic Old Mine Road. Nine miles north of the Visitor Center is the Depew Recreation Site, a popular summer beach and picnic ground along the river. Just beyond that lies Van Campens Glen, where a trail leads alongside a stream in a scenic gorge to upper and lower Van Campens falls. A mile or so north on the road (or by trail) is the Watergate Recreation Site, a popular picnicking and fishing spot with ponds set amid a large, open, grassy area (parking fee). Blue Mountain and Crater Lakes, on a turnoff north of Millbrook, offer swimming, picnicking, fishing, canoeing, and hiking amid deep forests.

Continuing north, you'll find Walpack Center, a small town along the Flat Brook, which is known for its trout fishing. Turn right into the town and continue across the brook. Just past the cemetery, turn right and travel a mile or so down a pot-holed gravel road to Buttermilk Falls, where a stream tumbles 75 feet down a steep, forested hillside. A wooden stairway climbs to two overlooks beside the falls, which is more dramatic in spring when water flows are greater.

LOCATION: Rt. 80, Exit 1. Also accessible on Millbrook Rd. from Blairstown and via Rts. 206 and 560 near Layton.
PHONE: 570-426-2452. **WEBSITE:** www.nps.gov/dewa.

On with the Show

The Growing Stage in Netcong offers four productions each season for families, from classics like *Peter and the Wolf* to presentations of new works. *(Photo courtesy of the Growing Stage)*

The following are theaters that put on series of live performances for children. Please note that performance times can vary significantly from one show to the next and that shows vary from one season to the other. Please call or check a theater's website for more specific show dates and times.

Growing Stage

The Main Stage part of this venue offers four productions each season for families. Some are classics and some are presentations of new works. Some recent shows have included *Busytown*, in which Huckle Cat takes the audience on a tour of his neighborhood and neighbors, including Farmer Pig and Grocer Cat. There was also *The Life and Adventures of Santa Claus*, a musical based on a book by the author of *The Wizard of Oz*, a work that has also been recently performed, as well as *James and the Giant Peach*. The Growing Stage is a professional member theater of the Actors' Equity Association.

> **LOCATION:** Rt. 183, 7 Ledgewood Ave., Netcong (Morris County).
> **HOURS:** Fri., 7:30; Sat. and Sun., 4. Call for performance schedule.
> **ADMISSION:** $$$$; children 14 and under, $$$. **PHONE:** 973-347-4946.
> **WEBSITE:** www.growingstage.com.

Broadway Theatre of Pitman

Set in a restored vaudeville theater that originally opened in 1926, this opulent facility once hosted such talents as Bob Hope, Abbott and Costello, George Burns and Gracie Allen, and Bing Crosby. Today it offers a wide range of stage productions and movies, including almost a dozen stage performances of children's stories every year. Among the recent productions have been *The Three Little Pigs, Charlotte's Web, Cinderella, The Little Mermaid, Alice in Wonderland, Winnie the Pooh, Doctor Dolittle,* and *Santa Claus Is Coming to Town.* Shows are staged from one to three days, usually Friday evenings and Saturdays.

> **LOCATION:** 43 S. Broadway, Pitman (Gloucester County).
> **HOURS:** Sat., 10; Sun., 10 and 1. **ADMISSION:** $$. **PHONE:** 856-384-8381.
> **WEBSITE:** www.thebroadwaytheatre.org.

Pax Amicus Castle Theatre

Pax Amicus, housed in a castle-like building on the shores of Budd Lake, provides a season of live theater for children. Performances include children's classics as well as adaptations and takeoffs on fairy tales. Some of the recent shows include such titles as *The Wizard of Oz, Babes in Toyland, A Fairy Tale Princess Tea Party,* and *Rapunzel, a Brush with Fate!*

LOCATION: 23 Lake Shore Dr., Budd Lake (Morris County).
HOURS: Performances typically are held Wed.–Sat. mornings and Fri.–Sat. evenings. **ADMISSION:** $$$. **PHONE:** 973-691-2100.
WEBSITE: www.paxamicus.com.

Villagers Theatre

Founded in 1960, this community theater strives to present both diversity and quality in its live performances. It's KidsVill Series offers family entertainment in the Black Box Theatre, particularly plays that incorporate a touch of music and dance. Among the recent shows have been *Seussical Jr., Cinderella, Disney's The Jungle Book, A Christmas Carol, Beauty and the Beast,* and *The Wizard of Oz.*

LOCATION: 475 DeMott Lane, Somerset (Somerset County).
HOURS: Fri., Sat., 8 P.M., and Sun., 2 P.M. Sat., 12 and 3, Sun., 12.
ADMISSION: $$. **PHONE:** 732-873-2710.
WEBSITE: www.villagerstheatre.net. (BP)

Community Theatre/Mayo Center for the Arts

This Morristown venue presents Kids Club, a series of live perform-ances for children that include both classics as well as shows that incorporate music and humor. These are usually one day only, mostly on Sundays, with one or two performances that day. Recent shows have included *Pinkalicious,* a fun musical about a girl who eats so many pink cupcakes that she turns pink; *Click, Clack, Moo,* a funny musical about farm animals on strike; *Beauty and the Beast, Char-lotte's Web,* the Berenstain Bears in *Family Matters: The Musical;* and *Winnie the Pooh.*

LOCATION: 100 South St., Morristown (Morris County).
HOURS: See website for scheduled dates and times.
ADMISSION: $$$. **PHONE:** 973-539-8008.
WEBSITE: www.mayoarts.org/genre_SundayKidsClub.htm.

Bickford Theatre

This theater at the Morris Museum features two series of live per-formances for kids. The Bayer Children's Theatre Series are single shows that include such diverse entertainment as a puppet theater, circus performers, and basketball antics. There's also the Bickford Summer Theatre Series for Children, which features live stage shows. Some of the recent works performed have included such fun shows as *Choo Choo Charlie's Magic Show, Buckaroo Bindlestiff's Wild West Jamboree,* and *Mammoth Follies*—the latter featuring dancing dinosaur puppets.

LOCATION: 6 Normandy Heights Rd. (Morris County).
HOURS: Days and times vary; shows start from 11 to 2:30.

ADMISSION: $$. PHONE: 973-971-3700.
WEBSITE: www.morrismuseum.org.

Kelsey Theatre

Kelsey Kids, a series of live performances at the Mercer County Community College theater, runs throughout the school year. Some of the recent live performances include such classic children's tales as *Pinocchio, Pippi Longstocking, The Ugly Duckling, Jack and the Beanstalk,* and *The Nutcracker.* Some shows run one day only; others run two or three days.

LOCATION: 1200 Old Trenton Rd., West Windsor (Mercer County).
HOURS: Fri. evening, Sat. morning and afternoon; Tue. evening.
ADMISSION: $$. PHONE: 609-586-4800.
WEBSITE: www.kelseytheatre.net.

Paper Mill Playhouse

The Children's Theater series at Paper Mill is designed for ages 3 through 12. These classics and adaptations of classics are designed as educational performances filled with audience participation. Shows are one performance only and are generally presented by visiting theater troupes. Among the recent presentations have been *Happily Ever After: A Cinderella Tale; A Christmas Carol; The Lion, the Witch and the Wardrobe; Click, Clack Moo;* and *Stuart Little.*

LOCATION: 22 Brookside Dr., Millburn (Essex County).
HOURS: Fall and spring, selected Sat., Sun., 10 A.M. ADMISSION: $$$.
PHONE: 973-376-4343. WEBSITE: www.papermill.org.

Premiere Stages

The Musical Fun Series at Premiere Stages during July offers professional theater designed for young audiences. Past performances have included such productions as *Cow and the Beanstalk* (told from the point of view of Jack's cow), *Happily Ever After* (based on Cinderella), and *Sword in the Stone* (about the boyhood days of King Arthur). As the name implies, the idea is that these live shows are entertaining and fun for kids.

LOCATION: Kean University Center's Little Theatre, 1000 Morris Ave., Union (Union County). HOURS: Selected Wed. and Thu. in July.
ADMISSION: $$$. PHONE: 908-737-7469. WEBSITE:
www.keanstage.com.

Studio Players

This community theater offers a regular schedule of children's plays from fall through spring called the Magic Trunk, which comprises half of this theater's season. Many of the performances are humorous twists on the classics. Among the plays presented recently have been *Cinderella! Cinderella!,* in which Cinderella is plain and her sisters are beautiful; *Snow White,* told from the Witch's viewpoint; *Little Red Riding Hood (and The Power Mutants); Beauty and the Beast;* and *Big Bad,* in which the Big Bad Wolf goes on trial. These shows typically run for 9 days.

> **LOCATION:** 14 Alvin Place, Montclair (Essex County).
> **HOURS:** Sat.–Sun. afternoons. **ADMISSION:** $$. **PHONE:** 973-744-9752.
> **WEBSITE:** www.studioplayhouse.org.

Surflight Theatre

During the summer, when Beach Haven is filled with vacationers, this theater puts on a season filled with classic children's stories. Among the recent performances have been *Snow White, Winnie the Pooh, The Little Mermaid, The Wizard of Oz, Peter Pan, The Princess and the Pea, Sleeping Beauty,* and *Beauty and the Beast.* There's also a Holiday Spectacular show production for kids in December. Kids can also pose for pictures with the actors.

> **LOCATION:** Beach and Engleside Aves., Beach Haven (Ocean County).
> **HOURS:** Late June–early Sep., Wed.–Sun., starting at 6.
> **ADMISSION:** $$. **PHONE:** 609-492-9477.
> **WEBSITE:** www.surflight.org/childrens.htm.

Ritz Theatre Company

The Ritz's Children's Series of plays features a lot of classic tales throughout the year, usually one a month. Shows typically run four days, ending with Saturday morning and afternoon shows. Recent children's shows have included *Rumpelstiltskin, Sleeping Beauty, The Ugly Duckling, Hansel and Gretel, Aladdin and Princess Jasmine, The Three Billy Goats Gruff, Treasure Island, The Sorcerer's Apprentice, Little Red Riding Hood, Chicken Little, The Jungle Book,* and *Peter and the Wolf.*

> **LOCATION:** 915 White Horse Pike, Haddon Heights (Camden County).
> **HOURS:** Wed., Fri. at 10 A M ; Sat. at 10 and 1. **ADMISSION:** $$.
> **PHONE:** 856-858-5230. **WEBSITE:** www.ritztheatreco.org.

Appel Farm Art and Music Center

The Family Matinee Series at this art center out in the country offers a variety of performances designed for kids and their parents. There's everything from a puppet theater presentation of fairy tales, acoustical songs for kids, and a musical adaptation of *Cinderella* to a dinosaur musical detective story, the *Velveteen Rabbit,* and other fun performances.

LOCATION: 457 Shirley Rd., Elmer (Salem County).
HOURS: Oct.–Mar., selected Sat., 2 P.M. **ADMISSION:** $$.
PHONE: 856-358-2472. **WEBSITE:** www.appelfarm.org.

Specialty Camps

Kids at the Buehler Challenger & Science Center's space camp can launch in the Shuttle and work in the Space Station and act as mission controllers or astronauts flying simulated space missions. *(Photo courtesy of Buehler Challenger & Science Center)*

Buehler Challenger & Science Center

Designed for kids in grades five through eight, Buehler's space camp lets kids learn about living and working in space. They investigate the prospects of life in the universe and learn how airplanes fly. They build and fly model rockets and work with teammates to build a Mars base or a futuristic airport or design a starship. They launch in the shuttle and work in the space station. They fly simulated space missions in the center's high-tech simulators. They also can act as mission controllers or astronauts flying simulated missions, including Rendezvous with Comet Halley, Return to the Moon, and Voyage to Mars. There's also a camp just for girls called Rocket Girls. One and two-week sessions are offered and are set up according to school grade.

> **LOCATION:** Lot G, Bergen County Community College campus, Paramus (Bergen County).
> **HOURS:** Late June–Early Aug., Mon.–Fri., 9–3.
> **ADMISSION:** Weekly tuition. **PHONE:** 201-262-0984.
> **WEBSITE:** www.bcsc.org.

Young Performers Workshop

Acting classes for children from 8 to 18 are held at Centenary College's new Lackland Center and are dedicated to the enrichment of youngsters through the theater. The program offers both formal training and production experience. An interview and an audition are required prior to the class. There's also a Tyro Theatre program for kids aged 6–11, broken into two age groups. This 2-week camp encompasses sessions over 10 days, with younger kids meeting in the morning and older ones in the afternoon. Kids learn acting games and improvisations inspired by fairy and folk tales as they learn about acting and theater.

> **LOCATION:** 715 Grand Ave., Hackettstown (Warren County).
> **HOURS:** A 5-week program beginning in July, culminating with the Summer Festival of Shows in August. (Spring and fall Saturday sessions are also offered.) **ADMISSION:** Camp tuition.
> **PHONE:** 908-979-0900. **WEBSITE:** www.centenarystageco.org.

Summer Theater Camp of Montclair

This day camp with Montclair and Cedar Grove locations focuses on acting, singing, dancing, theater games, rehearsal, and performance. A 4-week Mainstage Program for children aged 8–10 and 11–18 features full days, with morning spent in training, with instruction in yoga, acting, singing, dance, movement, and choreography. Afternoons are spent in rehearsal for a final show, which features a full set, sound, lighting, and costumes. All the World's a Stage program for kids aged 8–12 offers 2- and 3-week sessions, with half-day or full-day options. Activities include acting, singing, dancing, theater games, and rehearsal for a final show to be presented to family and friends. There's also mask making, costume and set creation, theater games, and Broadway music. Little Summer Stars offers the same session outline for kids aged 5–7, just geared for younger children.

> **LOCATION:** Unitarian Church of Montclair, 67 Church St., Montclair (Essex County). **HOURS:** 9–4:15. **ADMISSION:** Camp tuition. **PHONE:** 973-746-8686. **WEBSITE:** www.stagekids.us.

Artistic Expressions Art Day Camp

These are 2-week camps in which kids can spend their mornings or afternoons working on drawing, cartooning, painting, games, watercolors, and other artistic media. The focus is on helping kids develop fine art skills through the eye of a cartoonist, working to create images based on their favorite movies and TV cartoon shows. Children explore different artistic media, from drawing, water-colors, and T-shirt painting to pastels and clay. Classes are held at the Saddle River Valley Cultural Center in Upper Saddle River and at Temple Beth Haverim in Mahwah.

> **LOCATION:** Allendale (Bergen County). **HOURS:** Late June–late Aug., weekdays, 9:30–12:30 and 1:30–4:30. **ADMISSION:** Camp tuition. **PHONE:** 201-327-5772. **WEBSITE:** www.theartcamp.com.

Joe Kubert Cartoon Sketch Camp

One-week and one-month summer cartoon sketch camps are designed for young, aspiring cartoonists who are interested in cartooning, comic books, and commercial art. Kids learn the secrets of cartooning from comic book professionals at the Joe Kubert School of Cartoon & Graphic Art. Among the topics covered are basic drawing, drawing the human figure, narrative art, art methods and materials, layout and design, humor, and lettering. Each session also includes a free art kit.

> **LOCATION:** 37 Myrtle Ave., Dover (Morris County). **HOURS:** July, Aug., Mon.–Fri., 9–12. **ADMISSION:** Camp tuition. **PHONE:** 973-361-1327. **WEBSITE:** www.kubertsworld.com.

Sea Pirate Campground

This is not a sleep-away camp but an out of the ordinary campground with a lot of fun activities for kids and the entire family. There are numerous scheduled activities such as ceramics, arts and

Painting classes are just one of the many types of art classes available for kids to enjoy at the Montclair Art Museum's Summer Art Camp. *(Photo by Sarah Lubachevsky; courtesy of the Montclair Art Museum.)*

crafts, hay rides, deejays, and more. There are also more traditional camping activities, such as boat rentals, a swimming pool, fishing, and bingo. Special events include a chili cookoff, an antique and custom car show, a strawberry festival, and a crabfest.

LOCATION: Rt. 9, West Creek (Cape May County).
HOURS: Overnight campground. **ADMISSION:** Camping fee.
PHONE: 609-296-7400. **WEBSITE:** www.sea-pirate.com

Montclair Art Museum Summer Art

Summer Art with the Montclair Art Museum's Yard School of Art provides four 2-week sessions designed to encourage children's creativity in a variety of media, such as drawing, painting, sculpture, collage, ceramics, and printmaking. Visits to the museum's galleries are also included with the classes. Kids make art every day and learn about the history of art and its role in society, and each session ends with a student art exhibit. Kids are grouped in classes by age (5–7, 8–9, and 10–12) and create art in the museum's professional art studios, where they are instructed by experienced art teachers. Individ - ual sessions have such titles as America's Memories: Storytelling and Art, Dream Catching: The Art of Native America, Fantastic Finds: Recycling Reinvented, Team Sculpture, Fun with Papier-mâché, Cartoon Drawing, Claymation, Easel Painting, and Fashion

Illustration. There are also studio classes for kids aged 12–15 covering drawing, painting, sculpture, pottery, and watercolor.

LOCATION: 3 South Mountain Ave., Montclair (Essex County).
HOURS: 9:30–5. **ADMISSION:** Camp tuition. **PHONE:** 973-259-5139.
WEBSITE: www.montclairartmuseum.org. (BP)

Geller Kids Chess Camp

Chess master Arkady Geller has devoted his life to the development of chess programs for kids. His week-long instructional summer sessions are organized according to experience. Kids attend a variety of workshops and classes covering such topics as openings, end games, master games, tactics, and traps. They also have plenty of practice playing each other and participate in tournaments. There are also recreational breaks from chess with outdoor sports activities. Day and overnight options are available.

LOCATION: 862 DeGraw Ave., Forest Hill (North Newark) (Essex County). **HOURS:** Late July–mid-Aug., 9–5.
ADMISSION: Weekly tuition. Discounts for 2- and 3-week signups.
PHONE: 973-483-7927. **WEBSITE:** www.kidschesscamp.com.

USA Chess Camp

The largest chess camp in the United States is held by Active Learning Services, with more than ninety camps coast to coast. It offers a structured but fun environment with talented instructors designed to encourage kids aged 5–16 to learn and develop their chess-playing skills. No previous experience is needed as kids are grouped by age and ability. Camps last five days, and there are morning, afternoon, and all-day sessions available. The goal is to take each student to a new level of playing, which not only advances their knowledge of chess but also increases their ability to focus and think logically.

LOCATIONS: College of St. Elizabeth, 2 Convent Rd., Morristown (Morris County); Rutgers Preparatory School, 1345 Easton Ave., Somerset (Somerset County); and Dwight-Englewood School, 315 E. Palisade Ave., Englewood (Bergen County).
HOURS: Mid-July in Morristown and mid-Aug. in Somerset and Englewood. See website for exact dates. **ADMISSION:** Weekly tuition.
PHONE: 888-65-CHESS. **WEBSITE:** www.chesscamp.com.

Video Game Creation Camp

Active Learning Services also hosts a series of video gaming camps throughout the U.S., and this course can be combined with the chess camp or taken separately. Starting with introductory programming skills, campers progress to making their own unique game. Camp begins with an introduction to Game Maker software, including techniques for adding rooms, walls, backgrounds, music, and other effects. At the end of camp, attendees get access to a download site where they can get Game Maker Lite software, their own games, a custom walk-through guide, and a resource folder that will help them continue to develop their game and to create new ones at home. Designed for kids aged 8–15.

LOCATIONS: College of St. Elizabeth, 2 Convent Rd., Morristown (Morris County); Rutgers Preparatory School, 1345 Easton Ave., Somerset (Somerset County); and Dwight-Englewood School, 315 E. Palisade Ave., Englewood (Bergen County).
HOURS: Mid-July in Morristown and mid-Aug. in Englewood.
ADMISSION: Weekly tuition. PHONE: 281-257-0078.
WEBSITE: www.gamebuilderscamp.com/video.htm.

Wizards of the Mind Chess Camp

This week-long chess camp combines chess instruction with individual matches and tournaments. Classes are broken into different levels, from beginners to advanced. Morning sessions focus on chess instructions and match play, while afternoons are for tournament play followed by art and pool time to provide a variety of activities. Full-day and half-day sessions are offered.

LOCATION: 379 Morris Ave., Springfield (Union County).
HOURS: Late June–mid-Aug., Mon.–Fri., 9–5.
ADMISSION: Camp tuition. PHONE: 973-262-1395.
WEBSITE: www.wizardsofthemind.com.

Circus Arts Camp

This camp provides a fun introduction to the performing arts through the world of the circus for kids aged 7–14. Professional instruction is provided in skills that excite the imagination and build teamwork, coordination, and physical fitness. Mornings include such under-the-big-top activities as juggling, acting, balancing, clowning, dance, acrobalance, tumbling, plate spinning, ribbon twirling, and more. Afternoons are spent working on art projects for a circus set as well as prop, poster, and costume designs. There are also rehearsals for a Grand Circus Finale show that the kids put on for family and friends as well as for children and adults with cerebral palsy.

LOCATION: 1st Cerebral Palsy of NJ, 7 Sanford Ave., Belleville (Essex County). HOURS: Late June, Mon.–Fri., 9–3.
ADMISSION: Camp tuition. PHONE: 973-320-2741.
WEBSITE: www.jenniferslaw.com.

ID Tech Computer Camps

One-week computer camps for kids 7–17 are held at Princeton and Seton Hall Universities. Day campers study in computer labs, with customized curriculums for beginners to advanced learners. Twenty different courses range from creating video games and producing digital movies to designing Web pages and learning programming and robotics. The youngest kids start with Adventures in Game Design, in which they create their own video games. Other courses include Game Creation, 3D Game Modding, Web Design, Adventures in Robotics, and Digital Photography and Photoshop. There are both day and overnight camps. Along the way, kids can learn video game design, Flash animation, programming, video editing, and more.

> **LOCATION:** Princeton University, Princeton (Mercer County), and Seton Hall University, South Orange (Essex County).
> **HOURS:** Mid-June–mid-Aug. **ADMISSION:** Camp tuition. Multiweek packages available. **PHONE:** 888-709-TECH.
> **WEBSITE:** www.internaldrive.com.

Classic Thyme

Summer culinary cooking camps offer week-long, 5-day sessions for kids as young as 4 years old, introducing students to the culinary world and developing basic cooking skills they can use throughout their lives. The first day gets down to the business of cooking. Skill levels and food interests are quickly assessed and used to plan the week's activities and menus. There are four levels: Kids Culinary Cooking Camp is for children aged 4–6; Youth Cooking Camp for kids aged 7–9; Pre-teen Camp for those aged 10–12; and a Teen Camp. There are also two full-day intensive camps offered for kids aged 12 and up.

> **LOCATION:** 710 South Ave. West, Westfield (Union County).
> **HOURS:** Each level runs four to six times during the summer, with 2- to 2½-hour sessions. **ADMISSION:** Camp tuition.
> **PHONE:** 908-232-5445. **WEBSITE:** www.classicthyme.com.

Camp Invention

Camp Invention's SPARK program is full-day camp for children aged 6–12 that features five hands-on science classes a day taught by local teachers. The classes are Wondrous Innovations and Living Designs, which explores how animals are inventors; The Curious Cypher Club, in which kids solve a mystery and use codes to send messages; Bounce: An Atomic Journey, in which children investigate atoms and molecules and design their own experiments; Game On: Power Play in which they are challenged to use nontraditional equipment to play classic games; and I Can Invent: Edison's Workshop, in which they create and market a multistep machine.

LOCATION: Our Lady of Mount Carmel School, Tenafly (Bergen County). **HOURS:** Late June, Mon.–Fri., 8:30–3. **ADMISSION:** Camp tuition. **PHONE:** 800-968-4332. **WEBSITE:** www.campinvention.org.

New Jersey Audubon Natural History Camps

Kids have fun hiking through fields and forests as they focus on various aspects of nature during week-long day camp programs for kids aged 4–15 as well as overnight camps for middle schoolers. There are 3-hour morning and afternoon sessions as well as full-day sessions. Leaders use stories, games, natural treasure hunts, crafts, and songs to make learning about animals and plants fun, especially for younger children. Other sessions focus on conserving wildlife, monitoring amphibian populations, and designing a backyard habitat. Overnight programs travel to other locations, such as Barnegat Bay and the Mohican Outdoor Center.

LOCATIONS: Headquarters: Scherman-Hoffman Wildlife Sanctuaries, 11 Hardscrabble Rd., Bernardsville (Somerset County) (908-766-5787). Camps are also held at Weis Ecology Center, Ringwood (Passaic County) (973-835-2160); Lorrimer Sanctuary, Franklin Lakes (Bergen County) (201-891-2185); Essex County Environmental Center, Roseland (Essex County) (973-228-8776); Plainsboro Preserve, Plainsboro (Middlesex County) (609-897-9400); Rancocas Nature Center, Mount Holly (Burlington County) (609-261-2495); and the Nature Center of Cape May (Cape May County) (609-898-8848). **HOURS:** Late June–mid-Aug. **ADMISSION:** Camp tuition. **WEBSITE:** www.njaudubon.org/sectioneducation/summernaturecamps. aspx.

Kean Kids Summer Fun

Call it summer camp or call it a summer school for fun, the sessions offer a variety of subjects with hands-on, age-appropriate activities for kids aged 6–14. The classes run 3 or 4 days, and there are different sessions in the morning and in the afternoon. Past class topics have included creative writing workshops, crime scene investigation, robotics, kids' art, chess, and space and rocketry. There are usually around sixteen classes offered in all, including a special 2-week camp on Lego robotics.

LOCATION: Kean University, 1000 Morris Ave., Union (Union County). **HOURS:** Late June–early Aug., Mon.–Thu., 8:30–12:30 and 1:30–4:30. **ADMISSION:** Weekly tuition. **PHONE:** 908-737-3430. **WEBSITE:** www.kean.edu/~cont-ed/docs/Kean%20Kids%20Catalog.pdf.

The U.S. Sports Institute offers kids the chance to learn about a wide variety of sports in its all-sports camps.
(Photo courtesy of the U.S. Sports Institute)

UCC College for Kids

Union County College's College for Kids is designed for children aged 4–17, with a wide range of summer fun topics. Think of a community college adult school catalog, then make all the courses for kids and you get the idea. There are arts and crafts classes, kids' theater, singing, fun with fossils, astronomy, juggling, weird science, building a web page, comic book art, scrapbooking, and a lot more. There are also academic courses, especially math. But the emphasis is on fun learning for kids. There are four class periods throughout the day, and courses last 2 or 4 weeks. There are also week-long half-day science fun courses covering rockets, robotics, chemical magic, and "mad science" workshops.

LOCATION: Union County College, Cranford Campus, 1033 Springfield Ave., Cranford (Union County). **HOURS:** Mon.–Thu., 8:50–3:35. **ADMISSION:** Separate tuition for each class. **PHONE:** 908-709-7600. **WEBSITE:** www.ucc.edu.

U.S. Sports Institute

This organization offers three main programs: Multi Sports camps, Sports Squirts, and Single Sport camps. The multisports camp offers more than fifteen different sports from around the world. There are baseball, basketball, flag football, softball, soccer, and hockey as well as more uncommon ones like touch rugby, bocce, pilo polo, handball, and cricket. Campers receive technical instruction in each, and they play a realistic game in each sport. They learn body control timing, and accuracy while enjoying the variety of many sports. Single sports camps let kids specialize in the sport of their choice, including golf, tennis, lacrosse, field hockey, flag football, volleyball, basketball, cricket, and touch rubgy. Sports Squirts (ages 3–7) experience a different sport each day—soccer, tennis, golf, basketball, and T-ball—in a shortened version of the multi-sports camp. There's also a Parent & Me program for kids 1½–3½ years. Half-day and full-day camps are offered that last a week. The main location is in Bound Brook, but camps are held at a dozen additional locations throughout north and central New Jersey.

> **LOCATION:** 12 Maiden Lane, Suite 3, Bound Brook (Somerset County).
> **HOURS:** Mon.–Fri., 9:30-4. **ADMISSION:** Camp tuition.
> **PHONE:** 732-563-2520. **WEBSITE:** www.ussportsinstitute.com. (BP)

Newark Academy Summer Sports Institute

Highlighted by the Mott-Leeney Baseball Camp, the summer camps at this prep school cover a variety of other boys and girls sports, from basketball and lacrosse to fencing and soccer. The baseball camp runs for five one-week sessions; the others for one week each. There are indoor batting cages, daily games, and instructional films. Baseball instruction (for kids aged 5–14) includes pitching, catching, infield play, outfield play, hitting, and base running. The other sports instruction includes drills, exercises, team competition, and teaching of sport fundamentals.

> **LOCATION:** Newark Academy, 1 South Orange Ave., Livingston
> (Essex County). **HOURS:** Late June–early Aug., Mon.–Fri., 9–2:30.
> **ADMISSION:** Camp tuition. **PHONE:** 973-992-7000, ext. 212.
> **WEBSITE:** www.newarka.edu.

Middle Atlantic Baseball Camps at Drew University

These camps offer a week of instruction in the fundamentals of baseball, with hands-on training in all facets of the game. A lot of individual attention and instruction are provided, from hitting and pitching to fielding, as well as teaching players how they can better prepare themselves mentally and physically to create better practice habits and to enhance game performance.

> **LOCATION:** 36 Madison Ave., Madison (Morris County).
> **HOURS:** Early July. **ADMISSION:** Camp tuition.
> **PHONE:** 973-408-3000. **WEBSITE:**
> www.depts.drew.edu/ath/baseball/camps.php.

All Star Baseball Camp

This camp provides instruction on specific baseball skills such as bunting, base running, hitting, fielding, pickoffs, and relays. Intracamp games are held with instruction by coaches, and there are sessions in batting cages. Kids can also choose extra one-on-one help in developing baseball skills or they can pick alternative recreation and sports in addition to the baseball clinics. Major leaguers also appear at camp from time to time. Camps are held on the campus of Ramapo College, and there are dorms on campus for overnight campers. Five one-week camps are held throughout the summer.

LOCATION: P.O. Box 302, Mahwah (Bergen County).
ADMISSION: Camp tuition.
HOURS: Overnight/day camp, early July–early Aug., Sun.–Fri.
PHONE: 800-828-7414. **WEBSITE:** www.allstarbaseballcamp.com.

S.E.E. Camp

A combination science, creative arts, and recreation day camp for kids entering grades 1–8. There are two 2-week camps at three locations. Every day there are three 2-hour sessions covering Science and Nature, Sports and Games, and Theater and Art. The science program covers chemistry, physics, biology, archaeology, ecology, and aerodynamics. Kids do hands-on projects like fossil casting, performing chemical analysis, dissecting and studying sea creatures, rocket building and launching, survival tactics, and yo-yo physics and competition. Creative arts projects include making a memory album, jewelry design, fashion design, cartooning, tie-dyeing, painting, sculpting, and scenery design. There are also musical productions, and kids can develop their acting, playwrighting, singing, dancing, and stage setting experience.

LOCATIONS: Office: 764 Speedwell Ave., Suite 4, Morris Plains (Morris County). Camps are held at the Wilson School, 271 Boulevard, Mountain Lakes (Morris County); Oratory Prep, 1 Beverly Rd., Summit (Union County); and Elizabeth Avenue School, Franklin (Somerset County). **HOURS:** Late June–late July, Mon.–Fri., 9–4.
ADMISSION: Camp tuition. **PHONE:** 973-831-7779.
WEBSITE: www.seecamps.com.

Camp Glam

This series of one-week camps combine girly clinics along with developing the creative abilities, independence, and confidence of girls 4–12. Besides clinics on glamour, there are sessions to help girls develop their talents in arts and crafts, music and drama, gardening, cooking, scrapbooking, and dancing. There are also sessions on

At Camp Glam, girls 4–12 get to enjoy glamour clinics along with developing their creative abilities in arts and crafts, music and drama, gardening, cooking, scrapbooking, and dance.
(*Photo courtesy of Camp Glam*)

physical activities such as rock climbing, tumbling, swimming, and bounce. Glamour instructors conduct the clinics, which are adapted to the individual skills and abilities of individual camper groups. There's also a visit by an expert in a particular field (journalist, fashion designer, hair stylist) who shares her experience in a career field and serves as a role model for campers.

LOCATION: 1855 Hurffville Rd., Sewell (Gloucester County).
HOURS: Late June–late Aug. **ADMISSION:** Camp tuition.
PHONE: 856-401-8111. **WEBSITE:** www.sportsandmorefun.com.

Plays in the Park

The Childen's Theater Workshop is designed for kids aged 8–11. This program offers instruction in music, dancing, acting, and arts and crafts for creating stage scenery and props. There are three summer sessions that last 2 weeks each, taught by theater specialists, and they conclude with a final production. There's also one 2-week session for kids aged 12–15, which also concludes with a final production.

LOCATION: Warren Park Amphitheater, Florida Grove Rd., Woodbridge (Middlesex County).
HOURS: Early July–mid-Aug., Mon.–Fri., 9–noon.
ADMISSION: Camp tuition. **PHONE:** 732-745-3936.
WEBSITE: www.playsinthepark.com/kidsinthepark.html.

Kids Critter Camp

Campers in grades 2–6 learn to understand, enjoy, and value the relationship between people and companion animals through educational activities, creative arts and crafts, and outdoor games. Each day has a specific theme, with visitors, crafts, animals, and daily walks through the shelter, and an end-of-the-day story. Kids learn about animal safety and how to understand animal communication. Special guests might include a Seeing Eye dog and her blind owner, various service dogs, and some interesting wild animals and insects. There's also a visit with one of St. Hubert's therapy pet teams consisting of a dog, cat, or bunny and its owner to help them practice what they've learned about interaction with pets.

LOCATION: St. Hubert's Giralda, 575 Woodland Ave., Madison (Morris County).
HOURS: Call for dates. **ADMISSION:** Camp tuition.
PHONE: 973-377-8877. **WEBSITE:** www.sthuberts.org.

Stokes Forest Music Camp

Montclair State University's Cali School of Music offers students ages 10–17 an intensive musical experience combined with environmental and recreational activities. The camp runs two weeks, and students can attend two weeks, one week, or a one-week day camp. Lodging is in cabins at the New Jersey School of Conservation. Along with music, activities include arts and crafts, canoeing, theater, water ecology, and a confidence course. But the main focus is on music. Starting with an instrumental, vocal, or keyboard focus, students take part in a large ensemble, one or more chamber ensembles, a music theory class, and electives. There's also an optional private lesson. Ensembles include orchestra, band, jazz ensembles, rock band, chamber choir, and chamber ensembles. The camp presents a musical at the end of the first week and offers students a chance to participate in all aspects of rehearsing and presenting a show. There are also evening concerts by faculty, students, and guest artists for kids to enjoy.

LOCATION: Off Rt. 206 in Stokes State Forest (Sussex County).
HOURS: Mid–late July. **ADMISSION:** Camp tuition.
PHONE: 973-655-4443. **WEBSITE:** www.stokesmusiccamp.com.

Codey Arena Figure Skating Camp

Half-day and full-day camps for ages 6–15 are set up in three class levels based on competitive ability. The on-ice clinics are designed to meet a camper's age and skill level. Campers work with professional instructors who provide lessons in a number of aspects of figure skating. Clinics cover moves in the field, edgework, jumps and spins, interpretation, and introduction to dance/pairs. Off-ice clinics include pilates, yoga, ballet, nutrition, and strength and conditioning.

LOCATION: 560 Northfield Ave., West Orange (Essex County).
HOURS: Five weekly sessions, late June–July, Mon.–Fri., 9–4.
ADMISSION: Weekly tuition; half and full days available.
PHONE: 973-731-3828, ext. 229.

One-of-a-Kind Places

The Battleship *New Jersey* on the Camden waterfront offers guided and self-guided tours that are popular with kids. *(Photo by Patrick Sarver)*

Battleship *New Jersey*

The most decorated battleship in the United States, the *New Jersey*, with its turret guns bristling, is docked not far from the Adventure Aquarium and across the river from Philadelphia (whose shipyards gave birth to it). At 887 feet long, the *New Jersey* is one of the largest battleships ever built. Designed for a crew of 117 officers and 1,804 enlisted men in World War II, the ship had nineteen battle and campaign stars and served in World War II, Korea, Vietnam, and the Persian Gulf.

Highlights of the guided tour include the ship's 16-inch gun turrets, Admiral Halsey's original cabin, the communications center, two mess areas, and crew quarters. You can watch a launch of a tomahawk missile on video and see how it's tracked in a virtual combat engagement room. There's also a multiroom museum where you can learn about life and duties on board, see comparisons with battleships of other countries during World War II, and find out about homeland defense techniques. You also have the chance to crawl inside a gun turret, just as the crew did.

There are three types of tours: self-guided, guided, and firepower. All include a lot of walking and climbing on ladders, both outdoors and inside, which makes it fun for kids. Special tours and prices are available for school groups.

LOCATION: Delaware River Waterfront, Camden (Camden County).
HOURS: May–Labor Day, daily, 9:30–5; Sep.–Dec. & Apr., 9:30–3. Feb.–Mar., weekends only, 9:30–3.
ADMISSION: $$$$; children 6–11, $$$. Under 6 free.
PHONE: 866-877-6262. **WEBSITE:** www.battleshipnewjersey.org.

New Jersey Naval Museum

The New Jersey Naval Museum's USS *Ling 297* submarine is 312 feet long but only 27 feet wide, and when you consider that eighty-one men and twenty-four torpedoes were aboard during its active career in 1945, you realize that this is no place for someone with claustrophobia. Nowadays, most of the torpedoes and many of the berths have been removed to allow tour groups to move about. Indeed, the inside seems surprisingly spacious. Tickets are bought at the museum building, which also houses a number of war pictures and paraphernalia, including the periscope prism from a Japanese sub.

Tours last about 45 minutes. You begin in the torpedo room, which still features two deactivated torpedoes. These weapons were activated only after they left the tube; they also had to be aimed correctly, since a miss would give away the sub's position. Much of the time onboard the vessel was devoted to eating and cooking. When the Ling first left port, space was so dear that fresh fruit and vegetables had to be stacked in one of the showerheads. Tours include the Control Room, Maneuvering Room, Main Engine Room, sleeping quarters, and more; but the conning tower and its periscope are off-limits. You are allowed to handle certain equipment, including the wheels and gauges, and the guide sounds the diving signal, which may be memorable to some from a host of old war movies.

The Naval Museum grounds also has a Vietnam-era patrol boat, a World War II Japanese Kaiten II suicide torpedo, and a German Seehund two-man coastal defense sub.

LOCATION: 78 River Street, Hackensack (Bergen County).
HOURS: Weekends, 10–4. **ADMISSION:** $$. **PHONE:** 201-342-3268.
WEBSITE: www.njnm.com. (BP)

A. J. Meerwald

This 115-foot oyster schooner has been restored and is berthed in Bivalve on Delaware Bay, but it also visits other ports (such as Liberty State Park, Philadelphia, Burlington, Atlantic City, and Cape May) during warm weather. From spring through fall, it takes on paying passengers, who can help hoist the rigging and trim the sails. Typical trips last 2½ hours. There are also sunset sails. In spring and fall, it's booked for school groups. There's also a small museum at the home port, with displays on shipbuilding, oystering, and commercial fishing.

> **LOCATION:** 2800 High St., Bivalve (Cumberland County).
> **HOURS:** Morning, afternoon, or evening sails.
> **FARES:** $$$$$. Advance reservations recommended.
> **PHONE:** 856-785-2060. **WEBSITE:** www.ajmeerwald.org.

Atlantic City Cruises

Cruisn 1 is a double-deck boat that carries 100 passengers and has an enclosed bar and galley as well as plenty of open-air seating. Cruises range from morning skyline tours and marine mammal cruises to a harbor tour.

> **LOCATION:** Gardner's Basin, 800 N. New Hampshire Ave., Atlantic City (Atlantic County). **HOURS:** May–early Oct. **FARE:** $$$$ and up, depending on cruise type. Discount for ages 5–15. Under 5, free.
> **PHONE:** 609-347-7600. **WEBSITE:** www.atlanticcitycruises.com.

Sterling Hill Mining Museum

The last operating zinc mine in New Jersey went out of business in 1986, but the buildings are now a mining museum open for tours. (Just remember to wear a jacket and good shoes, because it's 56 degrees inside the mine and often damp.) Besides the primary zinc deposits there are over 300 kinds of minerals in this area, half of which are found nowhere else. Because the area around Ogdensburg and nearby Franklin has the world's largest deposits of fluorescent stones, an important stop on the tour is the "Rainbow Room." This is a wall that looks like ordinary rock, but when the tour guide switches on an ultraviolet light, the red-fluorescent calcite and green-fluorescent willemite begin to glow.

The Zobel Exhibit Hall was once used by miners to change clothing. Displays include dinosaur footprints, rows of zinc products, and a whole range of mining paraphernalia. There is also an impressive collection of rocks and minerals, including 700 fluorescent specimens from around the world; gold, copper, and silver specimens; and meteorites.

You can also look for minerals yourself at the Rock Discovery Center and collect up to six specimens. The mine tour is not recommended for children under six, but there is a Fossil Discovery Center, where kids can dig for "fossils" for an added fee (Apr.–Nov.).

LOCATION: 30 Plant St., Ogdensburg (Sussex County).
Rt. 517 to Brooks Flat Rd. to Plant Rd.
HOURS: Apr.–Nov., daily, 10–3; Mar. and Dec., weekends. Tours at 1.
Shop and mineral collection only on Jan. and Feb. weekends.
ADMISSION: $$. **PHONE:** 973-209-7212.
WEBSITE: www.sterlinghillminingmuseum.org.

Northlandz

Northlandz is a combination of the Great American Railway, doll museum, La Peep Dollhouse, art gallery, and a frontier-style music hall. All are housed in a Greeklike temple of a building that's a popular destination for grandparents, families, and railroad buffs.

The huge, largely HO-scale model railroad covers 52,000 square feet and uses enough wood to build forty-two houses and plenty of plaster to create small towns and cities among the great gorges of this huge layout. There are more than eighty trains and 8 miles of track that cut through looming mountains, deep quarries, and unique cityscapes. They go over bridges up to 40 feet long, above rivers, and past alpine scenes. Visitors walk about a mile as they travel on ramps that rise 3½ stories to view the massive layout from different angles. You see Pennsylvania coal-mining towns, horses grazing on sloping hills, and marching bands. Some scenes are built with humor in mind. A hotel "with a view" perches precariously over a deep gorge. For drama there's a deep canyon with a complete mining town set beneath the looming railroad bridge. Some towns are peopled with miniature figures, while farms may have horses and cows set out to pasture. Anyone with any interest in model railroads will find this place interesting—even if parts of the layout could use a few repairs here and there.

The La Peep Dollhouse is a series of ninety-four miniature rooms set into the wall, featuring home scenes including a library, indoor pool, and ballroom with doggie band. A doll museum of 150 large collectible dolls in fancy costume can be seen toward the end of the tour. The American Music Hall, in the style of a Western saloon, features a 2,000-pipe organ, which is played several times a day. In good weather, there's also an outdoor mini-railroad train you can ride for an extra fee.

LOCATION: 495 Rt. 202 South, Flemington (Hunterdon County),
2 miles north of Flemington Circle.

The Black River and Western Railroad is an old-time railroad that provides regular and themed rides between Ringoes and Flemington. *(Photo by Patrick Sarver)*

HOURS: Weekdays exc. Tue., 10:30–4; weekends, 10:30–5:30.
ADMISSION: $$$. Discounts: Seniors, children. Under 2 free.
PHONE: 908-782-4022. **WEBSITE:** www.northlandz.com.

The Model Railroad Club

This is a fun place for kids who like trains. There are HO, N, and Garden railroad layouts in an 11,000-square-foot building. The N-scale layout features a double-deck design, with trains traveling through detailed scenes that include a container port, passenger terminal, and industrial areas. The HO-scale setup has two sections, one 40 by 40 feet and another 60 by 80 feet. There is also an annual Light and Sound show and open house for three weekends in late November and early December. Model railroading classes and workshops are also offered.

LOCATION: 295 Jefferson Ave., Union (Union County). Off Rt. 22, behind Home Depot. **HOURS:** Sat., 1–4, and special show dates. **ADMISSION:** $; children, $. Slightly higher on show dates. **PHONE:** 908-964-9724. **WEBSITE:** www.tmrci.com.

Black River & Western Railroad

New Jersey's best known excursion trains (both steam engine and diesel) operate from Stangl Road in Flemington, next to the outlet shops of Liberty Village, and travel to Ringoes and back three to four times a day. You can also board in Ringoes, get off in Flemington, and return on a later train. The trip meanders through the woods and farms of scenic Hunterdon County.

HOURS: Sat., Sun., holidays, May–Oct. Special events include the Easter Bunny Express in April, and the Santa Express and North Pole Express from late November to early December. Other fun rides include the Great Train Robbery and Crazy Train Maze. **FARE:** $$$; children 3–12, $$. Under 3 free. **PHONE:** 908-782-9600 for boarding times. **WEBSITE:** www.brwrr.com and www.brrht.org.

Delaware River Railroad

Ride along the Delaware River to Belvidere behind a steam loco in historic open-window cars from the 1940s. There are Santa Claus, Pumpkin, Corn Maze, Mine, Thomas, and Easter Bunny train rides in season.

LOCATION: 100 Elizabeth St. (Market Square), Phillipsburg (Warren County). **HOURS:** Departs Sat.–Sun., 11, 12:30, 2, & 3. **FARE:** $$$. **PHONE:** 908-454-4433. **WEBSITE:** www.877trainride.com.

Cowtown Rodeo

This is a real rodeo on the Professional Rodeo Cowboys Association circuit. It features bareback riding, calf roping, saddle bronc riding, steer wrestling, brahma bull riding, team roping, and girls' barrel racing. It's held every Saturday night from the last weekend of May to the last weekend of September at 7:30 P.M., rain or shine. The arena holds 4,000 on outdoor bleacher seats.

LOCATION: 780 Rt. 40, Woodstown/Pilesgrove (Salem County). Eight miles East of Delaware Memorial Bridge, off Exit 1 of the N.J. Turnpike, or Exit 4 off Rt. 295. **ADMISSION:** $$$. Discount: Children 12 and under. **PHONE:** 856-769-3200. **WEBSITE:** www.cowtownrodeo.com.

Medieval Times

Combine a horse show, a dinner theater, and a Renaissance festival, put it all in a circuslike arena inside a huge stucco castle, and you have the New Jersey version of Medieval Times. Here you get not one but several jousts, a narrative of times gone by, and a chance to eat dinner without utensils.

When you enter the cavernous castle to buy your tickets, you are handed a paper hat with a special color. This will determine which section you sit in and which knight you root for. These colored hats really get you into cheering for a particular champion so you feel like you're part of the show.

After a chance to look at medieval artifacts and inspect a torture, you are ushered into the arena where chairs are set against long banquet tables. These are set in tiers so that everybody in the huge oval arena can see the show. First comes the soup, then chicken, potato, and barbecued ribs, plus dessert, coffee, or punch. Since you are supposed to eat this all with your fingers, the serving wench hands you a huge napkin to be tucked into your collar King Henry VIII style.

As for the show—there is a story of sorts about a king who's come back from the war and orders a tournament. The show includes some fancy prancing by the horses and a display of skills by the knights. Then it's on to the jousts. The knights not only fight on horseback but also engage in swordplay after being unhorsed. And, of course, there are several good knights and one bad apple—usually the green knight. After a few jousts and lots of clashing swords, the final victor is announced and the villain is sent to his doom. After the show, some families stay around until their knight shows up to autograph the picture or shield their kids have bought. This is a popular spot for preteen parties.

LOCATION: 149 Polito Ave., Lyndhurst (Bergen County).
HOURS: Wed., Thu., 7:30 P.M.; Fri., 8 P.M.; Sat. and Sun., 2, 4:30, and 8 P.M. (hours vary). **ADMISSION:** $$$$$$. **PHONE:** 888-WE-JOUST.
WEBSITE: www.medievaltimes.com/findcastles/lyndhurst.

Ocean City Ghost Tour

Stroll the streets of this resort town and listen to fascinating and historically documented tales of the unknown and the folklore of the Shore. Learn the untold secrets of the Boardwalk as well as mysterious encounters at the Flanders Hotel and appearances of the Jersey Devil. This 90-minute candlelight tour of downtown Ocean City (actual walking time is about 30 minutes) stops at eight haunted sites along the way. You'll learn about the shadows haunting the beaches at night and about the legends of buried treasure and the pirate ghosts left behind to guard it. Discover the eerie secret that lies beneath the waves where the *Sindia* went down on a stormy night in 1901 with a curse by a Golden Buddha and smuggled treasure aboard. Take a step beyond campfire ghost stories and see the actual places where supernatural events took place.

LOCATION: 9th St. and Asbury Ave. (City Hall), Ocean City (Cape May County).
HOURS: Late June–Labor Day, nightly, & Apr.–Halloween, Sat., 8 P.M.
ADMISSION: $$$; children 4–12, $$. Reservations required.
PHONE: 609-814-0199. **WEBSITE:** wwwghosttour.com/oceancity.html.

Cyber Robotics Learning Center

Kids get a fun introduction to robotics, basic programming, and electronic control and go on to advanced programming, mechanics, and design engineering at this center. The courses are designed to be used with the Lego Robotics Set, Robolab Software, and other robotics resources. Students keep notebooks of their work. There's a class for Pre-K, K, Grades 1–2, and Robotics for third grade and up, as well as advanced classes for high schoolers. The Science and Technology series, for example, uses hands-on learning about motorized machines. (Ten classes of 1½ hours each.) The Robotics Series includes Introduction to Robotics, Robotics Engineer, RoboChallenge, Robo Alien Adventure, and Cities and Transportation. In the last of these classes, students learn real-life applications of automated devices. They also explore traffic controls, traffic monitoring, intelligent vehicles, and city planning and work on projects related to these topics. There are eight classes of 2 hours each in this series. Besides the two main locations, after-school classes are also offered at a number of Bergen and Passaic County schools (see website for current list).

> **LOCATIONS:** 861 Main St., 1st Floor, Hackensack (Bergen County). Also at Christ Church, 105 Cottage Pl., Ridgewood.
> **HOURS:** Class times vary; call or see website for details.
> **ADMISSION:** Semester tuition. **PHONE:** 201-768-6111.
> **WEBSITE:** www.cyberroboticslearning.com. (BP) (SC)

Storming Robots

This center offers a place where kids can learn about robotics, automation, and the exploration of artificial intelligence based on their grade level. Kids learn engineering concepts, explore robotics using Lego robotics components, and learn programming to automate their robots. There are weekly classes for grades 2–12, set up into four age groups: MicRoBotics for grades 2 and 3; Stormbotics for grades 4–6 and for 7–8, and Senior for grades 9–12. Classes are set up as Robot Technology Clubs in which kids build robots from scratch and learn the fundamentals of mechanics, electronics, and programming. Sessions last 1½–2 hours and run for the fall and spring semesters. A one-month introductory trial period is also available. There are also independent 1½-hour workshops on Sundays as well as special full-day and week-long sessions on a variety of topics and projects such as building a flying saucer, a hazmat robot, and an FM radio.

> **LOCATION:** 3322 Rt. 22 W., Bldg. 4, Suite 402, Branchburg (Somerset County). **HOURS:** Wed.–Sun.

ADMISSION: Semester tuition. **PHONE:** 908-595-1010.
WEBSITE: www.stormingrobots.com.

International Chess Academy

This local center teaches kids how to play chess, from the basics to more advanced techniques, in ongoing 11-week sessions of one to three hours a week as well as holding weekly camps in summer. The academy also holds its own chess tournaments for students, and many students participate in a number of outside chess matches.

> **LOCATIONS:** 185 Court St., Teaneck, and 9–10 Saddle River Rd., Fair Lawn (Bergen County). **HOURS:** Teaneck: Mon. & Wed. evenings & Sat. Fair Lawn: Tue. & Thu. evening & Sat. **ADMISSION:** Semester tuition. **PHONE:** 201-833-1741 and 201-797-0330. **WEBSITE:** www.icanj.net. (SC)

Powerhouse Studios

A creative center that focuses mainly on providing fun and entertaining party settings and activities for kids. Party venues feature a series of unique television-style game shows and interactive programs for a wide range of ages. Entertainment specialists put together a fun program especially suited to individual parties. For example, the Wild 'n Wacky Challenge game show features competition with a boogie blaster, phoam booth, and pie wall—somebody always gets really messy. At the Playtime Forest with Milo the Dragon and friends, kids 3–6 can sing, dance, and play games and activities. The Hype is a pop culture game show with music, video, and live performances designed for middle and high schoolers. There are other shows as well as a game arcade.

> **LOCATIONS:** 7 Little Rd., East Hanover (Essex County), and 49 E. Midland Ave., Paramus (Bergen County).
> **HOURS:** By appointment. **ADMISSION:** Party fee.
> **PHONE:** 973-560-9560 and 201-265-9060.
> **WEBSITE:** www.powerhousestudios.tv.com. (BP)

Parteaz

This party place specializes in birthday tea parties for different age groups of girls. The themes are Princess (ages 4–6), Mermaid (ages 4–6), Glam (ages 6–10), Hollywood (ages 8–12), Tropical (ages 6–12), and Spa (ages 6–12). The first two parties include dress-up, a high tea, and crafts and games. The Glam party includes designing a customized spa body lotion to take home, and all partiers gets a goodie bag with "everything a totally glam girl needs." The Spa party includes a manicure and mini facial and creating personalized bath salts to take home in a goody bag. And the Hollywood party includes

There are a number of themed parties for girls, including a glam party that features a walk down the red carpet, at Parteaz in Maplewood. *(Photo courtesy of Parteaz)*

having hair styled and makeup applied, then playing a part from a movie or TV show, with an edited DVD of the performance as a keepsake of the event.

LOCATION: 1860 Springfield Ave., Maplewood (Essex County). **HOURS:** By appointment. **ADMISSION:** Party fee. **PHONE:** 973-447-0616. **WEBSITE:** www.parteaz.com. (BP) (SC)

Jersey Shore Pirates

Kids take a swashbuckling ride on the pirate ship *Sea Gypsy* on the Metedeconk River. Face painting and dress-up start half an hour before sailing time on the dock. There's an interactive treasure hunt, with kids learning to read a treasure map, discovering a secret message in a bottle, and working as a team to defeat an enemy pirate who has stolen the keys to the treasure by shooting water "cannons" at the foe.

LOCATION: Riverfront Marina, 281 Princeton Ave., Brick (Ocean County). HOURS: Sails daily, every hour and a half, 9:30–5. ADMISSION: $$$$; 2 and under, $$$. PHONE: 732-899-6100. WEBSITE: www.jerseyshorepirates.com. (BP)

Sparkle Diva Studios

Glam parties for girls create a little diva's paradise. There's a Mommy & Me Day at the Spa, and Little Diva Day at the Spa. It includes manicure, pedicure, facial, hair service, and "pink carpet" service. Little divas can enjoy a fun manicure and pedicure, followed by a fantastic fruit facial. For those who want the Always Sparkle treatment, the Glam Squad will transform girls into the Glamour Girls they want to be with their Sparkle Service.

LOCATION: 989 Burnt Tavern Rd., Brick (Ocean County). HOURS: Tue.–Fri., 10:30–6; Sat., 8–12; & Sun., 8–12 by appointment. ADMISSION: $$$$$$; varies with package. PHONE: 732-206-1100. WEBSITE: www.sparkledivastudios.com. (BP)

Sweet & Sassy

Why have a regular party when you can have a glam party? There are parties with eight themes, all designed for girls aged 4–13. They include glittery makeovers, free take-home gifts, themed activities, and time in the Cake Place room. Sweet & Sassy is a national franchise with four New Jersey locations; each is a combination salon, spa, and party place for girls. There's a child-friendly fashion runway, pop star and princess parties, and spa-inspired services. There are also haircuts, mini manicures, and ear piercing. Plus, there's a multicolored, purple, plush pedicure pit and a celebration area with globe lights, runway, and reflective disco ball. Mini manis and pedis include free nail art and finger or toe ring. Party themes include Magical Fairy, Enchanted Princess, Night on the Red Carpet, Fashion Diva, Pop Star, Designer Diva, VIP Pajama, and the Ultimate Spa party. And your party group can be picked up and chauffeured to and from the party in the hot pink Sweet & Sassy limo.

LOCATIONS: The Shoppes at North Brunswick, 764 Shoppes Blvd., North Brunswick (Middlesex County) (732-24-SWEET); The Shoppes at Old Bridge, Old Bridge (Middlesex County) (732-591-0020); 216 E. Ridgewood Ave., Ridgewood (Bergen County), 201-670-0123;

and Towne Place at Garden State Park, 957–961 Haddonfield Rd., Suite 1, Cherry Hill (Camden County) (856-665-7465). **HOURS:** By appointment. **ADMISSION:** Party package. **WEBSITE:** www.sweetandsassy.com. (BP)

Camden Children's Garden

One of the most interesting interactive education sites for kids is the Camden Children's Garden, which spruces up the outside of the Adventure Aquarium. There are lots of colorful play areas in this 4½-acre attraction, many of which aren't just about flowers or plants. The Dinosaur Garden, for instance, offers a prehistoric environment of rock walls, waterfalls, and huge trees—not to mention a 35-foot-long Apatosaurus, created from recycled automobile parts. Hand-painted benches and painted wooden violets add color to the nearby Violet Plaza, which also features an interactive water fountain. Kids can also learn and play in the Tree House and nearby underground maze (which is really above-ground and at eye level for children).

The Storybook Gardens have three little houses in the Three Little Pigs Garden as well as fanciful topiaries and a chair made out of yews where children can hide and play. A giant watering can fronts the Giant's Garden, which is filled with oversize plants and foliage, and a slide sends children down a rabbit hole into Alice in Wonderland's Garden. Besides the many interactive play areas, there is now a small carousel. The Railroad Garden (fanciful plants inside small boxcars) also offers a miniature train ride.

A statue of Walt Whitman is a fitting nod to the poet who lived his last years in this city. And the enclosed, heated butterfly house nearby allows you to experience the winged creatures and tropical plants year-round, and there's a small Spring Butterfly ride nearby.

Although this is primarily an outdoor garden, it does operate year-round. There are also many special events, including a Festival of Lights on Fridays and Saturdays in late November and December.

LOCATION: 3 Riverside Dr., Camden (Camden County). **HOURS:** Wed.–Fri., 10–4; weekends, 10–5. **ADMISSION:** $$; children 3–11, $. Under 3 free. **PHONE:** 856-365-8733. **WEBSITE:** www.camdenchildrensgarden.org.

MINOR LEAGUE BASEBALL

Throughout the state, there are stadiums have where minor league teams have lots of fans and draw sizable crowds. Some teams are affiliated with major league teams at the A or AA level. Most are in independent leagues. These are small versions of major league stadiums, with box and reserved seating. Many also offer lower-priced general admission tickets so you can sit on the grass or picnic down the lines beyond the stands. Seating capacity generally runs around 6,000. Here are the minor league teams that play in the state.

Camden Riversharks. Atlantic League (Indep.).
Campbell's Field, on the waterfront, Camden
(Camden County).
PHONE: 866-742-7579. WEBSITE: www.riversharks.com.

Lakewood Blue Claws. Southern Atlantic League (A).
A Phillies affiliate. FirstEnergy Park, Lakewood
(Ocean County). Take Rt. 70 West, go right on Rt. 623.
PHONE: 732-901-7000. WEBSITE: www.lakewoodblueclaws.com.

Newark Bears. Atlantic League (Indep.).
Bears & Eagles Riverfront Stadium, Bridge St., Newark
(Essex County).
PHONE: 973-848-1000. WEBSITE: www.newarkbears.com.

New Jersey Jackals. CanAm League (Indep.).
Yogi Berra Stadium, One Hall Drive, Little Falls
(Passaic County). On Montclair State University campus.
PHONE: 973-746-7434. WEBSITE: www.jackals.com.

Somerset Patriots. Atlantic League (Indep.).
TD Bank Ballpark, East Main St., Bridgewater
(Somerset County).
PHONE: 908-252-0700. WEBSITE: www.somersetpatriots.com

Sussex Skyhawks. CanAm League (Indep.).
Skylands Park, Rt. 565, Augusta (Sussex County).
Near junction of Rts. 206 and 15.
PHONE: 973-300-1000. WEBSITE: www.sussexskyhawks.com.

Trenton Thunder. Eastern League (AA).
A Yankees affiliate. Waterfront Park, Trenton
(Mercer County).
PHONE: 609-394-3300. WEBSITE: www.trentonthunder.com.

LIGHTHOUSES
Sandy Hook

The pure white column and red top of the oldest working lighthouse in America stands on a small grassy rise inside Fort Hancock, in the Gateway National Recreation Area. When it was built in 1764 it was 500 feet from the tip of Sandy Hook. Today, that distance is a mile and a half. A maximum of eight people at a time is led to the top, where the views include the New York skyline, the Verrazano Bridge, and the Highlands. There's a height minimum of 4 feet, so smaller children won't be able to make the climb.

LOCATION: Garden State Parkway, Exit 117, to Rt. 36 East to Sandy Hook exit. **HOURS:** 12–4:30 on weekends, Apr.–mid-Dec., plus weekdays, 1–4:30 in July and Aug. Sign-up sheet for tours at the keeper's quarters adjacent to the lighthouse. **ADMISSION:** Free. Parking fee for park in summer. **PHONE:** 732-872-5970. **WEBSITE:** www.nps.gov/gate/planyourvisit/sandy-hook-hours.htm.

Twin Lights

An unusual brownstone building that looks more like a castle than a lighthouse, Twin Lights is perched on a bluff in Highlands with a sweeping view of Sandy Hook and the ocean. The "twin" lights (one is square and one octagonal) are towers on either side of the main building. The first Fresnel lights were used here in 1841. The present fortresslike structure was built in 1862 and was the scene of many "firsts." The museum inside includes exhibits on early life-saving equipment and Marconi's demonstration of the wireless from this site. The spiral staircase involves only sixty-five steps and leads to an excellent view. Outside are a picnic area and several historical markers.

LOCATION: Lighthouse Rd., Highlands (Monmouth County). **HOURS:** In summer, daily, 10–4:30. Closed Mon. & Tue. rest of year. Call to confirm hours. **ADMISSION:** Donation requested. **PHONE:** 732-872-1814. **WEBSITE:** www.twin-lights.org.

Sea Girt

This lighthouse stands atop a four-story square brick tower in an L-shaped Victorian brick house in a residential area of Sea Girt. The interior has been restored and furnished according to the 1890s, when it was first commissioned.

LOCATION: Beacon Blvd. & Ocean Ave., Sea Girt (Monmouth County). Rt. 71 to Beacon Blvd. Left at end to Ocean Blvd. **HOURS:** Sun., 2–4. Call first. **ADMISSION:** Free. **PHONE:** 732-974-0514. **WEBSITE:** www.seagirtboro.com/lighthouse.html.

Barnegat

"Old Barney" guards the northern tip of Long Beach Island. Its classic red-and-white design stands against a backdrop of ocean and bay in a state park of the same name. You can climb the 217 steps to the top or simply walk around the esplanade and view the tip of Island

Beach State Park across the inlet. The park also includes some nature trails among the dunes, a maritime forest, a picnic pavilion, and a small Visitor Center with exhibits on the lighthouse and nature at the park. A private Barnegat Light Museum several blocks away at 5th and Central is open in the summer and has lots of material on the lighthouse.

LOCATION: Take Garden State Parkway, Exit 63, to Rt. 72 to Long Beach Island, then 9 miles north to Barnegat Light (Ocean County).
HOURS: Lighthouse: Summer, daily, 9–4:30; Nov.–Apr., weekends. Call for spring and fall hours. **ADMISSION:** Free. **PHONE:** 609-494-2016.
WEBSITE: www.state.nj.us/dep/parksandforests/parks/barnlig.html.

Absecon

Just northwest of the casino strip, this lighthouse stands on a sandy inland block surrounded by a fence. Painted pale yellow and black, it features a wrought-iron spiral staircase with 228 steps. Absecon, at 171 feet, is the tallest of the Jersey lights, and the view up top encompasses the beach, inlet, and ocean as well as the town. There's also a reconstructed keeper's house with displays of photos and artifacts about the lighthouse.

LOCATION: Pacific and Rhode Island Aves., Atlantic City (Atlantic County). **HOURS:** Thu.–Mon., 11–4; July & Aug., daily, 10–5.
ADMISSION: $. Under 4 free. Museum free. **PHONE:** 609-449-1360.
WEBSITE: www.abseconlighthouse.org.

Hereford Inlet

Surrounded by lovely gardens and a park, this building in North Wildwood sports a furnished interior and Victorian architecture that make it a landmark. Originally built in 1874, it has been restored to its Swiss Gothic style. The gardens are landscaped and include 200 varieties of flowers. There's a half-hour tour of the furnished "house" section, which includes exhibits on lighthouse history, shipwrecks, and the lifesaving service, as well as furnished rooms from the days when keepers lived there.

LOCATION: 1st & Central Aves., North Wildwood (Cape May County).
HOURS: Mid-May–mid-Oct., daily, 9–5; rest of year, Wed.–Sun., 10–4.
ADMISSION: $. **PHONE:** 609-522-4520.
WEBSITE: www.herefordlighthouse.org.

Cape May Point

This restored 1859 lighthouse is the center of a state park well known for bird-watching, a beach, and a nature center. There are several historic plaques on the way up the 199 steps of the black spiral staircase. The view from the top includes Delaware Bay, Sunset Beach, Cape May, and the amusement rides at Wildwood. At various times during the season, the "keepers on duty" allow you to meet the last keepers of the light at the top and ask questions about their life and times in the 1920s.

LOCATION: Off Sunset Rd., Cape May Point.

HOURS: Apr.–Nov., daily, 10–8; limited times rest of year.

ADMISSION: $. **PHONE:** Park: 609-884-2159. Tours: 609-884-5404.

WEBSITE: www.capemaymac.org.

Fairs and Festivals

The midway at State Fair Meadowlands is filled with rides and visitors during the event's three-week run in late June–early July.
(Photo by Steven Ikoguchi; courtesy of State Fair Meadowlands)

JANUARY

Winter Festival, Lambertville (Hunterdon County) and New Hope, PA. Last week of month. Storytelling, parade, kids' musical performance, kids' theater shows, art show, and children's activity center with an obstacle course, dinosaur moon-bounce, arts and crafts, and sports games.

PHONE: 215-862-5067. WEBSITE: www.winterfestival.net.

MARCH

St. Patrick's Day Parades, Belmar, Union, Kearny, Newark, Morristown, Seaside Heights, etc. Belmar's is in early March. Others on March 17 or the weekend before.

APRIL

New Jersey Folk Festival, New Brunswick (Middlesex County). Focus is on the folk life of an ethnic group. Includes two large children's activities tents. Also **Ag Field Day**. With a petting zoo, farm animal show, sea creature touch tank, potato sack race, and more. Held in late April.

PHONE: 732-932-5775.
WEBSITES: www.njfolkfest.rutgers.edu and www.agfieldday.rutgers.edu.

MAY

Native American Arts Festival, Rankokus Indian Reservation, Westampton (Burlington County). Artists, entertainers, food. Last weekend of the month. Second festival held in October.

PHONE: 609-261-4747. WEBSITE: www.powhatan.org.

Ocean Fun Days, Sandy Hook (Monmouth County) and Island Beach State Park (Ocean County). One day in each location, mid-month. Exhibits, classes, nature tours, and children's activities related to the coastal environment.

PHONE: 732-872-1300. WEBSITE: www.njmsc.org/oceanfunday.html.

JUNE

Appel Farm Arts and Music Festival, Elmer (Salem County). Early month. Concerts; children's village with puppet theater, magicians, jugglers, and storytellers; crafts area; and toddler area.

PHONE: 800-394-8478. WEBSITE: www.appelfarm.org/festival.

State Fair Meadowlands, 50 Rt. 120, East Rutherford (Bergen County), at the Meadowlands Fairground. Late June–early July. Amusements, kid zone, concerts, clowns, auto show, vendors, and more.

PHONE: 973-450-1073. WEBSITE: www.njfair.com.

Kids Kingdom Traveling Jubilee, Cedar Brook Park, Plainfield (June); Rahway River Park, Rahway (July); Mattano Park, Elizabeth (August); and Oak Ridge Park, Clark (September). Entertainment specifically for kids, headline talent, building Lego creations, hands-on science experiments, a bubblemania tent, video game trailer, pony rides, petting zoo, hayrides, face painting, sand art, and amusement rides.

PHONE: 201-653-2699. WEBSITE: www.thisisitproductions.com.

JULY

New Jersey Renaissance Kingdom, Red Mill Museum, Clinton (Hunterdon County). Two weekends, mid- to late month. Knights and ladies, village characters, storytellers, jesters, and lots of shows.

PHONE: 732-271-1119. WEBSITE: www.njkingdom.com.

Quik Chek New Jersey Festival of Ballooning, Solberg Airport, Branchburg (Somerset County). Mid- to late month. Balloon launches, rides, music, amusement rides, vendors, family fun pavilion.

PHONE: 973-882-5464. WEBSITE: www.balloonfestival.com.

AUGUST

New Jersey State Fair, Rt. 94, Augusta (Sussex County). At the Sussex County Fairgrounds. Ten days in early month. Farm animals, amusement rides, entertainment, vendors.

PHONE: 973-948-5500. WEBSITE: www.newjerseystatefair.org.

SEPTEMBER

Bloomfield Harvestfest Street Fair, Bloomfield (Essex County). Late month. Street festival with entertainment, vendors, amusement rides, crafts, pony rides, petting zoo, games, and JC's Traveling Kids Shindig.

PHONE: 201-653-2699. WEBSITE: www.thisisitproductions.com.

Edison Fall Family Spectacular, Municipal Complex, Edison (Middlesex County). Late month. National and local musicians, children's amusements, pony rides, petting zoo, arts and crafts, classic car show, and large fireworks finale.

PHONE: 201-653-2699. WEBSITE: www.thisisitproductions.com.

OCTOBER

Ultrasonic Superfantastic Family Day, Hoboken (Hudson County). Early month. Hands-on arts and crafts, performances, costumed characters, interactive science and nature experiences, amusement ride midway, hay maze, pumpkin picking and decorating.

PHONE: 201-653-2699. **WEBSITE:** www.thisisitproductions.com.

Eighteenth-Century Field Day, Fort Mercer, National Park (Gloucester County). Third Sunday. Revolutionary encampment, battle re-enactment, colonial crafts and trades demonstrations, glassblowing, music.

PHONE: 856-853-5120.
WEBSITE: www.co.gloucester.nj.us/government/departments/ parksnrec/redbank.cfm.

Index

Page number in italics refer to illustrations.

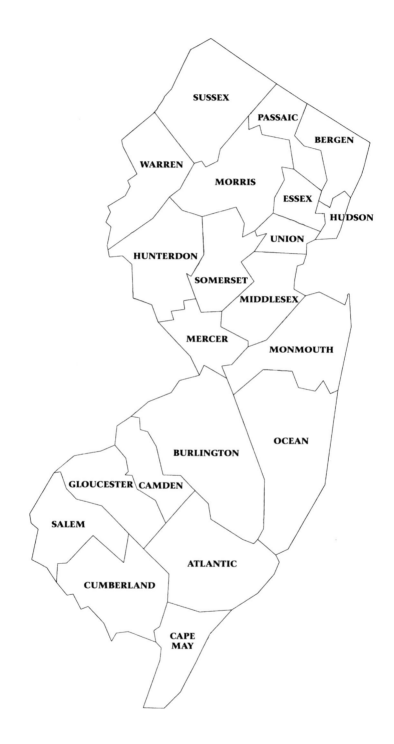

Index by New Jersey County

About the Author

Patrick Sarver is a former executive editor of *New Jersey Monthly* and of *Rutgers Magazine*. He has served as the editor of *Vista/USA*, the Exxon Travel Club magazine, where he was also a contributor to the Exxon Travel Guides. He is currently editorial director of the PFM Group and resides in Bernardsville, New Jersey. He is also the author of *New Jersey Day Trips*, published by Rutgers University Press.